THE GREAT SADNESS
INDIGENOUS ANGLING AND THE LOSS OF HOME

THE GREAT SADNESS
INDIGENOUS ANGLING AND THE LOSS OF HOME

By

Roger Emile Stouff

SHADOWFIRE BOOKS, LLC

PUBLISHED IN THE UNITED STATES OF AMERICA

THE GREAT SADNESS

SHADOWFIRE
BOOKS, LLC

SHADOWFIRE BOOKS, LLC

www.shadowfirebooks.com

Books By Roger Emile Stouff

Native Waters: A Few Moments in a Small Wooden Boat
An indigenous fly fisher's journey across water and time
A Memoir

The Great Sadness: Indigenous Angling and the Loss of Home
A Memoir

Chasing Thunderbirds
Illustrated by Gary Drinkwater
Short Stories

Books By Roger Emile Stouff and Kenneth R. Brown

For There Is Still The Sky
Book One in the Allidian Saga
A fantasy novel

The Dark Lands
Book Two in the Allidian Saga
A fantasy novel

The Thunderchild Fables
A science-fiction novel

Firekill
A science-fiction novel

This is for Siti. A world of water, slowly dying.
This is for Co'ktangi, grown shallow and thin.
This is for Peach Coulee, but a shadow of its former midnight.
For Little Pass, Big Pass, Sandy Cove, Round Island, Bird Island
and Buffalo Cove.
For Sawmill Bayou, Bayou Jean Lewis, Cotton Canal and Crewboat
Chute.
And this is for the Long River, the Atchafalaya, which struggles on.

Table of Contents

FOREWORD

The Chitimacha could always tell if they were going to have company, rain, good news or bad news. They had a tiny bird they called kich *in the Chitimacha language. It is better known as the wren today. The little bird would come close to the house and sing or chirp its messages that only an Indian could understand...*
Taunte Pauline Paul...often said the little bird does not come and talk anymore. It might know all the older Indians are gone who could talk to it.
– Faye Stouff, *Sacred Beliefs of the Chitimacha Indians*
(Nashoba teḳ Press)

There was a morning I sat sipping hot, black coffee with my mother on a cypress bench on her front porch. It was early spring in the year that I never saw or heard *kich,* the year wind and water became rough beasts. We admired her prized zinnias, roses and gardenias, and she told me that a strange thing had happened. During the night she opened her eyes to find a man standing over her bed, features obscured by near-darkness. When she drew a startled breath, he backed away, across the bedroom floor and out the door into the hall. She never saw him again. Her sister worried there had been an intruder in the house, but I reassured Mom against that notion.

"It was just one of the old folks coming 'round to check on you," I said. "They check up on me from time to time, too."

We sat clutching cups of steaming-hot Cajun coffee and watched the breeze flirt with the zinnias in front of that little house on the reservation; I thought of old people visiting a world that they had departed years or decades before. I know they do it —my father's people have always known—but that other part of me, the part that is not indigenous to North America, stubbornly whispers that this is impossible. Human beings die and go to heaven or hell, that fraction of me insists, and any apparitions we may see or sense on earth are the work of the devil, a deception by Ol' Scratch. I wonder at such a dichotomy of cultures: that one should believe in worlds interacting, mingling and coalescing, while the other conceives worlds as separate, barriers between them, never, ever merging. No small wonder such a clash ensued on this soil five centuries ago. I marvel sometimes that the latter culture, with so many self-inflicted, crippling wounds managed to dominate most of the known world.

Earlier that morning I fished for eager and willing redears, shellcrackers they're called elsewhere, but here in south Louisiana we call them chinquapin. They flung themselves merrily at every gold bead-headed Jitterbee nymph fly I presented with a little five-weight fly rod. I even landed a few respectable bass that didn't find the nymph too meager. I was in sight of the bone-white clam shell remnants of *Co'ktangi*, the ancient worship place of my people, where our holiest and most honored were interred.

"Did you keep any fish?" my mother asked me between sips of coffee. She is small and worn, a little Cajun lady with silver hair and a gravely voice; she was once four-feet eleven-inches but the years have stolen two inches away from her, a fact that has become a forbidden topic of conversation.

I smiled and broke the sad news. She frowned back with that familiar look of incomprehension and, at the same time, resignation. Catch-and-release fishing is something her generation will not grasp in their lifetimes. Raised poor on her father's farm and later a wife living modestly with her husband, fish were for the table, and whatever sport came with the catching was a bonus. I take her a batch of panfish now and then, but the bass go back into the lake.

She's eighty-two years old as of this writing. There's still enough gumption in her to grow beautiful roses and fret over her gardenias when the white flies descend from muggy, scorching Louisiana skies. There's a shadow of loneliness over both of us. I perceive it from time to time, purple spots lurking behind her eyes, and now and then, with a glance, I am sure she sees them stalking behind mine. Of the core family, we are all that remain. Growing up, my entire world revolved around my parents and paternal grandparents. I was estranged from my mother's parents, segregated by language barriers since they spoke virtually no English. I remember them fondly as kind but mysterious folks. My mother and her siblings refused to teach their children Cajun French. In those days, before the fad of Cajun cuisine and fascination with its culture, to be Acadian was an embarrassment, and our parents tried to shield us from that. So did my Chitimacha forebears. They burdened me with a dizzying requirement to learn about the old people and the old ways, but with a stern warning to adapt, survive in a world that shuns indigenous ideals and beliefs. I was born, then, of two of the most oppressed people in Louisiana.

I embrace a sort of smug satisfaction in that.

Spring and summer days of my youth, we fished. We cut river cane along the shores of the Atchafalaya River for the old people to make baskets. We built boats, we hunted buried treasure along Peach Coulee on Lake Fausse Point Our house stood on the banks of Bayou Teche on the reservation. The Teche took its name from Chitimacha, meaning "snake." If I had been closer to my Acadian relations, perhaps we'd have run crawfish traps, pulled seines for shrimp, trapped fur-bearers in the marsh.

But as my mother and I sat there that morning, the absence of my father and my grandparents on both sides lay heavy and sullen over us. One by one, time has eroded them from the earth, like water beating on stone, like wind moving across clay shores. And the unspoken bears even more heavily on our brows: that some day she won't be here either, and I'll be left with nothing but diminishing water, ghosts and voices I can't quite make out through the obstinance of that non-native part of me.

On days when I can go to the water, drifting between the cypress and tupelo of *Co'ktangi* in my father's wooden bateau, the loneliness creeps over me, displacing some fraction of the peace only these ancestral waters could once provide. There on *Co'ktangi ha'ne het ci'ne,* the "pond lily worship place" of my father's people, an ancient and powerful place where a little magic stubbornly persists. *Siti imaxa* were people of water, and though that was the year water would rise up and bring suffering under skies full of unseen, silent messengers, I still seek it out. It is home, and these are the days spent there, the far end of eons and generations of my own kind upon those waters.

The majority of these notions were written as my newspaper column and chronicle in those essays a year in the life of a fisherman, a Louisianan and a Native American. Many thanks are due. Foremost among the many are Allan Von Werder, publisher of the *St. Mary and Franklin Banner-Tribune* and managing editor Vanessa Pritchett; readers of "From the Other Side"; my darling mother, Lydia Marie Gaudet Stouff, always a source of inspiration and laughter that spirits away the blues; Frank Musso, as dear a friend as any miscreant writer could ever hope for; Harry

Boyd, Louisiana bamboo rodmaker, a craftsman and gentleman in every sense of the word; Deanna Travis of Fly Anglers Online; Pete Cooper Jr., Francis Todd, David Naquin, Joe Kipp, Gary Henderson, Larry Offner, Glenn Cormier, Lamon Miller, Carlos Snellgrove, Mick Faherty; my boys, Matthan Christopher and Blaise Michael; my brother Larry Richard; all the Stouffs in Texas, California and New Orleans; and of course, Susan, the bright star by which I steer.

One: Between the Ice and the Sky

Once the people lived to be old, old—sometimes eight or nine hundred years. Once a girl, just about a hundred years old, got sick and was about to die. They hated to see her die so young so decided they would go find out how to make her live.

A great many people agreed to go—several hundred, both men and women. They took everything with them. They even took corn to plant, so that if they ran out of food they could stop and raise a crop. And they did this. Then their food gave out and they stopped and raised a crop of corn, killed game and dried meat, then they went on again.

After a very long time, they came to the Cold Country. Here many of them died; some were crushed between the ice and sky. One man who died was not even buried, and the buzzards ate him.

Finally those who were left alive got through the Cold Country. When they got on the other side, they met the spirit of the man who had not been buried. They asked him if he could tell them where to go to find out how to keep people from dying. He told them to go on a certain way and they would come to a house. By this house they would see an old man. If they would ask this old man he would tell them what to do.

After while they come to the old man, and they asked him how to keep people from dying. Now, this old man was Nete'schmeesh, chief of the spirits (This was before they knew anything about Koot-na'hin. Kootna'hin is our name for the white man's God).

The old man told them that the world was getting so full of people that the old ones had to die to make room for the young ones. From that time on, people would never again live to be so old. But he showed them all the herbs that would cure sick people, but after people got old, they must die in spite of these.

Then they asked the old man how they would get back to their country. He told them to go until they come to the edge, where they could look down on their country. Then they would have to jump off. But he told them he would turn them into anything they wanted to be. So one said he would be a squirrel. He was turned into a squirrel, but when he jumped down, he was crushed to death. Several others chose the forms of different animals, but were

crushed to death. Then one said he would take the form of an eagle;
he got down safely. The next said he would be a spider, and he spun
his web down and was saved. All of the people had died before they
got there except eight, and only four got down safely.
When these four got back, the girl was dead. They had been gone a
very long time. But after that, people knew what herbs to use to cure
sickness. Only the very old people died. But nobody lived to be much
over a hundred any more.
(As told to and documented by Caroline Dorman)

The Great Sadness

I fish where Indian warriors once stalked hardwood oak forests and paddled dugouts through stands of red cypress older than the cathedrals of Europe; where enormous stepped-pyramids rose from clam shell islands off the coast of what would become Louisiana.

Four centuries ago, within sight of where I cast a bee-shaped, bead-head nymph fly to eager, ferocious bluegill thick as a Puritan bible, a man stood on a hard-pack beach of white clam shell and confronted a future few of his forefathers could have imagined, but some prophesied. Their dreams told them of the change to come.

The fish were eager and obliging of the fly rod, predictions of a great spring, better than I'd seen in years. Besides bluegill, there were huge chinquapin taking a little red-black variegated Jitterbee, and just moments before a largemouth in the three-pound neighborhood happily threw an Accardo popper back at my face as he danced for me on his tail. Maybe I fouled the hook set. Perhaps I was distracted, thinking of the man on the shell beach in the distant past.

He was *na'ta*, chief of his village of *Siti imaxa*, "people of the many waters." The hair on his head was likely pulled back tight. His knees were scarred with fish fins and then tattooed. Deer skins and feathers of egret, turkey and, since he was a chief, eagle adorned him. There his people lived for eight thousand years, and there they remained when great wooden ships with parchment-colored sails approached the village from the Atchafalaya River. The Spaniards had made their way up from the Gulf of Mexico, and from their teak decks and iron helmets, they stared back at the tawny people there on the clam shell reef along the lake shore

His name is forgotten, that *na'ta* who stood firm against the first Europeans to reach the indigenous lands and waters of *Siti imaxa*. It was likely Desoto who piloted ships through a nation that claimed territory roughly one-third the current state of present-day Louisiana and tens of thousands of warriors strong. That day, unexpected by most save some dream-wizened shamans, that powerful chief jabbed the butt of his spear into the clam shell and forbade the Conquistadors to come ashore. The Spaniards tried, blade and ball. They were quickly and soundly beaten back, retreating along Grand Lake and back to the river. It would be many decades before such strangers would return, but these would be Frenchmen, and the world of that *na'ta* would change forever.

Perhaps it's at that clam shell beach where Creation begins for me, but my father's fathers came from Natchez, an offshoot of that great Mississippi nation. Here they merged with a more ancient people who left archaeological evidence along the brackish, marshy Louisiana coast back eight millennia. To be certain, they were fishermen. Middens and mounds are littered with piscatorial remains. They used the bones of bowfin for body ornaments and the formidable scales of the garfish for arrow points in a land where there was no stone. Some of these garfish grew over a hundred pounds, and those scales served as spear points. They set weighted traps for bowfin, gar and catfish.

But now I use a split-bamboo fly rod to probe for panfish and largemouth bass. There's an affinity with the cane rod. *Siti imaxa* harvested native river cane, split and peeled into the fine, thin strips of the "power fibers" to weave baskets so tight they held water without application of pitch. Like my old Goodwin Granger Co. rod of Tonkin cane, those baskets achieved worldwide fame. The culms of the local cane grew to sixty feet tall, three or four inches around. My grandfather and I would hike deep into the woods to find an upland ridge near water to harvest cane. Everything Chitimacha did was near water. People of the many waters.

We sat in a cane patch where there was no undergrowth beneath the canopy of leaves, surrounded solely by dry, creamy yellow stalks, chewing sandwiches my grandma made for us. He had polio when he was a boy so was spared the fate his brothers endured, hauled off to Carlisle Indian School where their hair was cut and they were beaten for speaking *Siti imaxa.* Annihilation by assimilation.

"This is where God lives," he said.

The cane is gone, except for a few small patches dutifully guarded by the handful of remaining basket weavers, but I still look for it along the lake shore when I fish from the boat. I look for it just as I look for that *na'ta* and the world he knew before he glimpsed sails through the thick, moss-draped tree tops.

Some indigenous people call that moment all those centuries ago the beginning of the Great Sadness. The last moment before they could suspect or imagine that they were going away. Where the chief stood, commercial fishermen and recreational anglers like me back their boats into Grand Lake, which we called *Siti,* and head into the remnants of a river basin grown shallow and thin from silt and the meddling influence of man on the natural world. That village—once teeming with families cooking and singing songs long forgotten—is a boat launch now, privately owned. Shards of pottery are pulverized under pickup truck tires, unnoticed. Some I've found there still bear the finger and thumb prints of their makers, fired into the clay.

Back End of the Canal

Chasing bream across the north shore of *Co'ktangi* in autumn, the boat drifted upon a short, wide canal cut into the north bank of that shallow bay near the lake. Loggers likely left the canal there prior to 1929 during a dark age when nearly all the old growth cypress in Louisiana was felled, until at last the Great Depression stilled the saws and silenced the mills. *Co'ktangi* was a pivotal point for the deforestation of St. Mary Parish, and the many thousands of logs floated out of that small bay of Grand Lake staggers the imagination.

It was late in the day, and the sun hung over my left shoulder. The boat brought me to the mouth of that canal, probably used to stash logs awaiting transport to one of the mills that dotted the parish from one end to the other. The scouring of south Louisiana partially happened here, cypress trees thousands of years old were toppled and floated to any of dozens of local mills. The canal is covered by a thick canopy of second-growth cypress now, choked by European and Asian invaders such as Chinese tallow. Though I knew it was no more than fifty yards from mouth to end, I could see only darkness in its depths. I made a few half-hearted casts into the jaws of the canal, but the black bugger at the end of my leader went unnoticed. The boat touched stem to a sunken log and waited there for me to push it free. I have caught several respectable largemouth bass at the mouth of that canal over a lifetime of fishing the cove with my father. He has since gone to his Creator, but I drift along *Co'ktangi* still, alone now in the wooden bateau he built two years before I was born, casting for fish as well as lifelines.

The darkness at the end of that canal held my attention. Late in the day, when skies are clear and dusk nears, the Atchafalaya River basin turns golden and green, quiet, breezeless and still. Here and there, egrets perch on ancient, worm-ridden logs, peck at bugs in rotting stumps. Beetles flush out from the decay, dive away into the water before the birds can snatch them up. A water moccasin coils within a patch of irises, and far, far behind me, I hear the splash of a largemouth, perhaps the one I missed moments before. He took me for a twisting, churning ride into the back of *Co'ktangi* before breaking my tippet on an unseen stump.

Down there, at the end of that dark canal there seemed to be another world. A world of twilight, where the margins of the present and past, the dividers separating this world from the next and that which has come before, are feeble and thin. When these bodies of water were a giant lake, before the levee was built in response to the flood of 1927, and farther back still when there was no one here but Chitimacha, a metropolis spread out over the higher ground. My ancestors, who harvested *Rangia* clam for food and used the shells for footpaths and village foundations, peek unblinking from layers of fallen cypress needles. Down at the end of that short canal, in the blackness, I can almost see the way it was. Lodged there against a log, the bow of the boat held firm, I can almost see all my relations since before there was time.

It looks like a tunnel, a cave, a passage. With a push of my paddle, the bateau drifts free, and I negotiate it around the log, then point the bow into the canal. With deft determination in the quest for erudition, I fade from the sunlit world into the darkness of the ages, lifted along by green-black water. The mingling limbs are like the arms of lovers, locked in embrace. Not a twinkle of light comes from above, but the glow of the cove is behind me, golden. The boat drifts a moment then settles quietly, almost in reverence. It has carried me to that cove many times over my life, though in distant days I sat in the back of the boat, and it was my father who sat forward, paddling with one hand and casting with the other. That part of me which stubbornly insists upon existing as a twenty-first century man removes the wooly bugger from the leader, replacing it with a black rubber spider. The part of me that persists in the here-and-now plays out a little slack and carefully sends a roll cast to the back corner of that dim canal's termination.

It is a sadness that a people who lived their lives in the light of day, who played and worked and hunted and fished a world of water under the full face of the sun now lurk in shadows at the back end of shallow canals. That people who lit the way to Creation by keeping an eternal flame afire not far from here should be cloaked in darkness at the end of their days. Most of all that I should flee choking deadlines, chattering offices and ringing phones to drift into a world of distant forebears...and feel I should roll cast a fly to a corner of their resting-place to make sense of the thin world left to me.

I glance behind me, and the waters of the cove are bright. Ahead of me, the foam spider is motionless, neglected. Past the end of the little canal, I peer into darkness and a shadow, a patch of darkness blacker than the rest, darts away behind an overturned cypress, mangled roots facing me like a den of snakes. I think of *Neka sama*, the "new devil," which moved across the swamps from west to east each year, whistling and making a sound as if pounding on a hollow log with a tree branch. Does *Neka sama* still lurk in the darkness at the end of that canal, afraid of the light and the deadly illumination of disbelief? A beast once so feared that children were huddled close to the breast when the whistling and pounding was heard far off, now a prisoner. Does *Neka sama* lurk here, looking out at the bright cove beyond, hear and watch the speeding, noisy boats, smelling the noxious fumes of two-cycle engines? It may snarl softly at fishermen who pass by it, casting into the canal's mouth, uncertain why they are suddenly so uneasy. They quicken their trolling motors to pass it.

When a people fade into the darkness at the back end of shallow canals, do they take their monsters with them, or do they persist, half-real?

I move the spider to the opposite corner with a careful twitch sideways. The ripples of its fall expand outward, touching darkness. There are no fish here, but then, I never catch much with rubber spiders. Perhaps that's why I tied it on. The darkness is all I may hook, and the soft, fluid motions within it, as breaths drawn from behind curtains, like fingers tapping on a drum. I take in the line and back the boat out slowly, receding from the shadows, and sunlight basks over the stern, moves amidships and finally floods me with warmth.

No breeze could penetrate the thicket behind that canal from the northwest. No wind could find its way through the dense growth. But it came nonetheless, pushing the boat just a little more, fondling my hair, tugging at my clothes. Then I was back on *Co'ktangi*, the ancient worship place of my father's people, and the air was still, that exhalation from the back end of the canal abbreviated and done. There were whispers on the breeze; my perceptions were keen to them. I could not understand the words, the language, but somewhere deep in my spirit the meaning was clear.

Do not forget.

Perhaps that's why the black back ends of shallow canals on *Co'ktangi* fascinate me so. I am just a wayward son who came home in the nick of time before disbelief erased entire slices of the world into darkness. Perhaps there's no one left who can see. No one who desires to see.

It is nearing sunset. I start the engine and idle out of *Co'ktangi* slowly, the prop kicking up mud from the shallow bottom. Instead of turning south for home, I guide the boat north, down the borrow pit that was excavated to build the Atchafalaya Basin Protection Levee to protect us from revered waters after the Great Flood of 1927. Less than a tenth of a mile and the pit opens up into Lake Fausse Point, once part of *Siti*, that the Spaniards named Lake of the Chitimachas. The surface is smooth as crystal, holding silent secrets. I throttle up a bit, not too fast, circle the lake once, breathing in the dusk. I soak up the oranges and greens and saturated silvers deep within me. The hues find illnesses and regrets, soothe them like grandmothers' medicines. I know that I am moving through barely two feet of water. The levee has caused it to fill up with sediment, like darkness under a cypress canopy. I dare not slow down or I'll be idling out of the lake as well, churning mud like faded memory.

My circumference of the lake complete, I return to the channel and make my way home. I pass *Co'ktangi* on my way, and it seems translucent, fading. I think that perhaps it might vanish each night, only returning at dawn. Farther down, I turn south at the floodgate system, installed to vent the overflow of water should the Atchafalaya threaten to tear down the stinging violation of the levee. On south, under the bridge, I turn west again and make my way home. It's nearly dark. Back on *Co'ktangi*, if it's even still there, I imagine the canal is completely cloaked now. Perhaps the entire cove is covered by darkness. Are ancestors dancing there, wraiths on the surface of the water, lifting themselves through the trees and into the stars just twinkling on high?

We once occupied these waters and lands from east to west, from the Gulf to the junction of the two great rivers, but now we are spread thin across time and space, sullen, hidden from the sun in the back ends of dark canals.

Crawfish created this world. It was all water first. A great, silver-blue sphere. The Creator commanded Crawfish to bring mud from below, mound it, bring it to the surface and create earth. There was great silence, then. The wind, perhaps, moaned or whistled, but the seas had no land to lap against, no surf to break. Not until Crawfish obeyed the Great Spirit and sundered perfection. Over countless millennia, Crawfish labored and the land rose up. Rains fell over it, rivers formed and shaped it, carved it, spread the seeds of plants. Near the end of Crawfish's labors, the Mississippi fanned back and forth, laying the land of my ancestors. They came from Natchez, my father's people. There was some sort of rift, some manner of division. They touched a brand to the eternal flame that burned for so long at Grand Village and moved south, carrying the flame with them, to be attended night and day, never allowed to expire, for that would mean the end of all things. Perhaps this ending would mean water would again engulf the world as it had twice before. When they came here, they found not only a more ancient people but also the only graceful, poetic balance of water and land in all of creation: these majestic swamps and marshes, the towering salt domes and great shell reefs, the rivers slicing courses through the earth, the abundance, the safety. They looked upon that great lake, named it *Siti*, and themselves forever more became *Siti imaxa*, people of the many waters.

It was a land of incredible bounty, for *Siti* ran some eighty miles northwest to southeast, and twenty or more miles wide in some places. A land of extravagant riches that allowed the Chitimacha to build majestic mounds in celebration of Crawfish' obedience to the Creator. Its uplands were hardwood forests devoid of understory, its lakes deep as glacial fjords, the swamps thick with primordial magic. Like many tribes along the Mississippi Valley, the struggle for life was unheard of among them; everything that the nation needed was provided by the movement and richness of water.

Years ago, too many to recall without wincing, my father and I drifted up to that same little canal. It seemed brighter then, but it may have been the season. Some places are brighter in spring than they are in summer; some darker in autumn than in winter.

He guided us up, stealthily, broad back tensed, thick arm silently working the paddle. He had warned me with a stern look and a firm word to be quiet as we approached.

"There's a nest of goggle-eye in there that'll feed your mama for a week, if we don't spook 'em," he said.

He certainly impressed the imperative of silence upon me. My mama, it was said by those who know her well, would readily fight a circular saw for a mess of cornmeal-fried goggle-eye, the venerable *Lepomis gulosus*. I was young enough to be armed with a little spin cast setup rather than a fly rod but old enough to be trusted to bait the hook with earthworms myself. Everything was just-made, new, as I was, in a world just unfolding, just brightening, just awakening. I had no notion of antiquity, galleons and *na'ta*, no thought of pre-existence to my birth. That morning, as we left the boat launch, the sun might well have been peeking over that cypress-lined horizon for the very first time. Dad paddled us up, and the silence was so absolute it seemed I could swing the tip of my little rod through it and see the slashes.

"There," he whispered, pointing with his own rod to a big cypress with dozens of knees. "Put it in *there.*"

I wanted to impress him. Wanted to gain his approval. Most of all, I *did not* want to cast my cork and impaled earthworm into the limbs of the cypress tree. He would not retrieve them for me and disturb the goggle-eye nest, scattering its denizens to the other side of the lake. He would not approach it until he had caught every big goggle-eye from beneath that tree, an endeavor that might take an hour during which I would sit in red-faced shame. A disgrace to my genetics. A dishonor to a long and distinguished lineage of fisherman, within a nation of fishermen on both sides of my genes.

I made the cast, and the rig landed about six inches shy of the trunk of the tree. Before I could gloat and seek praise, though, my red and white cork vanished and I snatched the rod back, which sent my cork and worm flying over my head.

He sighed, and I felt my face redden.

"Don't worry, don't worry," he said. "Get in there again!" He was holding his own rod and reel in his left hand—he was a southpaw—and I think it was trembling.

I cast again.

And landed in the exact same place.

The cork plunged, and I reared back, making the boat roll in protest.

"Got him!" my father cheered, and promptly cast his rig into the same nest, leaving me to land my prize while he shared in the bounty. An irresistible force pulled back, and rushed away, towing me at least in spirit with it, across not only an expanse of water but a corridor of time. I have been pursuing that force ever since and that journey to the ancestry of my grandfathers' waters continues.

True to the nature of parents descended from people born of water—Chitimacha and Cajun—my grandfather built my first boat. He used it for a time then gave it to me when I was twelve. He was a general contractor by trade, but less the boat builder my father was. The bateau was slightly askew somewhere amid-

ships, and tended to pull to the right under power. By the time I
was fifteen-years-old, my best friend and I never missed a fair day
to make the hour-long trip to the lake for a day of fishing, back
in a time when you could let fifteen-year-old boys take off in a
boat without worry.

Drifting between cypress trunks big around as the boat, we
hauled in remarkable catches of bluegill and bass in four or five
feet of black-green water. Now and then we'd see small reefs of
shell against the bank, overgrown with briars and palmettos. Indian home sites, most likely, or hunting camps. Now and then, a
little mottled-brown bird would rest nearby and screech at us.
Perhaps the call should have been no different than any other,
but something about it made me stop, listen:

Chuee! Chuee!

It was like that first goggle-eye, pulling me through the centuries as it struggled against my line. It conjured...something.
Something I couldn't quite identify or was really sure I believed
in. I related the experience to my grandmother and she reached
out across the kitchen table, strewn with split river cane and a
half-made basket, and she touched my hand with a look of wonder.

"Those days are so far away now," she said. She was the last
medicine woman and a vast repository of our ways. "Gone, like
season's ending but no other followed. First the Spaniards, then
the French...it doesn't really matter anymore, unless you believe.
In days long gone, *kich* would talk to us. It would come in
spring. Every spring, to tell us if friends were coming, or enemies, or danger. Your great-grandma was the last one to really
understand it. I do, a little. She taught me a little. You have been
blessed, boy."

Then she spent some time telling me how to understand it.
She told me the sounds it made that meant visitors were coming,
or enemies, or death. I was fifteen, fishing out of a twisted
wooden bateau and until then not much had been said about
such things. It was a shame to be an Indian. As with my mother's
Cajun ancestry, my parents and grandparents wanted me to survive in the world, and to do that, I had to be like everybody else.

When the Taino people of Hispanolia refused to be the good,
civilized Westernized subjects of the Crown as Christopher
Columbus required of them, he threw them in chains and made

them dig gold out of the mountains, and when they refused to work, he lined them up and shot, strangled, stabbed or set war dogs upon them. In Columbus' estimation, then, if the Taino were not "like everybody else" they were not being murdered at all, they were simply being punished by horrible, grisly means of death.

Those deeds were repeated a thousand, ten thousand times over the centuries. In an effort to make Native America "like everybody else" the United States forcibly removed Indian children from their homes and parents and sent them to boarding schools in places like Carlisle, Penn., where their hair was cut, they were dressed in non-Native clothing and beaten if they spoke a word of their languages. "Like everybody else" apparently does not include prohibition of kidnapping and abuse. The United States thought Indians were enough removed from being "like everybody else" that they forced the Cherokee to the Trail of Tears, where every other member of that forced march died.

I might seem as close to "like everybody else" as you can get, really. I don't look very Native, thanks to those predominant white genes in my blood. In fact, I'm more white-blooded than I am red-blooded, pardon the pun. Everybody else insists on asking me "how much Indian" I am, instead of asking me how I was raised and what is in my heart. No one asks an African-American or an Asian-American "how much" they are. No one asks a tawny-skinned, black-hair-in-braids Indian man with high cheekbones and a long, sharp nose "how much Indian" he is, though he might answer that he was raised in New York City and never stepped foot on a reservation or ate a piece of fry bread in his life.

What would be expected of me, to be "like everybody else?" I just can't figure it out. Should I forget that five hundred years ago my ancestors numbered in the tens of thousands and occupied a third of what would become the State of Louisiana? Should I forget that an ancestor of mine named Soulier Rouge was a mercenary soldier who fought on behalf of many Native nations in Louisiana and beyond against becoming "like everybody else?" Should I forget, then, that an ancestor named Long Panther journeyed to make peace with Gov. Bienville to end many years of hostilities in an agreement that guaranteed *Siti imaxa* would remain who they were? Should I, then, forget that my relations were sent to that school in Carlisle and they tried to make them "like everybody else" with scissors and belts and canes?

"That's all in the past," I'm told, and maybe that's quite true. It's all in *my* past, and nobody's going to take any of it away by making me "like everybody else." Ever.

Who are "they" that I should be "just like everybody else?" Many of them don't even know who they are, where they came from, often don't even care. I do. But we all know that they are referring to sovereignty, of course. That's the thing. The right to govern ourselves, insofar as Congress says we can. We're fine and cute when we're selling trinkets at pow-wows, dancing to *oooh* and *ahhh* over, and rudely pointed at with fingers. But sovereignty? Didn't Andrew Jackson take care of that little annoyance?

Blood the same as mine spilled to make sure I would be who I am. Treaties were signed, broken and wars fought to make sure I am who I am, and maybe my skin is not brown and my hair is not black. Maybe my cheekbones are not as chiseled as some glorified Hollywood expectations seem to require, my nose not as sharp, thin and hawk-like as some art gallery prints might imply.

But what I am, what all of us living Chitimacha are, is a descendant of Long Panther, who shook hands and smoked the calumet with Jean-Baptiste Le Moyne, Sieur de Bienville; I am a descendant of Soulier Rouge, given the name "red shoes" by a young white boy whom he called friend, and who struck terror into the hearts and souls of those who tried to make his people "like everybody else"; I am a great-grandson of Delphine Arnis, last Chitimacha-blood medicine woman; I am a descendant of Emile Anatole Stouff, last bloodline chief of the tribe, who passed it on to my father just briefly, and Nicholas Leonard Stouff then became first elected tribal chairman. I am a bearer of the flame.

Thin Places

"Always watch where you are going. Otherwise, you may step on a piece of the Forest that was left out by mistake."—A.A. Milne

There is a canal on the north shore of Lake Fausse Point called Peach Coulee. It is a place of mystery and stirring, restless ghosts.

No one is sure why it was named Peach Coulee. It is a natural canal, not one of the many man-made channels cut during the logging days of Louisiana. Its east bank is, for quite a stretch, topped by prehistoric construction. Winding from the lake down the coulee's shallow spine, off the boat's starboard gunnel there are occasional glimpses of white shell peeking out like bleached bone. I have never found a piece of broken pottery on that shell embankment. Unlike most of the other ancient Chitimacha sites I have located and visited, I cannot guess its purpose or use. The mound faces west, but flanked by water. Traditionally, southeastern tribes believed the "good" directions were east, where the sun rises, and south, where warming winds come from. Cold from the north and sunset to the west make those directions less than desirable and most ancestral sites faced the "good" direction. When it was necessary to face a "bad" direction, they placed water between themselves and the evil on the horizon, because evil cannot pass over water.

But the Indians avoided the place in recent memory, told stories about it to frighten the young away. My grandfather hunted pirate's treasure there, for it was long-rumored that Jean Lafitte used Peach Coulee as a hideout. My grandfather said that when he was a young boy, the very tip of a ship's mast was visible at the mouth of the coulee. Over the decades it sank into the mud and vanished. He said that, during the Great Depression, he and one of his friends picked Spanish moss from the overhanging limbs along the lake, and while in Peach Coulee, they noticed a cypress knee shaped like a saddle. Nearby was a pile of oyster shell.

"Looks like some old Indian sat down for his lunch there," he laughed. They passed the spot for months each time they picked moss in Peach Coulee. Finally he got to wondering about that spot, and went back to find it, but both the cypress knee and shell were gone.

There are many stories about Peach Coulee. Most I disregard as fabrication, though who am I to judge another man's stories? Tales of headless women, monstrous beasts with red eyes, hanging nooses strung from tree limbs, wooden crucifixes that appear and disappear at random. I know that it is a place of power, though I have never seen anything within. Yet it is always silent within Peach Coulee, no birds, no croaking frogs. My father and I took many fine bass and bluegill from Peach Coulee, but we never stayed there long. Trees sway and twist in the breeze within Peach Coulee, except that there is no breeze.

Many ages ago, a Chitimacha family was tending to their daily fare when a white deer appeared near them. Though it was forbidden to harm such an animal, they killed, cooked and ate it. After their hunger was satiated, the old people say, each member of the family stood up, as if in a trance, and walked deliberately into the lake, never to be heard from again, at least in their human form. Yet it is said among my people that they sometimes emerge from the lake as balls of fire, penance for their crime being eternity in such form.

And when I was a teenager, my friends and I would camp on the eastern shore of Lake Fausse Point Nearly every time we were there, late at night, we saw them: four bright lights, circling over the northern shore of the lake, over Peach Coulee. They danced there, almost jubilant, almost frenzied. We could never explain their source.

An old fisherman, heading home late with a skiff full of dying catfish, stopped near our campsite as we watched the lights dance over Peach Coulee. We were teenagers, hiding our beer and smoking cigarettes out by the lake where the only eyes were those of nutria and the occasional waterfowl. He scared the bejeezus out of us, approaching from across the lake in the shadows of the moon. He drifted up to the bank and called in a way that was little more than a guttural growl; we nearly leaped out of our skins.

"It's thin there," he said, looking over the lake at the lights dancing above Peach Coulee after we had settled down, offered him a beer. "Thin," he repeated, taking the beer and then he nodded to us knowingly and took his leave.

I didn't know what he meant at the time, but I think I do now. There are places where the boundaries between this world and the next, the separations of the seen and the unseen, are not so substantial. I first heard the quavering voice of the old fisherman use *thin* to describe such locations. Peach Coulee is one of the thin places, and now and then, the comfortable lines we depend on to organize and make safe our world bend, converge and overlap.

There are times when I wonder if the old fisherman who stopped by that night came from within the lines of comfort, or behind the thin places.

I go there still, chasing fish. The coulee forks not far from the lake, and the east channel eventually ends at a rise in the topography. My grandfather said there was a farmhouse there, though it had long been abandoned even when he was a boy. He stumbled on it while treasure hunting.

He met an old black gentleman who told him a story at the local waterin' hole one night. When the man was but a lad, a group of white people were digging a massive pit somewhere at the back of Peach Coulee. They had erected a tall fence around the site, and he was not allowed within.

As he stood there, the man told my grandfather decades later, he suddenly noticed a small woman by his side. She said to him, in a language he should not have understood but somehow did, "What are you doing here? This is not for you," and she promptly picked him up and threw him over the fence.

At the exact moment he fell to the ground the men digging the pit leaped from it, screaming in terror, running. The young bystander, his own experience with the small woman now compounded by the mass hysteria, fled with them. Later, he told my grandfather, he learned that the white men in the pit had looked up from its depths, and they saw soldiers in uniforms standing around the edge. They were firing down into the pit with muskets, though the diggers heard no sound. Yet, when they looked at each other, they saw horrifying wounds.

My grandfather suspected those were military uniforms, perhaps French or even Spanish. Convinced that there had been a treasure excavation ongoing, my grandfather asked the old man if he remembered where that spot was in the back of Peach Coulee. He said he did, and promised to take my grandfather there. They set a time of six o'clock, after my grandfather got off work.

He was half an hour late. Walking up the driveway, he met someone coming out of the house.

"Where's Mister Beau?" my grandfather asked. I don't know what his name really was; that was never passed down to me.

The other man shook his head sadly, hat grasped in his hand

in respect.

"He died at six o'clock," he said.

I go to Peach Coulee when I can. It does not frighten me, though I do not go at night. When I reach the edge of the finger of clam shell lining the east bank, I sprinkle tobacco over the ancient embankment and into the green-black water. Whatever spirits linger there seem to be appeased. I fish the channel down to the fork, follow it as far as there is enough water to float the boat. There are big bluegill there in the spring, coming into the shallows to spawn, and in the summer, the occasional old and seasoned largemouth lurks under a canopy of overhanging cypress limbs. They like the hard pack shell along the east bank.

Now and then, when the trees sway in air still as stone, or when silence becomes deafening enough to raise the hair on the back of my neck, I understand that this is still one of the thin places. It causes me no alarm. It is but one part, a facet of the whole, of my world. Within range is *Co'ktangi*, the religious center of my people's entire nation, where wispy turkey-buzzard men still dance and tend the bones of the dead under starless skies. To the west is an enormous village, its name forgotten, where broken pottery lies brown and tan and yellow under the lapping movement of the lake. To the southeast is *Amat'pan namu*, a great village where the Spanish first arrived in galleons almost five hundred years ago, and a *na'ta* stood against them and rallied the warriors from villages all around to turn the invaders away. For a time.

But when the water is high and the color of stained parchment, I ponder over maps and search for hidden sloughs and canals, ponds tucked away in farm fields I might be able to get permission to fish, little remnants of much larger lakes deep in the swamp, hopefully on public land. The digital age has simplified this: rather than trek to the parish courthouse to dig out maps from various agriculture, forestry and tax assessment agencies, attention to Louisiana's coastal erosion problems has yielded a plethora of online mapping resources. Stunning satellite imagery is now available to the general public.

So I sit with a cup of coffee, hot and black like Cajun dreams, and look them over, searching for sparkles of water. The winter had been none too severe, really, but not mild. There had been no hard freeze of the severity necessary to keep the water hyacinth and hydrilla at bay. Scrolling and mousing and clicking my way around St. Mary Parish from a synchronous orbit above the planet, I laugh when I consider what my grandfathers must think of their descendant searching so for fish.

My father told me that back deep in the swamps of Peach Coulee, my grandfather had gone squirrel hunting and found an old farm. Nothing there to really indicate it except neat rows in the soil, large trees growing from them, and a bit of old brick, enough evidence to convince him it had been there. It's all private land now and there are signs all along Peach Coulee forbidding entry, despite my ancestral claims to it. There's not much public land in Louisiana. Just ownership and leases and signs. I thought of challenging their black letters and white backgrounds, thought of arguing with their plywood and nails but shrugged it off as yet another byproduct of the Great Sadness that began five centuries ago.

I found a little pond on the map. It was well into the woods, across what appeared to be relatively high ground, or at the worst nothing a good pair of knee-high rubber boots couldn't handle. It was, I thought, worth going to take a look at and late winter was the best time, with the snakes down and duck and deer season just over.

One day when the weather was not quite so cold I readied myself. I have a sort of backpack that is a tackle bag where I keep all my gear. I slipped a rod tube containing my vintage bamboo Granger Victory fly rod into the straps on its side, along with a graphite backup rod. Thick rubber boots—usually called Cajun Nikes here—and a small caliber pistol on my hip just in case. A hand-held GPS I left at home; it would be useless in the dense cypress and tupelo stands, but I brought a trusted compass. I was a little worried about my pickup, but found a nice niche in the tree line to conceal it from all but the most curious of passersby.

I hoisted my pack on my back, put my fedora on my head and headed into the brown jungle. Within moments the truck was out of sight, and then the road, and the distant drone of occasional passing vehicles. Moments after that, there were no reminders on the ground: no beer cans, no worm buckets, no orange plastic tape on the trees. I understood again the lure of hunting: it gives a man something to do between fishing seasons. I am not much of a hunter, except a few teenage years shooting quail with a .410 shotgun before completely giving it up for fishing. I disdained the notion of sitting in a deer stand or a duck blind freezing to death for hours on end. But as a distraction until the fishing gets good again, well, I guess there's at least that much to say for hunting.

A couple of wild hogs, big and brown and snorting, scared up within fifty feet of me and, chortling angrily, stalked off while I stood there with my hand on my pistol. Wild hogs can either be timid or ferocious. These two big sows were apparently somewhere in between, because they grudgingly took their leave at my intrusion, but scolded me harshly as they departed.

I checked my compass to make sure I had not strayed off course: perfect, still. I nodded smugly at my woodsman's abilities, but reminded myself that being too confident amounts to tempting fate. On I went, noticing huge fallen cypress logs that would bring thousands of dollars for their heartwood, and smiled with satisfaction that they'd never, ever be harvested or see the blade. A pair of wood ducks took flight as I passed, whistling. Now and then, though, the bright red and brass of an expended shotgun shell on the ground reminded me that I was still far too close to civilization, far too lodged in linear time.

Something rumbled to the northwest and I cursed angrily. I had the good sense to check the weather forecast before departure, and there had been only a small chance of rain for the day. The adage, "If you don't like the weather, stick around a minute," may have been adopted by other members of the Union, but it was definitely birthed in Louisiana. I was probably nearly halfway to the pond, if it indeed really existed and was not merely a low spot in the woods no more than three inches deep. The canopy of cypress was thick though defrocked for the winter. I decided to continue, congratulating myself for packing my rain gear in my bag.

It's tempting to imagine that I was seeing the swamp like it was five hundred years ago, but I knew better. All the trees around me were second- and third-growth after the lumberjacks deforested Louisiana of cypress and most of its oak. Who knows what spirits they freed or banished from the trees, depending on its nature, with their saws? After that, invasive and secondary species had settled in, forever changing the landscape. But I could dream, perhaps, that it was something like this. In fact, I saw few signs of invasive plants so deep in the woods. Perhaps they did not do so well under the thick canopy of even successional growth cypress and tupelo, as these were larger trees than I expected. Now and then a palmetto patch sprouted, green against the stark brown backdrop, and I was, as always, glad to see it. Chitimacha covered their huts with these plants, a natural-made shingle of the finest kind. The gutter-shaped fronds displace water neatly. But I knew these woods. It was near here, on the way to Peach Coulee, that friends of mine found a wooden cross nailed to a tree and a hangman's noose below it. It was not far from here that there were wild hogs big as men, one of those same lads' father said, and another shot a squirrel that screamed like a man until it broke its neck in the fall.

It's thin there. Thin.

At last I detected an opening in the distance and the familiar smell of swamp water. I reminded myself it still might be nothing but a puddle, or it might be choked full of water hyacinth since the aerials were shot. But I emerged from the trees and there it was, a little pond, perhaps just less than an acre, nestled into the woods. I saw no bobbers, no monofilament line and no cellophane. Could it possibly have gone unnoticed? I had walked perhaps forty minutes to reach it, and since it was public land all the way and I had seen the few shotgun shells farther back, it would seem like someone should have been here. Bass fishermen, bait fisherman, a duck blind in a patch of reeds. But I saw nothing to indicate anyone had been there since my ancestors were unfettered.

Poking around with a fallen tree branch revealed the pond had some depth to it, and I was so encouraged and excited I dropped the mid section of my rod twice trying to mate the ferrules. I had the tip on in three tries and strung it up. There were no signs of life on the surface, no rises, but that meant little. It was midday, temperatures hovering around fifty-five. I had no room for a back cast but the pond was shaped oddly enough that I could stand sideways to it and work various juts and points along its margins. I opted for a small Clouser minnow, about a size six, to descend slowly and probe the pond's depths.

It was, at last, to this place that brawling goggle-eye had taken me, beginning that journey so many years ago when I made two perfect casts against the trunk of that old cypress tree growing at the mouth of a bright canal. A waypoint, anyway. A stopover in the journey. Of course I hadn't known then where I was going, but Havilah Babcock once remarked that there'll come a time in every man's life when he'll either go fishing, or do something worse. The powerful, royal-blue and green goggle-eye had put me on the right side of the law, at least.

Rumbling to the northwest again troubled me, and over the trees I could see the sky darkening. Forty or so minutes back to the truck. I had my boots on. Would the lightning be ground-contacting? Lightning is always unpredictable, of course. But I couldn't turn from this little pond, now that I was there. My grandfather claimed that if you find pirate's treasure you mustn't leave it. It would vanish before you returned. You mustn't curse or turn your back on it, he said. I was afraid this little pond—its potential still unknown—would dissipate into some marginal place if I departed, turned back by a little rain and thunder. Notions like that may defy sensibilities reared and honed on city streets and in office buildings and urban sprawl, but they are at home in the swamp. They are indigenous where places are barely real, places were my ancestors might dance, in the back ends of dark canals. It can only be sensed in the wilds, the power and substance of such notions.

I focused on my fishing. *If I were a vintage bamboo fly rod,* I mused, *I'd like to be a Granger.* No doubt about it, when it came to the classics I never held one I liked more than a Granger. Some might say it's long and heavy at nine feet, and to be certain, the Victory's tip-top might well have been touching the darkening clouds above me. I set the Clouser into a patch of reeds, let it settle for a moment then began a slow, steady strip in. A Granger, I mused, has no illusions of grandeur such as a Leonard might harbor, but holds its head higher than a hardware-store bin Montague, for goodness sake. It would probably share a beer with a Heddon, make fun of blue-blood Winstons and sadly mourn the plight of the common rods piling up in hardware stores everywhere.

Thunder rattled and a gust of wind twisted the bare cypress tops. I swung the Clouser out and set it back a little over to the right from its previous spot, stripped in slowly. Nothing. Perhaps the cold had put any fish down? The pond might have been deeper in the center. I sent the Clouser there next with a pathetic roll cast, letting it settle longer, tried a different strip, much slower, much longer between pulls.

A glimpse of something out the corner of my eye made me look up, but I couldn't be sure it was anything more than a roll of the clouds, a billow expanding and collapsing, churning along as the thunderhead moved just north of me. I could tell by the flow of clouds that it would likely miss my location by only half a mile, tops. I was hopeful, anyway.

Another cast into the pond, fanning. I stripped slowly, but I realized the water was shallow there. Hidden there in the trees with little sunlight throughout the day, it would be colder than an exposed pond. Largemouth and bream within would be sluggish, reluctant. And the threatening shadow of the clouds darted across the curve of the Granger's nickel silver ferrules.

I took the rod down. The storm worried me, and a dozen casts had produced nothing. I decided to return when the weather warmed but before the snakes became active again. I was sure there had to be something there in that secluded little pond. When the cane was back in the sock and tube, I looked up at the clouds again and it might have been great wings up there, gargantuan and black, or it might have been a purple spot on my cornea. I don't know.

But I do know that I didn't go back that spring because the fishing elsewhere was so excellent. I did go in the fall, but whether because of the storms that had wracked Louisiana that summer or some thinness of being, I could never find it again. Gone, as if it had never existed at all.

James Wilson defined something indigenous people have always known, but could not express in the white man's words: the notion of time, and how it's perceived based on many cultural influences.

Therein lay one of the major sticking points of worldview between the indigenous people of North America and the Christians of all flavors who came to these shores. For us, time is a circle, always coming back to where it was. That does not mean events repeat and loop endlessly, but yes, what has gone before will come again, in a sense.

The Western world lives in linear time, time that moves in a straight line. Thus, time begins at the Creation, is intersected at one point by the Birth and again at the Resurrection, ending finally at the Revelations. I'm not arguing theology; I'm outlining a difference in perceptions of the continuum two peoples lived within.

But those of us who are 'Breeds live in a paradoxical world that's even more difficult for Westerners to understand than it is for us to live in, if you can believe that. The linear world is a path from here to there, or if you will, from birth to death, notwithstanding what lies beyond mortality. In fact, Christianity can have it no other way: if Christian time were circular, there could be no end of days, for there is never an ending.

Indigenous people never conceived of an end of days. Even the Aztec knew that their civilization would collapse and they would vanish in the year One Reed, when the white-bearded serpent, Quetzalcoatl, returned to destroy them. This came to pass exactly as prophesied, except that Quetzalcoatl was the conquistador Hernan Cortez, and it was he who brought about the demise of Aztec civilization. Someone thinking in linear time would presume that the Aztecs got it all wrong. The Aztecs knew without a doubt they had got it right.

Because even though the Aztec empire ended, they did not conceive it "the end of the world." The world would go on, others would follow, just as they themselves had followed others.

My grandfather, "educated" by nuns and taught' by old Indians, later gave up the church. Many decades later, a new Baptist minister came to Charenton and visited him at the old house.

"Preacher," my grandpa said, testing him as he tested everyone, "what if I told you I had given up the white man's religion and went back to the old Indian ways?"

"That'd be fine," the preacher said. "You know, my Lord died for all people."

The old man considered this and seemed to find some logic or truth in it. He became a Baptist and remained one until he died.

But that old Indian man could step behind an oak tree and you couldn't find him until he reappeared in his wood shop some hours later. He could slip into a patch of basket cane and hide behind a single stalk. I didn't understand it for most of my life, but I finally think I know that he moved between circular time and linear time at will. Between a world where only angels and demons can perform such acts, and one where the power of the earth is accessible to each of us.

He learned to walk a thin line many indigenous people can't, so they die from exhaustion and loneliness. It happens all the time, you just can't see it because it's hidden on the reservations and on the slopes of mountains. My father learned it, too. I am still an apprentice, I suppose. If I am unknowingly moving between models of time, it is unconscious.

So here I am, raised southern Baptist, but a container of what old ways they passed down to me. My father was buried in a blue suit with a crisp white shirt, clutching an eagle feather and wearing a bolo tie. My brother put cedar and tobacco and food in the grave to sustain him on the journey while the preacher read Scripture promising everlasting life. A dichotomy? Are the two the antithesis of each other?

"My Lord died for all people," the preacher said, and then he followed my grandfather and my father all over the Southeast, talking to school children about Indians and Indian ways. He did missionary work for Indians in Central America. He presided over the funerals of my grandfather, grandmother and father and wept for all.

He, too, seemed to know the path to the bridge.

I continue to search for a way to straddle the discordant sides of this being. The difficulty I have is finding harmony, balance, and peace. It's not some literary inner turmoil or anything so wildly romantic as all that. It's just a search for a talent to unite my left-brain and my right brain, to fuse gene pools evolved on two continents, and to make a treaty between clashing spiritualities.

Sometimes I lie awake talking to my grandfather, and I ask him why he didn't teach me that magic. He doesn't answer. That part of time hasn't come around again yet. He came to me once, though. He came to me as part of a bargain we made early on, in which he promised he'd let me know if there was, indeed, something there beyond the final closing of the eyes and last breath. He fulfilled his promise.

Here I am, on the inside, looking out through the spectacles that have perched on my nose since I was two. One lens is measured in diopters; the other is smeared with war paint. I can't see through either with much clarity.

Beads, Stilettos and Black Iron Pots

Here at the delta of the Atchafalaya River, when the fishing is good there is none better. When it is off, however, it is completely, absolutely *off*. We learn here quickly to go when it's good and let nothing stand in our way. When it's off, well, we tend to other things neglected while we were on the water. To understand the nature of home waters, it is also necessary to comprehend the face of the landscape around them. The Atchafalaya, formed by the convergence of the Red River and the Mississippi River, is subject to the sediment and quantity of all the water lifted by melt-off and rain from the north. It can be temperamental and vicious.

When the river runs high and muddy, when the cold descends, that's when we pass the time until spring by taking care of the things we should have done instead of fishing.

Moving stuff around always precedes renovations to the old family house. Most of those things have migrated upstairs, which will be the last room of the house I remodel. There are boxes and boxes of things up there, some mine, mostly things that were here already. I've come to view them as component pieces of a whole, so to speak. The house itself is the bones and flesh of a lifetime; the things boxed up around its innards are its blood, organs and heart. Lots of it is probably better off in a landfill, but far too sentimental to be parted from. Much more, though, is purely precious treasure. These are the things in tattered boxes that spill out when they swell from soaking up rain outside the window. Though merely a family house built in the 1840s by an Indian chief, it is a storehouse of treasures valuable only to its kin.

There's a beaded purse, purple and silver, which belonged to my great-grandmother. It is in fair condition for its age. There's a machete my grandfather carried when he worked on the Panama Canal, the blade black as the wooden handle. He told me that, when workers moved through the jungles, they kept a machete balanced with the back of the blade on their shoulder, sharp edge out. That way, he said, if one of Panama's many dangerous snakes fell upon them in a suffocating stranglehold, they could cut it off with the machete.

I don't know where it came from, but an old and not very skillfully carved walking cane has a removable handle which, when separated, reveals a stiletto about ten inches long. My grandparents always warned me to leave it be, because the tip was dipped in poison, they said. I don't know if that's true, but I don't fool around with it much, clumsy as I am.

My grandfather's old footstool is there, upstairs. It's something he built, brown wood paneling sides with black claw feet and a homemade brown cushion on the lid. The top opens and inside was a wonderland he would let me pick through now and then. Old pocket watches, broken Zippo lighters, bullets of every imaginable caliber. Feathers, turquoise and silver. There were cigarette papers, tobacco tins and a couple of old pipes. Even today when I open that stool, the smells of tobacco drifts out like a cloud of memory.

There's an Edison Amberola, the old cylinder-type phonograph. When I was a kid, it was a great delight for my grandmother to wind it up with the handle on the side and lower the arm that held the reed needle to the cylinder. Tinny music would play from the front of the Amberola. It was the one antique I always begged my grandmother to leave to me. She got rid of many others in her later years, for reasons unknown, but kept the Edison for me.

An old black Derby, frayed at the edge of the brim, was my great-grandfather's on my grandmother's side, if I recall correctly. He must have had a small head, because if I try to wear it, it sits on my skull comically. Great-grandpa Rogers was gone before I was born, but my great-uncle, Luther Rogers, painted portraits of the old man and great-grandma Rogers. They hung in the living room most of my life, but are mysteriously missing now. I wish I knew where they were.

Beads are everywhere. And river cane to make baskets. Boxes of beads, old coffee cans of beads, cake tins of beads, beads in Tupperware containers, beads still on their strings from the factory, purchased in bulk. There is river cane, thin strips coiled in tight loops, lying bundled like a witch's broom, in natural beige or dyed red and black. Elements of art, left behind when the makers joined the Creator, the art they were intended to become unfulfilled.

A framed painting of a vase with red roses, which my grandmother did early in her life. On the back, she penned, "Alpha and Omega," and it took me some time to realize that the title of this painting did not refer to the subject, but rather her decision that it would be the first and the last painting she would ever attempt.

There is a blowgun, a spear, bow and arrow, *atlatl*, a U.S. Cavalry sword and a Spanish sword. There are tools everywhere, too. Hand planes, brace and bits, saws, squares, compasses, a slide rule, other tools I can't begin to fathom the purpose of. They are in the wood shed, which was my grandfather's last standing workshop among several, but many have slipped into the house over the years, into the corners of closets, into kitchen cabinets and drawers, into the bathroom, under the bed. They are black or rusty, most well-worn and well-used. They seem to have lives of their own in their slinking movements, slow and imperceptible. They are seldom where I remember them being when I need one, and often show up in the most unlikely of places that I *know* I did not put them in. Stanley No. 8s turn up in clothes closets, spoke shaves in dresser drawers and drill bits in silverware cabinets. Mysterious, very mysterious.

It's difficult to move such things from one place to another without becoming enamored of them. In a small cardboard box are tiny, delicate teacups I can't guess the age of; in another, silverware with the family name on the handles, hinting at some forgotten prosperity in the lineage. Old suitcases are full of photographs. I open brittle leather lids and the faces stare out at me in grayscale singularity. Some of them I know, some I can guess about, many I haven't a clue. There are people, family, friends, passersby in the crafts shop my grandparents operated. There are dogs, cats and horses, and I know some of them are Sookie, Crazy Cat, Prissy and Bootsie. Sometimes I find myself in grayscale in an old suitcase, an infant in a crib, a bespectacled toddler holding myself upright at the marble coffee table that used to be in the living room, a chubby pre-adolescent astride a Shetland pony named Nancy. When I am feeling lost I look inside old suitcases to find myself again.

Bibles abound, huge ones which make me groan to lift them, hardback-sized ones with spidered spines, miniature ones in red, brown and yellow, in King James or Modern English. Correspondences from when my grandfather was chief fill a box, discussions with Philadelphia, Miss., Washington, D.C. and Baton Rouge over a new school, health services, sovereignty and museum pieces. There are pocketknives, most broken, nearly every place I look.

But I put them aside, and work some detail molding back into the living room, along the wainscot, near the stair alcove, at the entrance to the kitchen. By nightfall I grow weary and hungry. I pull out a small black iron skillet, remembering it belonged to Delphine, my great-grandmother. It is well-seasoned, jet-black and with a pleasant sheen, and cooks eggs like magic. Watching my eggs fry in it, bubbling and sizzling, leaping now and then at an edge as a bubble of oil pops, I think that this whole house and its contents are like that. Well-seasoned. Nurtured and cared for.

It's a simple place, really. Built by poor Indians in a time when there was nothing much here but poverty and prejudice. There's nothing grand or resplendent about it. Just a little cottage by the bayou, short of space at times, with simple lines and rough-hewn bones. But like an open suitcase, a cushioned footstool, a cigar box, this old house accumulated the mementos of its occupants over the decades, held them close and cherished. It is a humble home, its contents trivial in passing, but treasures within a pirate's sea chest to me.

A little detail molding, here and there, but it seems to grow, the house does. It seems to draw a breath, as if given air, seems to sigh in relief, as if administered medication. When I touch the things stored in boxes and old footstools, we handle them together, reliving memories I never shared.

Oh! Bobwhite!

Then there are the guns.

In the moving and packing and cleaning, I found the little gun in a corner of a room, with a few cousins. Leaning in a corner like a clutch of old men, some drunk but most just aged and staggering under the weight of forgetfulness. All I could feel from them was shame.

I dug out the little shotgun first, caked with dust, and my heart sank at the ocher hue of the barrel. Next came a pair of old twenty-twos, a Winchester and a Remington, both single-shot bolt actions; then a bolt four-ten shotgun; pulling up the rear, a hammered twelve-gauge side-by-side. Family lore has it that it killed three men, all by the hands of my ancestors. My father referred to it as Mankiller, and had last used it to dispatch the neighbor's chickens that had grown fond of my father's fishing worm beds in the back yard.

In the workshop, I scrutinized the little crack-barrel four-ten with regret. My grandfather gave it to me. It was his brother's. Marked "Volunteer" it was probably of Iver Johnson manufacture. Maybe a Savage. Certainly it was very old, like the rest of them.

When had I last handled it? Probably when I moved into my grandmother's house, an inheritance stretching back some 160 years. The house was built by my great-great-great uncle, an Indian chief, and had remained in the family.

A decade earlier, I fled the remains of a broken life and taken refuge in that house, and the old guns came with me. They sat there, forgotten, until that day I sifted through the flotsam and jetsam of the past to find them leaning in a corner like weary, battle-worn soldiers.

My grandfather stood on the porch of that same house when he gave me the four-ten. I was twelve. I was given a BB gun when I was eight, a Benjamin pellet rifle when I was ten and the little four-ten followed. I was afraid of it, and he was mightily disappointed that I didn't have the courage to pull the trigger. He would go to his Creator before I found the will to fire the first round, and learned it wasn't nearly as intimidating or loud as I feared.

Steel wool and gun oil relieved it of rust, and stock oil revived the walnut. Restoring the cold bluing is a long process and requires great patience, but retribution was due.

Not long after I learned to shoot it, my father donated a worn carpenter's belt and bag to my forays afield. "Head out to the cane fields," he said. Though I had never known him to hunt, a devout fisherman by all I knew of him, he spoke with convincing authority. "Walk the ditch banks and the fence rows. You'll scare up some quail out there, I'll bet."

No dog, but I didn't know anything about dogs and bird hunting then. I tucked away his tutelage and set out, out into a world where it was still safe to let a fourteen-year-old boy loose with a shotgun and an old carpenter's pouch in search of quail in the sugar cane fields of south Louisiana. I was addicted after the first adventure! Right as rain, there were quail out there, Gentleman Bob, as Havilah Babcock called him. The first covey erupted at my feet when I stepped into it, and the great explosion of deafening wings and swarming birds nearly made me run away. I didn't even fire.

But there were more coveys and before long I learned to pick a bird rather than try to shoot all of them at once with a single-shot gun. Not much longer than that I was bringing home a dozen birds every trip, which my mother would smother down in onions and gravy and serve over rice.

Now and then I'd run into a farmer, and he'd tell me the locations of a few respectable communities of bobwhites to plunder. Usually he'd send me home with a few ears of fresh corn or turnips. Even if I never saw him, sitting on his tractor in the distance, to be sure he saw me. If I were handling my gun in an unsafe way, or shot a mocking bird, my father would know it before I got home. That was my world, my era, back when I shouldered that little four-ten.

Bluing the gun took days. In between sessions, I started talking up quail hunting with my buddies who roam afield.

"There's very few quail left," they told me, and my heart sank lower into my chest. "Been gone for years."

I couldn't fathom it. I turned to the great realm of cyberspace to verify the awful truth: Bob was mostly gone, had been in steady decline since the 1980s. New farming practices and a preponderance of fire ants, bobcats and coyotes, among other predators, had done the little gentleman in.

It was unthinkable. What is the South without Bob? As empty as a Jack Daniels bottle turned on end. As silent as a burned-out plantation home. As lonely as an elderly statesman, the landed gentry, holed up in a rest home.

After I outgrew the little four-ten, thinking I would venture into waterfowl, I acquired a Savage Fox in sixteen gauge. A beautiful old side-by-side, but I didn't make it to the duck blind until my twenties, where I learned that sitting idle for hours in thirty-degree weather was not for me. Besides, where was the explosive flight at my feet? The drumming wings? Where, after all, was Bob?

There was no pitting in the metal of the little shotgun, and I was glad of that. It was choked full, and belatedly I realized my adequate marksmanship had been cultivated by shooting wild exploding quail with a little shotgun that might as well have been a rifle at close range. By the time I hit my adolescence, though, with an eight-cylinder Mustang and girls bounding all over high school, the hunting diminished, then stopped altogether. My father's addiction to fishing, particularly bull-nosed bream on the fly rod, became my own. By the time I was in my early twenties, the guns were put away or sold.

Dismissing college, I took a job with a newspaper in town and started a career that filled me with interest in politics and government. I moved to the city, found it was not to my liking, and came home. I made a stint in radio news, but returned to my first love, the broad-sheet press. I married, became a father, and divorced, fleeing to my grandmother's house on the reservation. My grandparents left this world, and my father followed. Long chains of events, long roads between that last quail hunt and finding old soldiers in a corner of the junk room.

In that time, Bob had departed, too. Now mostly found on hunting refuges for hundreds of dollars a day, or crowded public wildlife management areas.

The little four-ten, and all its kin, revived beautifully. I took a box of two-and-a-half inch shells to the bayouside and fired off a few rounds, and the slight recoil and the smoke and the oil conjured me back to my days with Bob. They say quail were thick as mosquitoes in the South before I was born. Now he's scarce as hen's teeth.

The few land owners I spoke to cast their eyes down, stuck their hands in their pockets and kicked at the dirt sheepishly.

"You know," they said. "Lawsuits, insurance and all that. You understand."

I understood. No place for quail in this New South. No place for little four-ten shotguns. No place for a man to follow the boy he once was along a fence row or ditch bank. The old haunts swarm with four-wheelers now, not Bob in frantic flight. I wander anyway to some of the public places, and listen. It's not silent, but it might as well be. There's no familiarity to it in the absence of the shrill call: *Bob-WHITE! Bob-WHITE!* I miss him as much as I do my own blood.

But one fall day, the guns oiled and safely tucked away with remembrance, I loaded my wooden pirogue into the back of the truck, searching for out-of-the-way bayous or borrow pits or ponds to fly fish. Out behind a vast woodland along an old dirt road, I stopped to survey a wet spot through the trees. As I walked back, I stopped dead in my tracks.

Illusion, I thought. A trick of time. But there it was again. And again.

Bob-WHITE! Bob-WHITE!

I smiled to myself, and the boy that once was smiled back.

Yet so far as legacy goes that part of the South is gone. Relegated to history books and memory. The gentleman's bird, the little statesman, only found in abundance near the pens where he was raised, or the public lands where he struggles to maintain a foothold.

Remnants of Bob, here and there, hither and yon. Like a pair of magnolias standing roadside at the entrance of a long-vanished plantation, or a rusting and rotting sugar mill in a thicket of Chinese tallow, or a dried-up marsh and silted bayou, Bob is a vestige of a South that has folded itself up and withered. Fast retreating the way of memory.

My South is a much, much lonelier place without him at every turn. Too bereft of his melody. Far and away darkened by his near-absence.

And of course there are the rods. Many of them. Lengths, weights, purposes all differ. At the heart of this cadre of fly rods are the bamboo.

What raises bamboo rods above all others, to those who suffer them and suffer admiration for them, remains mysterious. Like wooden boats, there is appreciation of the craft, but that's only the start of it. In the same way a wooden boat feels warmer, more inviting and secure, the bamboo fly rod feels more natural in the hand. A better fit. There are physical properties espoused by champions of these rods, their sensitivity, the feel of a fish unlike any graphite rod can offer, but this is merely icing on an already delicious cake.

They demand from me patience and synchronicity, but offer in reward elation and insight. An entire line will probably never shoot from the tip of any rod in my hand, for I'm simply not that great at casting. Some of these rods may be misfits, some may be bullies, some graceful sprites, but each is a connection to an art and saturation within the fishing that is so integral in a life. Among those who do not understand fly fishing in general and bamboo in particular always comes the query, "How many fly rods do you need?" in amazement at my collection, humble as it is. It is difficult to explain the personalities of each rod in the rack to the uninitiated, and even among those who are familiar with the nuances of modern rods there are often blank stares when the subject of bamboo rises.

It's all a matter of choice and preference, of course, and the choice for me is very often but not exclusively bamboo. Never would I fish with another angler and express even the slightest disdain for his tackle. A fellow fisherman, regardless of the tools used, who is gentle, patient, cognizant of conservation and respectful of his partner, is a welcome companion. What we share is communal; our only difference is the path we take to divinity. But isn't that the way of all individual lives? The bamboo rod came as a surprise to me. In a lifetime spent tethered to a lifeline of water, the separation from those who do not have water behind their eyes was always clear. The fly rod and spin tackle were always part of my childhood, but the long wand was put aside during my teenage years and not picked up again for two decades. That first season was spent relearning most of the things my father had taught me, finding rhythm again, and learning to hear. The first cane to come into my hands was a Montague Splitswitch, a combo rod that could be used for fly or spin fishing. Long, heavy and similar in action to a piece of firewood, the Splitswitch lit the fire of cane nonetheless. The music of the fly rod took on new movements, different arrangements, and the things bamboo said to me were more lyrical, glowing with warmth. There is symmetry and convergence. There is saturation and immersion.

In fact, I have grown to dislike the trend of featherweight rods. I like a little heft to my rods, I like to feel them in my hand. No, I'm not talking broomsticks. But a rod so slight as to hardly make itself known to my hand is too light. Give just a little substance, just a little meaning in a rod.

Today's bamboo rods are in most ways far superior to those of the past, but owe much to the makers of those golden years. While new tapers are constantly being developed, the tried-and-true remains the cornerstone of the rod maker's craft. New adhesives, hardware and tools have elevated the bamboo fly rod to new heights, but the classic rods of the past are like wise old ancestors, aloof and self-satisfied. Commanding what some consider princely prices, the modern rods represent the craftsman's dedication, time and careful scrutiny to his art. There is no price applicable to this. They are not turning out thousands of rods a year like those that came out of the Granger and Heddon shops. The price tag of a bamboo rod by a modern maker stands as testament to the finest in craftsmanship and dedication.

It's my father's curse, all this talk of guns and rods and wildness.

"Give a man a fish or a quail and you feed him for a day. Give a man a fly rod, a shotgun and a bird dog and he won't amount to a damn," someone said.

I'm wondering if my father knew he cursed me. Put a hex on me that I'll never, ever shake.

I'm desiccated. I'm drying out. I can't sleep right. I sleep *all* night, but I don't feel rested; the only place I can sit calmly is at the office, and I suspect that's because of the psychological shackles and the dumbing-down of the fluorescent lights. At home I can be sitting in my chair and, without warning, suddenly leap up, almost leaving my skin behind, and race for the bayou behind the house with the dog. I can't fish it, the time is wrong, but being near it is mildly reassuring.

It's tough going through life as a prisoner. A prisoner to all things that keep me away from water. Not even just water exclusively. Just...the great wide open. Out there. Far and away.

Ah, I'm ruined. So miserably disturbed. It's all my father's fault. He led me out to the lake and set me loose in the fields.

Did he intend it? No, of course not. My father had great expectations for me. He gave me the most sage advice any parent could ever offer. He said, "Boy, I don't give a damn what you do, just as long as you get rich."

But somehow he didn't see the contradiction in his actions: on the one hand urging me toward higher education and a career in some six-digit salaried position...and then placing a burgundy, willowy six-weight fiberglass fly rod in my hand when I was old enough to competently cast it without snatching off either of our ears with a hook.

I'm surprised he didn't realize what he had done, really. He was greatly disappointed in me after high school when I spent a month in college and promptly decided that dormitories and journalism professors who had never stepped into a newspaper in their lives offered me nothing but lost time afield. Yet he signed off for me to acquire a Savage Fox sixteen-gauge to go find quail when I was old enough to be trusted not to blow my dang-fool head off with it.

Mamas, don't let your babies grow up to be outdoorsmen. It's kinda like Harry Middleton wrote, when at twelve-years-old he asked his grandfather to teach him to fly fish. His grandfather wailed and fretted, vowing that never, ever would he corrupt the boy by doing such a horrid, hateful thing.

Nick Stouff also doled out his wisdom along with fly rods and shotguns, without recognizing the dichotomy. No cognizance of the disparity. I'm sure, if he had his way, he would never have put such a *gris-gris* on me. Oh, he'd have much druthered to have a doctor in the family, I suppose. A lawyer, or at least a good veterinarian. The idea of making a living as a writer escaped him. Come to think of it, I've been at it thirty years now, and it escapes me, too.

My father was a good man. He would not have condemned me to gazing through the glass slits of the concrete bunker of the newspaper at the sky and the few trees I can see; he wouldn't have dreamed of sending me off to city council meetings at six in the evening, when I could be taking advantage of the long summer hours to tempt stump-knocker bluegill with a carefully tied fly at dusk; or in the shorter, auburn light of winter, searching for quail in some cane or corn field or pasture near the Rez.

I wonder if what my father intended was for me to get well-off enough to go "out there" anytime I wanted; certainly it can be said that I failed at comprehending his instruction. But being the victim in this debacle, I make a plea for misdirection, as well as beg forgiveness on behalf of the old man: he didn't realize what he was doing to me, so neither of us can be held accountable.

My adopted brother gave a part of Dad's eulogy at the funeral. He spoke of how our dad reminded him so much of his true father who passed away years before.

"I can imagine the two of them meeting up there," he said.

"The one says to the other, 'Thanks for taking care of that boy all these years.' And the other replies, 'No problem. So...how's the fishing?'"

Testament to a man who figured it all out, and expected the Hereafter to be as it should be. Somehow, I missed a nuance of merging the two ideals: fiscal security with being far and away. I don't know. But I was hooked when I was three or four and we'd be out in the boat and owls would perch nearby in the cypress trees and call, *Who? Who? Who?*

He taught me to say, "It's just me and Daddy!" and, remarkably, the owls would fall silent, satisfied with the answer.

Maybe I missed a chapter in the lesson on "the good life" but I was simpleton enough to believe that the best life was paddling through *Co'ktangi* when rain came, and if there was a bit of a surface film on the water the falling droplets would create thousands of bubbles that stayed for long, beautiful, translucent minutes; the covey of quail erupting at my feet from browned corn stubble in a morning misted like the whole world had just been born; fleeing a thunderstorm in a tiny wooden bateau when the lake stood up on its hind legs, and the swells were so high that, between them, we could see only sky—the only time I ever saw fear etched on my father's face.

Who's to know? I'd like to think that he'd be proud I can now cast a five-weight fly rod approaching seventy or so feet. That I shot at least three clays out of every four with a side-by-side four-ten not long ago. He'd likely be disappointed in my efforts to save for my retirement, something he was diligent about, and frown and shake his head at how close my checkbook consistently skirts the edge of disaster.

"One day, standing in a river with my fly rod, I'll have the courage to admit my life," author Jim Harrison said. Maybe, one day on Sawmill Bayou or far, far back at the end of a dark canal off *Co'ktangi*, or somewhere in the Rockies, I'll uncover the magic to make sense of mine. Perhaps my father will send an owl to comfort me. The bird will perch in a tree, great yellow eyes staring unblinking, and inquire, *Who? Who? Who?* I'll give the same answer I did all those many, many years ago: *Just me and Daddy.*

And maybe then I'll find that, as he intended, I am rich after all.

Study to Be Quiet

And the down-turn of his wrist
When the flies drop in the stream;
A man who does not exist,
A man who is but a dream;
And cried, 'Before I am old
I shall have written him one
poem maybe as cold
And passionate as the dawn.'
–Yeats, "The Fisherman"

If I compose anything in this life, through words or—far less likely given my complete lack of ear—music, it can never compare with the compositions I find out there. Far and away.

This angling passion has led me on journeys I could not have imagined as a wee lad, barely old enough to hold an old fiberglass spin cast rod with a green Johnson Century reel. I could barely hold it, since my arms were poking out from my sides around the orange life preserver I had to wear until I learned to swim, which was an iffy proposition since I was born with problematic ears prone to infection. Perhaps the damage to my ears, and the surgeries before I was two, hobbled whatever instinct for music I might have inherited from my father's side of the family, almost all of them musicians to one degree or another.

But my umbilical to water has towed me far into the Rockies of Montana; Elkmont, Tremont and the Little Pigeon River in Tennessee; and countless waters here in Louisiana.

What Thoreau said, about men going fishing without realizing it isn't fish they are after, didn't ring true for me until I was well into my adult life. Now, with fewer years ahead than there are behind, I try my best to express in conversation and on these pages that my fishing is in itself a means to an end. Solace, companionship of true friends, wild water, trees, four-footed observers, all are the true catches of the day.

I didn't understand until after he was gone that my father was that way. Certainly food for the table was important, but there was a man who was happiest on the water. I know it now, though it took the accumulation of years on the dusty shelves of my memory for me to discern that truth.

He was adamant about silence, supposedly to not scare the

fish, but now I know he demanded it so that the spell would not be broken. Study to be quiet, Thessalonians advises. My father was teaching me reverence for all things wondrous; as we drifted between stunningly old and beautiful cypress trees, paddling an old wooden boat through backwater sloughs and hidden lakes, he tethered me to sun and air and water and sky.

Then came a time where I touched no water except that in the bath or the kitchen sink for almost a decade, and those years I can confidently say were the worst of my life. When finally I returned to grace he was gone, and I believe that when his spirit left his body he asked heaven to hold on just a moment; he drifted across cane fields and cypress stands to the ancient worship place at *Co'ktangi*, in the night, hovered there for a time, ethereal, silent. Only then did he continue, only then did he believe his days in this world were done.

If I compose anything more in the days remaining to me, it will never convey the way my father and I are linked by water.

People ask me, "Why do you fish?" and I say I fish to get away from it all, but I think I'm lying. I think I fish because I'm seeking something. A bit of wild, silver magic I hadn't realized I was searching for until it was gone. I'm slowly learning the words again. They are not whispered by tongues, scribed on paper; rather they are enunciated by waves lapping against lake shores, by green needles rubbing each other in a spring breeze, but most of all, by quiet.

Because you can't go there and be loud and raucous. Not if you expect the magic to stay rather than shrink away in dismay. The fish don't really care how loud you are, but the very thing you're after out there, the thing that sends you driving hundreds of miles and throwing yourself headlong off the side of a safe, mapped road into a thicket of trees where you can hear laughing water, or deep into a blackwater canal...that thing despises riot and turbulence and noise.

I'd like to believe my father is out there, in the water, in the air, in the trees with me. In fact, I guess I do, because despite my Baptist upbringing, I still think all my relations are here, with me, not in the clouds playing harps or surrounded by some disembodied white light. They are in the breeze, along the horizon, mingling with the dawn. I'd like to think of him as part of all this because that's the way we believed before the Great Sadness.

And if I live my life with sanctity, I'd like to follow my father. Into the ethereal, into the Great Mystery. I'd be no happier than if someone drops my old, frail and dead body into a river and lets me become what I've always been: water. A part of something ceaseless in movement, enveloping in love and permeating into the very heart of the earth. At last, then, I'll have composed something that will be worth knowing.

Vanished

Like the Stanley planes moving here and there, or old carved pipes in tobacco-musty footstools, I feel like I'm vanishing sometimes too. In the same way that if that stool remained closed for years, decades, its contents would vanish. In that same way that the home of Chitimacha is vanishing. Someday, one fine twilight eve, I think I might vanish without knowing it.

My grandfather knew how. I think my father might have known, too, how to paddle down a winding slough in the back of Peach Coulee and, in some way, vanish at least from the here-and-now. He didn't share that knowledge with me, if he did possess it. My grandfather didn't either, but he had a key. For a man nearly crippled by polio and who walked with a limp and never swiftly, he could appear from nowhere, and be gone from sight if you turned away for just an instant.

Someone told me I'm like Billy Pilgrim in Kurt Vonnegut's *Slaughterhouse Five*, who could unstick himself in time. Perhaps that's also why maps have fascinated me since I was old enough to unfold one and lay it on the floor, tracing the lines of borders and roads and rivers with a forefinger that has grown and aged over the decades, but still loves following lines on maps. I cannot go where my grandfather and perhaps my father went, at the back end of dark canals or in the shade of a low-hanging, light-blocking oak branch, but I think my spirit has been making ready to vanish for a long, long time. How can someone so entwined with the water not vanish with it?

From the first days of looking in wonder at maps, red tennis-shoed feet waving in the air, brow furrowed over names I could scarcely pronounce my soul was making ready to vanish. I see hints of it throughout the house, signs of making ready to disappear, in things I have no need of otherwise. There are three compasses in the house, ranging from a tiny, quarter-sized one on a key chain to a cheap plastic job from a department store to an ornate brass nautical model in a walnut box I bought at a wooden boat show because I heard sea wind and smelled salt air when I picked it up. The key chain was a gift from one wanderer to another; I remember vividly walking through the sporting goods aisle of a department store, throwing into my basket a few fly rod poppers, some fly leaders...and a cheap plastic compass. I go few places in this life that I need a compass. But off the edge of the map, where there be dragons...

The signs of my vanishing are everywhere. I bought a good hunting knife in a sheath at a gun show here in town five years ago, though I don't need one. I carry a pocket knife when I'm outdoors and I have a fillet knife when I need to clean fish...but I have no use for a hunting knife with a long blade. Yet it calls me sometimes when I have not unsheathed it in too long; it speaks with a cold, steel voice and I take it to the shop and hone its edge sharp again. It seems to long for buckskin fringe and beads. But then it goes back in its sheath, to await the vanishing. I wonder if there are more dangers along the way, and I think sometimes I will acquire an old Fox double-barrel shotgun, or a Winchester lever-action rifle, but I shake myself and resist. Try to stay here. Try not to think of the edge of the map...

Where am I going? I don't know. But it is inevitable, I think. Tomorrow. Next week. A half-century from now. Backward or forward. Who knows? A butane-powered torch, no bigger than a disposable lighter, in my tackle bag, for fire. There's a flashlight that runs for a hundred hours; a bag of fire sticks; maps and maps and maps and more maps. They accumulate at their edges, you see. I buy a map and I wonder what is beyond its edge, so I find another that takes up at the edge where the previous left off... then another, and before I know it I have traveled across Harry Middleton's trout on Starlight Creek in the Ozarks, I have gone through the Grand Banks, to Hemingway's Africa and the Far East when it was a mysterious, fabled place and before I know it, I've circled the globe and gone from pole to pole, and I am back at the edge of the first map I started with.

My best friend and I took off in my little boat to *Co'ktangi* one spring Saturday morning, and my father left simultaneously in his little boat. We saw him winding down Sawmill Bayou and followed, sure he would point out—willingly or not—where we might find the fish. But do you know, we paddled the entire length of that backwater canal and never found him, and when we returned to the mouth of the bayou, he was fishing the edge of the cove just beyond? With a live well full of fish, too. We never even heard a single splash.

But they never taught me those magics, never gave me those keys. In the same way that my mother's people would not teach me French, so it was with the *Siti imaxa*. It had been made an embarrassment. It was beaten out of them at Carlisle School. It was prayed out of them in wooden pews and it was ridiculed from them on oil platforms and carbon black plants. Can anyone blame them for not passing it on to their children?

I wish they had. I would endure all they did and more to know where those keys are. What's on the edge of the maps that don't go completely around the world. In the places where there are dragons.

But one day I'll know. A little mottled-brown bird might tell me. Or a song in the swamp. Or maybe I'll just vanish all on my own, and the only thing that will save me from falling off the edge of the world will be my cheap plastic department store compass, a talisman, charged with the power of sheer belief; maybe the only light I'll find in some dark, damp forest where yellow eyes stare out from the thick blackness will be my little hundred-hour flashlight, or a fire lit with my butane torch. I'd like to know what's in the spots you can never quite see beneath bridges; where the shadows go when they shrink into nothingness in the noonday sun. I think my ancestors are in there, all of them killed by small pox blankets and gunshots and knives in the dark. They're all in those little dark places under blades of grass and behind thickets of briar. Sometime they rustle the brush as I pass to get my attention, to get me to notice them.

I might vanish some twilight eve. Don't worry if I do. I'll be fine. I've been preparing for it all my life, without even knowing it.

Time was nobody fished Lake Fausse Point and *Co'ktangi* much. Just me, my dad and a few locals. But the state built a big park on the north end of the lake, with cabins for rent, a boat landing and recreational facilities. There's even talk of another such park, but more elaborate, at Eagle Point on the western shore of the lake. The personal watercraft are abundant. When I was growing up, dad and I rarely encountered another vessel. Now the state is paving the levee road as a hurricane evacuation route, also making access to the lake much easier. I don't really know why. The fishing is always good but the catching is usually pretty dismal.

It may have been one day when I was about ten that folks outside our local area started taking an interest in these waters, and it might have been the fault of my father and I. We were coming down the levee road after a great fishing trip. Near the exit back to blacktop, the Louisiana Department of Wildlife and Fisheries had set up a checkpoint.

The agent was friendly. "We're not looking to cite anyone," he said. "We just want to get an idea what the fishery is like down here."

Dad obliged by lifting the bench seats of the old wooden bateau. The live well was beneath, and it was nearly full of bluegill, more than a hundred of them, headed for our freezer.

The agent's eyes grew pan-sized. Dad said, "We had a fair day."

It was a few years later that more people started coming to Lake Fausse Point and development of the recreational facilities began. Then we began to have to contend with game wardens persistently inspecting creels which were far, far less than in my youth. The pressure of increased numbers of anglers, recreational vessel traffic and the constant sedimentation of the lake has taken a terrible toll.

But I return there when I can, not because the fishing is phenomenal by any stretch of the imagination. In fact, it's grown pretty bleak in recent years with all the environmental changes the lake has suffered. But I was born there, in a way. A father who had absolutely no interest in sports certainly raised me there. In my absence from it for a decade, my spirit grew shallow, too. When at last I returned, I thought that the rest of my days would be spent exploring its diminishing body. The collecting sediment moves the lake bottom upward, the water rushes out, and margins between the thin places grow stronger. We are aging together, this old lake and I, approaching a certain mortality that neither of us can avoid. If I am to have a companion in death, I can think of none better.

During the waning years of a souring marriage, I fished little, constricted and forbidden. After it, I spent several years finding my way again, and seldom went to the water. Eventually I met Susan, knew I had found the one I had searched for so long, and about a year later I woke one morning with my eyes wide and glassy, pupils dilated.

"What's wrong?" she asked upon seeing me, the condition having persisted.

"Fishing," I said like a man in a dream.

"What?"

"*Fishing!*" I rasped, breathless, and giggled. It was upon me. The fever. The obsession. I was lost to it again, a goggle-eye on the end of my line years ago, decades before, pulling with irresistible force and brutish but graceful power.

Susan was a trooper. She deserves plenty of credit. She accepted this sudden change in my personality and lifestyle with a shrug. She fishes with me every season until the weather gets too hot, even going out in the boat on some bone-chilling days where we caught nary a fish, but we were *out there*.

The Way of Memory

My father's people called themselves *Siti imaxa*. Our word for the lake where we made our home was *Siti* and *imaxa* means roughly "those who live on" so the translation is "people of the many waters." Today this is pronounced Chitimacha.

We occupied what would become the State of Louisiana from west of present-day Lafayette to New Orleans, and from Baton Rouge to the Gulf of Mexico. The central "capital" of the nation was at *Tkasi'tunshki*, near Bayou Teche, close to the shores of *Siti*, which would be called by the Spanish explorers "Lake of the Chetimache" and also by the French, but they later referred to it as Grand Lake.

An early map of Louisiana reveals Grand Lake to have been a massive body of water stretching from St. Martinville to Morgan City, roughly eighty miles in a line from northwest to southeast. If this area had anything akin to the Great Lakes, this was it.

In 1927, the worst flooding ever in Louisiana's history wiped out thousands of homes and untold millions in real estate. Many people died. The U.S. Army Corps of Engineers, desperate to provide a safer environment for residents here, conceived and began construction of the Atchafalaya Basin Protection Levee. It took many years to complete, but once finished, it was intended to block the mighty Atchafalaya River Basin from overflowing into the residential and commercial areas below.

While the Corps' intentions were honest, the result was disastrous. Over the more than half-century since the levee was completed, the basin has filled with sediment trapped between the levees to the east and west of it, unable to complete its natural transit to the Gulf of Mexico. A 1973 topographic map of the same area shows the levee and the network of canals and ponds north of it that was once gargantuan Grand Lake. This map is thirty years old. Far less water would be visible on an updated map.

When I was but a lad, I could stand on the shell beach at Grand Lake and could not see across to the other side. In just the thirty years since, a line of willow trees has emerged. Grand Lake is dying, filling up with sediment diverted from the Mississippi River. Worse yet, the same thing happens on the west side of the levee. Lake Fausse Point and *Co'ktangi* are dying as well.

Looking at the historic map, it is easy to imagine thousands of my ancestors living along the shores of that magnificent lake. They built mounds of clam shell from the species *rangia* to keep their feet out of the mud. We fished here, built temple mounds here. One, on an island just off the coast, held a stepped pyramid shell mound, the base big as four football fields arranged into a square. This was mostly ravaged for the value of the shell early at the turn of the century, and the United States armed forces finished its destruction by using it for target practice during World War I.

The concept of home waters is indelible among anglers, and among non-anglers who are simply most content there. My life is inexorably linked to these waters, and as they slowly diminish over time, I feel they are aging in time with me. Together, *Siti* and I are approaching the end of our days.

Co'ktangi once ran four or five feet deep, but now at normal water range I am lucky to find two feet of water. Most places it is less than that. Lake Fausse Point averaged four to six feet deep; now it is often less than three. The earth is slowly swelling beneath it, pushing these ancestral waters aside and eventually dry land will emerge and the world of water that has sustained my people for eight thousand years will vanish.

To the north, Grand Lake is but a series of channels and canals, with a few small ponds struggling on. The Atchafalaya, the "long river" in the Choctaw tongue, carries much of its sediment to the bay, making the delta the only actively growing one on the continent. But the rest of the sediment filters into the basin, filling it up, and the water is again displaced.

The land continues to rise up, displacing the water, and soon my liquid world will vanish. When I look at that old map, I see a young man, in his prime, strong and healthy. Like photographs of me years ago. Like my nation. Once we numbered in the tens of thousands. Now we are grown thin, like the lake. The nation will survive, I suspect, but this old lake and I are thinning much more rapidly. In time, we will simply fade out of existence, our water displaced, and dry earth will cover our final resting place. To become the purple spots in someone else's eyes, someone who may remember us fondly.

The state has entered into intergovernmental agreements with federal agencies in an attempt to save the basin in its entirety, but I fear it may be too late for *Siti*. The millions of dollars necessary, even if acquired, may not be enough to resuscitate it. After the 2005 hurricane season and the billions in destruction, I fear that basin restoration has been moved to a distant back burner.

Now I spend as much time with it as I can. Like visiting the terminally ill. We sing dirges together, *Siti* and I. We share old memories, though like the old, our recollections are growing thin, and purple spots are dancing, dancing before our eyes.

Together, that old lake and I, we go the way of memory. This is the finality of the Great Sadness. When I say such a thing to most people, their eyes glaze over and the fluids in their brains make new connections. There is so much more, they say. There is family, there is progress, success, gain, accomplishment. There is wealth and fame, there is even love. Yet what remains undiscovered and incomprehensible to them is that love is exactly what torments me with the thinning, the aging of the two of us. Don't they realize that thousands of my ancestors lie beside its fading waters? They don't understand that for eight thousand years I have been here. When I drift along the lake and the sun catches the refraction of the water, convergences interact between time and legacy. Gnarled, sunken tree limbs are shadows under the surface, but they seem to me like skeletal fingers, reaching, pleading to be remembered, to no longer be forsaken as rubbish and offal.

I am at its bedside, holding its hand as the moments tick away toward the inevitable. Sometimes there is a wish, silent but resounding, that my own life will flicker first. To exist without it, no matter how short a time, would be to exist without spirit. To exist without love. The boats skim across it, fisherman cast lines into its heart, run traps and trotlines. There are camps along its margins, teens swim there. Hunters lurk its banks in search of ducks, squirrel, deer. But do they know its soul? They are like the intimates in my own life: existing on the periphery, but do they know what lies undiscovered deep within? Would they be surprised to find the essence of me is not some non-corporeal energy, not some misty spirit or glowing light, but an endless, timeless expanse of water?

I drift along its surface, letting it take me where stories are. I probe its depths, searching for creation in the details of demise. Each year, the mud below it is closer to the surface. Rising, displacing the water, pushing aside part of me. How to mourn it? It cannot be, unless you have waded the remnants of a shell mound and picked up pottery with adolescent toes, wiped the silt from it to reveal etched designs, fragments of paint, and thumbprints of its maker in the fired clay. Cannot, unless you have seen the bones of your ancestors lying atop the ground at its lapping edge, beside crumpled tin cans, discarded bottles and rotting cardboard. Simply cannot, unless you have known the love of it and for it.

There was a young Chitimacha maiden immortalized by poet James Smith in an 1851 issue of the *Planter's Banner* in Franklin, La., a forebear to the newspaper I work for today:
The Indian maid sat beside the gate
When the shadows of night were gath'ring late
Thick and black the clouds cluster'd fast around,
And the winds spoke from far with a hollow sound.
The maiden she asked with a downcast eye
For some drug that might calm her fever high.

"Here! here!" she said, "I fear it will break!"
And giving her wild, black locks a shake,
Her tawny hand on her brow she placed,
Which throbbed like the heart of the hare that is chased.
The drug was given, but there she sat—
That child of the wilderness—desolate!
One of the last of the ancient band,
Unto whom the God had first giv'n the land.
"Maid of the sad eye—lady in right—
Where in thy pain, sleepest thou to-night?
Who among those who thy heritage keep,
Will give thee thy nurture and couch to sleep?
Where wilt thou to-night thy sick rest take?"
She answered gently— "I sleep by the lake."
"Nay, maiden, nay; far is the lake,
And wildly the clouds in the bleak skies break.
Canst thou alone find thy night-way home?"
Mildly she said— "See the people come!"
Methought 'twas some couch, that object black,
On which they would carry the sick girl back;—
But no—neither couch nor litter had they;
There were two or three women and an old man grey,
And one wild-eyed boy walked beside a squaw,
With the bright forest glance of the Chitimachas;
For he felt not yet in his bosom brave—
That his doom was to be the white man's slave—
To lead in the land where his sires were chief—
A life without joy, except that 'tis brief—
To prowl about, though the lord in right,
Like a lean dog hounding for carrion at night!
I turned to the maid;—she her brother had ta'en,
A babe in her arms, but she staggered again!
So I sprang to her side and said, "On, no!
Thou art weak, thou art sick—thou must not go.
Rest thee to-night, (e)ve (?) will safe thee keep;
Thy couch shall be soft—thou shalt soundly sleep."
"Sleep," said the maiden, "I may not take:
I cannot sleep, save I sleep by the lake:
For low and soft there the ripples break—
If I hear not them, no sleep can I take;

And forever since I slept there when a child,
Its sad murmur calms this fever wild."
No words spake they, but they onward went—
Straight was the foot-print, the body bent;
They looked not up to the wild-tossed sky,
For forward and earthward turned was the eye.
Sad is thy heart, thou poor forest child!
Dark and bleak is the night and the path is wild!
Sadly she looked, and she said again
She would come if away passed not the pain.
The time went on—seven day were o'er,
And I marvel'd the maiden came no more;
So I went to the place where the wigwams stood,
To see how fared the sick child of the wood.
By an old dead thorn tree the mother sate,
With a cold, blank gaze—Disconsolate.
Gently and lowly I asked her to tell
How the maiden fared—was her fever well?
No word spake she, but she shook her head
So again I asked how the maiden sped.
"She sleeps," she said; "she hath now no pain;
The fever has pass'd—my child wakes not again.
Sees't thou yon mound, where the white shells rise—
Beneath that my heart and my daughter lies;
And I come here to listen the sad lake swell,
Because 'tis the sound she loved so well !"
They had buried her there, without prayer or knell
On the bank of the lake that she loved so well;
For when winds are high springs the cold wave's spray
O'er the Indian grave-mound of Granavoley;
And no more by the wood or the river we saw
The sad-eyed maid of the Chitimachas.

I stand at the lake shore knowing something no one who
came before me for eight thousand years could ever have known,
could ever have even imagined: that one day all this will be gone.
That all this is dying. My ancestors could not have conceived it,
could never have dreamed it in the blackest of their nightmares.

Here is what has been left for me to discover: there is finality.
There are endings, nothing is perpetual, nothing is eternal. When

the lake and the Atchafalaya Basin are gone, their bones will bleach white under the sun, and at last, the circle will be rent, slashed. A broken circle is incomplete, no longer a circle. That is when time ends. Sometimes the creel of home waters is full to the lid with sadnesses as well as joys.

Two: Waiting for Spring

When its hails, God wishes to put fish and clams and everything back into the bayou and into the lake. That is why the ice precipitates.

That old traveler asked the Indians, "Don't you have anything to eat?" The Indians asked the old man, "Why do you want to know that?" The old man told the Indians, "I ask you again; if you want anything, I shall put clams back into the lake." Then he caused it to hail. (Thus) he put fish and everything back into the water. Then the Indians had something to eat.

That is why the ice precipitates every now and then. It comes about in order to put fish back into the water for the people.
(Benjamin Paul, Chitimacha, American Philosophical Society recordings)

I fish where a boy named Ustupu was cursed by bad medicine, doomed to chase his six great hunting dogs across the heavens for eternity; where an old couple was turned into bears; where the devil *Neka sama* reaches out from the fire to snatch children into the hearth. I fish where three dozen villages and thirty thousand warriors thrived for eight millennia; where a huge snake was killed by many, many braves and the death throes and weight of its carcass formed Bayou Teche.

They built huts on the water's edge from palmetto fronds over dome-shaped frameworks of cottonwood bent into arches. Though deer, rabbit and other game were on the menu along with the fish, they apparently seldom ate crustaceans. Crawfish, after all, created the world when the Creator ordered him to go down into that sphere of water to bring up the land so that *Siti imaxa* might exist there. Nor would they take flounder from the saltwater marshes along the coast, for such a creature was surely sacred since both eyes faced upward toward the Creator.

Flounder notwithstanding, I wet-wade the shell reefs in Atchafalaya Bay with a modern seven-weight bamboo rod built by Harry Boyd of Winnsboro. Near where I hooked several rat reds and one bull that took me within a few feet of the reel's arbor and long minutes later spat back a gold bendback fly within as many feet of my rod tip, a similar reef towered. That stepped-pyramid mound my ancestors constructed from oyster and clam shell. The military bombed it into rubble for target practice in the early part of the twentieth century, but none of the fifty or sixty surviving Chitimacha were there to mourn it.

Over the last half-century, the oil industry sliced and diced the marsh into irregular rectangles, dismantling it a piece at a time. Dredges pulled the great clam and oyster reefs up and redeposited them in driveways, roadbeds and building foundations. While the basin filled up, the coast was vanishing.

Now and then I take the little wooden bateau, make a long voyage up the basin to Bayou Portage. Of the four sacred, powerful trees that marked the boundaries of the nation, the last grew there and it was certainly a cypress. It was known as the Raintree. In times of drought, Chitimacha would carefully and with great ceremony take limbs from it, say the words and sing the songs of our forefathers, the baptize them into the lake to bring rain. It grew there for centuries until the waterway—altered, diverted, and rerouted by the meddling hands of bureaucracy—undermined its roots and it toppled into the flow. The rain began almost immediately, and didn't stop for many months.

My old grandpa was adamant about most things in our oral tradition. No matter how fantastic or scoffed upon by non-Indians, and he was sure that the collapse of the Raintree caused the catastrophic flooding of that year, 1927.

Right as rain, he would nod, there in the cane break as we lunched. *Right as rain.*

The basin contracted and thinned after that, when fear of another flood prompted construction of the Atchafalaya Basin Protection Levee and strangled that ancestral lake into a gasping, lethargic web of channels. Later the oil industry would arrive with steel rigs and hard hats, cut pipeline and crew boat channels, breaking the marsh into dying segments. Sandbars dissect the basin, infested with Chinese tallow and other non-indigenous species.

My father and I chased largemouth when there was more water here. Six-pounders were common then, rod-twisting beasts that leaped and danced on their tails like native largemouth should, unlike the introduced Florida strains that are quickly eradicating indigenous populations. Mere brutes, those bass are behemoths without finesse. It appalls me that Louisiana spends oodles of money to eradicate invasive species such as hydrilla, but imports Florida largemouth deliberately.

Big Cats

Still groggy, I pulled on pants and slipped a shirt over a too-rotund body for a boy of twelve. There was just the barest hint of light through the windows of my bedroom. The twilight of dawn left the world blue-gray. Blue and white sneakers went on my feet and I grabbed the bag of snacks and soft drinks my mom packed for me Before I came into his life, dad never took a drink or so much as a cracker fishing with him, and he'd stay out there from dawn to dusk. The pitter-patter of little feet between the gunwales might not have changed his viewpoint much, but mom made sure I had sustenance for the long day ahead.

The boat was already out of the boat shed and hitched to the old Mercury Comet dad used as his work car. I rode with him to Bayou Teche, right behind our house, and he negotiated the car and trailer in an awkwardly small space between a large ditch and a derelict shotgun shack, watching out for a half-filled water well nearby. Once the boat was backed into the water, he'd push it out while I held the bowline, and we'd board.

It was a short trip to Lake Fausse Point from home. The old Mercury 110, a nine-point-eight horsepower engine of 1963 vintage, cranked without hesitation. I had learned early on to sit to the left of the forward bench seat in the bateau, since dad sat to the right so that he could manipulate the tiller arm of the outboard with his left arm and see clearly what was ahead of us.

Still yawning, I held the bowline tightly in my hand. I always was required to wear a life vest when the boat was in motion, but was allowed to take it off when he cut the engine. I noted carefully how he dodged floating debris; even if something was not from a distance clearly an obstacle he steered around it. Perhaps it was no more than a floating elephant ear, but he took no chances. The boat, build by his own hand in 1962, was strong and sturdy, but my father was cautious to a fault.

The old Mercury—for it was nearing fourteen years of age by then—hummed happily, and sent a spray to either side of the bateau's stern as we went. I loved that time of morning, even back then. So quiet and still, with just a faint hint of mist still hovering over the water and the sun just peeking over the trees to the east. From the time I was old enough to sit up straight without assistance, that boat had been my happy playground. That's not to suggest that I might have been deprived in other facets of toddlerhood. But in that boat I was happiest. When sufficient manual dexterity came to me, a rod was placed in my hands, and when I advanced a bit more, the box of worms was passed to me to deal with all on my own.

We went to the lake proper, finding a stand of trees knee-deep in the green-black water. Both our rods were identical, unknown fiberglass makes upon which were set Johnson Century reels loaded with eight-pound line. At the end of the monofilament was a small bobber, just large enough to stay afloat above the weight of a small Idaho spinner and size eight hook upon which an earthworm from dad's worm beds was impaled.

The spinner and worm combination is still perhaps the most deadly freshwater system I have ever fished. The gentle roll of the spinner's spoon creates an irresistible flash, and the wiggling worm sends fish over the edge of temptation. When they prefer their bait a bit more lively, dad would remove the bobber and pitch the combination like a spinner bait, working it carefully over brush and logs. I have probably caught more bass on an Idaho spinner and earthworm than anything else.

Once the engine fell silent, we changed spots in the boat, dad in the front so he could paddle easily. He would paddle us around the lake all day without complaint, guiding the boat with one hand and casting with the other. It didn't take long for us to fall upon a nest of big bream. Tucked between a circle of cypress knees, they ravaged the spinner and worm the instant it hit the water. Orange-breasted, green and silver, long goggle-eye, they came out quick and splashing.

My father chuckled and spoke to the fish he caught. "Come on in here, big fella, you might as well give it up," he'd say to one hand-sized perch. "Where you going, boy, you have to get in here with your brothers," he'd say to another. All the while chuckling happily, the nameless rod bending nicely, the Johnson reel sure and trusted. He caught two, perhaps three, to my one, pausing only to light a cigar or sacrifice another worm to the day. Perhaps this is why I still talk to my fish as they come to hand, and chuckle happily with each.

I threw my bobber, spinner and worm into the fray again, and it darted off like lightning. I set the hook as he taught me to do years and years before, expecting the jaunty, frantic pull of a big chinquapin on the other end. But the force that suddenly tugged back was overwhelming. I reared the rod back, and would have guessed I had hooked into a log, had not the line been rushing out of the circle of cypress knees toward deeper water.

Dad saw what was happening and said, "Hold on to him, boy! What the hell have you got there?"

Far as I knew, it was an underwater locomotive. "Let loose some drag," he said, and I spun the dial on the Johnson reel. The monster beneath the water shot off faster. Dad spun the boat around with his paddle so that my line barely cleared the bow.

"Tug at him," he said.

I did, and just then, the fish surfaced: slick and blue-gray, like the skies outside my window just a few hours earlier, the grandpappy of the Lake Fausse Point channel catfish rolled, showed us his belly, and was off again, leaving the Johnson screaming and myself terrorized.

Dad paddled frantically. "Hold onto him, that's enough catfish to eat for a month," he said. We chased the catfish into the deeper waters of the lake. All I could do was hold on, let him strip line, not even trying to reel. Once again he surfaced, splashed water across our bow like an enemy warship, and dove.

The fish made for a lone cypress far from the treeline, out in the deep water. Gnarled knees surrounded it.

"Lean on him, boy," dad said softly, still paddling like a madman. "Put some pressure on him."

"Take it!" I pleaded.

"You got him, just don't let go!"

I leaned on the fish, and he leaned back, bowing the rod like a slender willow branch.

"If he gets in there, we'll lose him," dad said, meaning the lone cypress tree and gauntlet of knees.

I thought he had gone daft. The fish we had glimpsed twice must have been bigger than me. He'd not even fit between the bench seats of the bateau. We'd have to gaff him and tow him home. But I leaned on him, felt the jerking in my white-knuckled hand through the rod handle as the catfish tried to shake away the hook.

But no force I knew of would stop him, and he made it to the trees. I felt a sudden lurch of effort, then my line went slack, the rod straightened and the Johnson fell quiet.

The big fish splashed around once between the cypress knees, and then all was silent.

My father looked over at the tree for a time, then turned to me and grinned.

"We'll call this 'the one that got away,'" he said with a grin.

I shakily asked him to hand me a soft drink and an oatmeal creme pie.

I sit in the front of the boat now. It's the same boat, built in 1962, two years before I was born. The paddles are there, but are only backup to the electric trolling motor dad started using when he got older. Small as the boat is, the little trolling motor moves it along nicely with only about twelve pounds of thrust.

From the front of the boat, looking aft, I sometimes get confused. I only sat there when the boat was under power, clad in my bulky orange life vest, holding the bowline. I am sitting in duality now. If I look aft, I expect to see him. But when I am sitting at the tiller of the engine, I expect to see myself forward. Yet in both glances, he should be there, in his proper place opposite me.

Perhaps this is why my father is almost always on my mind when I fish. The relics of father and son stretch beyond the passing of the former. Yet it confuses me when I sit alone in that old boat, fishing from the forward bench seat, guiding the trolling motor. With each bream or bass taken from the base of a cypress tree, I expect to hear words from where I am. A remark on the fish, its size, color. I say them to myself instead. When later in my life I watched myself on national television, catching cutthroat and rainbow trout in Montana, I had to laugh when I talked to the fish even then. Just like he did. Half the time, I don't even realize I'm doing so.

When my mother and I sat on her front porch, looking out over her zinnias and roses, remarking on their size, their color, and speaking of visitors, I was aware that the house is different now, replaced after Hurricane Andrew. The cypress bench was a

Mother's Day gift I made for her in my shop. The entire landscape of that childhood home is changed, but we still exist there. We are aware of the absences there as surely as I am in that wooden bateau. Change comes, sometimes it comes quickly, sometimes gradually. We deal with it as we may.

Forty-two years of life for a wooden bateau borders on miraculous, though it has survived so long because it has been cared for. I hope that I can pass it down to my son, and in turn that he will take care of it as well. Sometimes I fear taking it out, that a disaster is in the making. Yet boats are born to be on the water, and to confine it to dry land for the sake of safety is unthinkable. A tiger in a cage is only the shadow of a tiger.

This is how the Creator made the world. It's all in the details. My world was made with details of wooden boats, lake water and clam shell In the grip of winter, slower time and murky water, they still sustain me as I await spring.

Once, before he went to his Creator, I wrote a column about dad's little bateau.

"Boy, you really put one on me, didn't you?" he said when I saw him that evening. It wasn't a complaint, it wasn't an annoyance. It was his way. He was modest and humble at his essence, but secreted that humility behind a jocular veil of bravado.

Time and again, his influences I thought didn't stick come through in my life. We spent a large part of my adolescence disagreeing on most everything, and that lasted well into my twenties. I don't guess we were that unusual in that regard, but I am glad that our fences were mended before he left us. Still, those times haunt me, the waste of them. I absorb all the blame.

But I do think of him every day. I walk the land I grew up on, live in the house my grandparents lived in. He is everywhere, really. In every room, every square foot of the grass, every linear inch of the bayouside. Then, as now. His tools are in my workshop, Stanley planes and Disston hand saws; spokeshaves and draw knives, pocket knives and chisels. I can't pour a patch of epoxy without thinking of him. A pile of sawdust smells like him when he came into the house after working in his own shop all day. The grip of my favorite crosscut saw is darker than the rest of the wood handle. Darkened by the oils from his hands.

There's a nagging leak in the stern of the little boat. No surprise, really. It's forty-five years old. But I can't locate it, and I am reluctant to use it much until I eliminate it. That leak would have obsessed him. It would have been unthinkable that his boat leaked. The well-regarded lie that all wooden boats leak was coined by people who never owned a boat Nick Stouff built. Dad's boats did not leak, and if he were here, he'd have found and sealed that leak astern post-haste. I will find it. But I am not the boatsman he was, nor the builder. His blood is in its frames from a splinter or a knife edge, his sweat in the plywood, his enthusiasm and pride in the sheer.

When the pup's bounding around for my attention and I reach down to rub his ear, I know my father would have loved him. My father loved a good dog like few other things. He even liked cats.

He had a passion for horses. Like an Indian man should. We rode all the time when I was a boy, when we weren't fishing, of course. His quarter-horse, Tee-Boy, had a leather bridle adorned with silver and turquoise and abalone. An Indian man's horse should have no less. Tee-Boy wore it proudly, and though he was just a quarter horse trotting along the cane roads around Charenton, he seemed to carry his head a little higher to show his silver, his blue stones.

Make no mistake about it, my father was an Indian man. Most folks in Franklin didn't even know there was a reservation just ten miles away then. I was raised very sheltered, to be honest, and when I turned my back on what heritage had been handed down to me for nearly twenty years, his heart broke.

I shall never be the Indian man my father was. My father bristled at being asked "How much Indian are you?" and would inquire in return, "How much Pilgrim are you?"

"Only people in the country who gotta live by fractions," he'd complain, back when I listened to what he said. Understand, back then, there was no casino, no intergovernmental agreements, just shotgun houses and bad roads. He gave his "talks" as he called them in schools across the state. My godchild several years ago was studying Louisiana history in grade school and came across a photo of the old man in his textbook. He excitedly announced that he knew the chief, and the teacher didn't believe him. His mother had to call the school and inform a disappointingly skeptical educational system that, indeed, the boy knew Mr. Stouff well.

He was interviewed by journalists from across the globe, ar-chaeologists, anthropologists, researchers, ethnographers, you name it. He was an Indian man, remarkably, that people listened to. Except for me. For almost two decades, I didn't listen to a single word.

He was stubborn. Oh, how that man was stubborn! I come by my own obstinacy honestly, to be sure. We were stubborn in an-tithesis of each other, and locked horns until we avoided each other to avoid the clashes. Finally, I had the heart and courage to come back around, and in the last years of his life—heart failing, breathing shallow—it was like I had never been gone at all. That is a warrior and a chief. That is the way of kindness and dignity.

"Sit down a minute," he said as I was leaving his house one evening in December. So I sat. We talked. Nothing important. I don't even remember what topics. Small talk, mostly. The weather. The fishing. Whatever. Just visiting.

Two, three weeks later I stood at his coffin. He was in a dark blue suit and a white, crisp shirt, but there was no cloth necktie. Not on an Indian man. He wore an abalone bolo in the shape of an arrow, the shell set in silver. His hands were folded across his chest, and held an eagle feather. He was pale. So pale. He had been sick so long, but didn't suffer pain, at least. In the next world, I knew, his skin would be the earthen hue of an Indian man again. Even then, as I stood by his coffin, he was joyous, learning songs not sung on this earth for a hundred years.

I keep his medicine bag close by. It's a small leather satchel, with buckskin fringe, no bigger than a thick trade paperback book. I don't know what's in it because it's *his* medicine bag. I have never opened it. It's full of the things that made him strong, kept him close to the water and protected him from the bad in the world. I can't possess his magic, but I can borrow from it be-cause the same blood flows in my veins.

Someday I'll have my own. Full of the things that strengthen and protect me. I haven't started to collect it. I'm a little lost over it, because I don't know what should be in there. He died before he could teach me. I thought of putting it in his coffin with him, but he had his abalone bolo tie on and the eagle feath-er in his hands, both full of power, and when I thought of pla-cing the bag at his side, the resonance of a tuning fork spoke in a deep voice slightly tinged with the accent of a man raised in

Texas:

Keep it. I know the way.

The look on his face, as he fished Bayou Teche in the last days of his health, the sadness in them, reappeared and manifested itself. When he was too old to go to the water, too sick with emphysema and congestive heart disease, he began to dry out. I could see it: a Chitimacha man can't be away from the water. He'll dry out. He turned pale, and the Indian man became brittle. He looked less like an Indian man than he did a white man near his death, so dry was he.

I let myself imagine what that bag contains sometimes. Almost assuredly alligator teeth, probably crowned with silver. Alligators are powerful, and in a tooth that power can be borrowed, made your own. I'll bet there is sage and sweetgrass in there, cedar and tobacco, but it's probably so dry I'll never catch the scent of it.

Perhaps there's a piece of flint, so if he ever found himself in a dark place off the edge of a map he could strike a spark off the blade of his knife and bring fire. I'll bet there's a fish hook in there, not for catching, but for remembering.

It's too small. It can't hold all the things I imagine if I think with the non-indigenous part of me. But the Indian man knows that the whole universe could fit in that bag, because so-called "laws" of time and space are only valid if you believe in them.

There might, I thought, be a King Edward cigar in the medicine bag. A red handkerchief. A pocket knife and a few nuggets of turquoise. Maybe some of the candies Mom kept in a jar for him. He had a sweet tooth something fierce, all his life.

Or maybe it contains sawdust and the ribbons of thin wood that curled out of the throat of his hand planes. I'll bet there's a few coins in there, too. Like the silver half-dime I keep close by, should I ever need to pay the Boatman for passage.

I don't know what's in there, but it nourishes me, keeps me whole. It remains unopened. I don't know what's in there. I don't want to know what's in there. Maybe it's the last mystery I have. The last map-edge. If I opened it, I'd have nothing left.

So when people ask me, "How much Indian are you?" all I can say is, "Not as much as my father was," and leave them to think I'm just talking about fractions again.

The paychecks that sustain me when I am not in wildness are earned at my job as a reporter in the city of Franklin, the seat of St. Mary Parish. Beyond the doors of this old house, past the waters of *Siti,* I know Franklin. It's the town where I work, where I have friends and family. I know its concrete streets intimately, peek into the downtown alleys that, at dusk, move with restless shadows of their own. The state undertook a major reconstruction of west Main Street not long ago, and in demolishing the decrepit concrete on that end of town, layers and layers of previous roads were revealed. It reminded me that there is a city beneath the city I see each day. Franklin is a small community, under eight thousand in population, but old and distinguished by a predominantly European heritage distinctly different from the surrounding French-Acadian parishes of Louisiana. The Germans, English and Italians came to Franklin, occupied its east Main Street antebellum homes, constructed its famed "White Way" boulevard of elegant lamp posts. Travel to Acadian towns such as Abbeville or Pierre Part and the Cajun accent is everywhere. It is not absent in Franklin, but it is a bit less pronounced, pardon the pun.

I know this town. My mother brought me here to get groceries, shop for clothes, pick up medication at the pharmacy where, if I behaved well, she bought me ice cream. I know the face of downtown, changed over my life, but still full of reminders of bygone days in the storefronts of buildings a century old. Once called "the little Natchez" and nationally recognized as one of America's most charming small towns, Franklin is a historic and beautiful community that has weathered hard times, most recently the fabled oil bust of the mid-1980s.

Founded in 1808 as Carlin's Settlement, Franklin became the parish seat in 1811 and the first incorporated town in St. Mary Parish. Though early settlers included French, German, Danish and Irish, the town's culture and architecture is heavily influenced by the unusually large numbers of English who chose to settle there after the Louisiana Purchase. Numerous large sugar plantations arose in the area, and with the development of steamboats, Franklin became an interior sugar port. By the 1830s, Bayou Teche was the main street of Acadiana, with one plantation after another along its banks.

The area's sugar cane planters were among the South's wealthiest agriculturists. This is reflected in the grand plantation homes and mansions they built in Franklin and the surrounding countryside. Most of these magnificent structures are still standing and well-preserved, giving Franklin its unique architectural flavor. Franklin's Historic District is listed on the National Register of Historic Places and encompasses over four hundred noteworthy structures. Many of the spectacular Greek Revival antebellum homes are along the live oak arcade on the East Main Boulevard. East Main Street retains its distinctive turn-of-the-century iron street light standards, which have become a symbol of the picturesque town.

Though a small city, Franklin has produced more than its share of statesmen, including five governors of Louisiana, four United States senators, a Chief Justice and a Lieutenant Governor. Franklin was also the boyhood home of Jefferson Davis, president of the Confederacy.

During the Civil War, the Battle of Irish Bend was fought near Franklin on April 14, 1863. Though eventually forced to retreat, the badly outnumbered Confederate forces cost the Union troops significant losses. Four hundred men were killed or wounded in the confrontation, which proved to be an important point in stopping the Union drive to invade Texas

Reminders of my own history are here. The Teche Theater, the only surviving example of Franklin's movie houses, was built partly by my biological grandfather, Nicholas Stouff Sr. It has undergone a remarkable restoration from derelict dismay, destroyed again by a hurricane just after completion, and completely renovated once more. It is now used for local theatrical productions and other community events.

It is nearly impossible to drive down any street in south Louisiana and not see a boat in a yard. With so much water available, people make the most of it. Franklin is no different, and neither is the rest of St. Mary Parish. Boats are everywhere, tiny john boats, expensive bass boats, tugs, cruisers, shrimpers, yachts, even the occasional sailboat. To find wood among these denizens is rare. Now and then I stumble upon a plywood bateau or skiff, but such finds are infrequent.

Derelict wooden boats lie along Bayou Teche as it winds its way through St. Mary Parish. They lay on their sides, rotting in half, or mostly sunken, only their proud bows cracking under the heat of the Louisiana sun. They are small fishing boats, pirogues, cruisers, even one finely planked shrimp boat of some forty feet. There are few things more beautiful than a wooden shrimp boat, its booms extended, against the sunset in the Gulf of Mexico. Such sights make me long for days when hundreds of these vessels set out each morning for the shrimp that seemed as abundant as the cod of the northeast, returning in the evening laden below their waterlines. One of the last of Morgan City's wooden shrimp boats sits on the boulevard of Brashear Avenue, white and elegant, but hopelessly stranded, shipwrecked along a busy city boulevard. Along Front Street, where the city's docks are, the fiberglass and steel shrimp boats line up, elegant in their own way, but somehow cold, somehow lacking the subtle touch of warmth that even a painted wooden boat conjures.

A proud Louisiana boat building tradition once covered this state across its coast. There are few of the old boat builders left. Each year, at the wooden boat festival at Madisonville, well over a hundred wooden vessels are displayed along the Tchefuncte River. While these handsome Chris Craft yachts and runabouts, streamline sailboats and proud schooners are a joy to behold, there are usually only a handful of traditional Louisiana craft to be found.

It remains something of a mystery that a culture such as the Acadians possess would so disdain the wooden boat today. The anglers and commercial fishermen, the recreational boaters and owners of personal watercraft, they elevate plastic and metal above all else. Wooden boats are to be appreciated safely on the river in Madisonville once a year in the fall. Sleek Carolina Skiffs, Rangers bass boats and all manner of aluminum hulls are the marks of distinction, while wood is a signal of eccentricity.

Here in the coastal parishes of Louisiana, wooden boats are to boat building what fly fishing is to angling: the mark of the eccentric, to a degree, but to their advocates, a finer and deeper immersion in the joys of the disciplines. A bamboo fly rod in a fiberglass boat rebels against its surroundings, but in a well-crafted wooden skiff seems to embrace the world within.

When some of us look into the open hull of a wooden boat—skiff, launch, utility, it makes no difference—we are seeing things alien to the confines of a fiberglass vessel. The frames, thick oak or fir or cypress, mahogany or cedar, lock the boat—and ourselves—firmly in another place, another time. The chines, sheers and longitudinals sweep through a world that has no sense of artistry, only function. Here we can see in the mind's eye a world before the obsession of permanence, the neglect of care. People who fashion wooden boats and those who use them do not wish to be buried in hermetically sealed stainless steel coffins painted faux mahogany. The notion of perpetual imprisonment in such a device is chilling and unsettling.

What modern man will leave behind when he has faded from the world at last is refuse. Nuclear waste, strip-mined mountains, rusting steel skyscrapers and crumbling concrete highways. Our neglect will outlive us, for we are far more concerned with such things as apartment houses, tin-can cars and fiberglass boats. Our homes are temporary despite the fact that we have built them of materials that do not rot or decay. Our cars are disposable, and our boats can too easily be parked on trailers in the back yard, or left in the slip of the marina, without need for attention. When we die, our makings will continue, but our names will be forgotten.

Perhaps, then, it is the very limited longevity of the wooden boat that appeals to us, in light of our own mortality. While we may marvel at the long-lived wonders of Stonehenge, ancient European cathedrals, and talk of leaving behind something that will outlive us, assembly-line cars, mold-poured fiberglass boats and prefabricated houses do not seem to qualify.

In his boats, or his Native crafts, in anything my father fashioned by his own hands he lived by a simple creed: if it was not good enough to put his name on it, it would never leave his shop. Marking a boat with a brand name means little; the faces behind it are nameless, featureless. Brand names stand only for corporate legality. The hands of the men and women who fashioned it, even by pouring or spraying fiberglass into a mold, are lost for all time.

It should not be surprising, then, that wooden boats are such a vital part of this world through which I make my way. The wooden boat is as essential to the quest for an authentic life as green-black lake water and ancient lore. Here in south Louisiana, we know little of hanging a garboard, steam-bending frames and searching for oak thwarts in living trees. Our craft are decidedly utilitarian, born of the need to survive and prosper in a swampy, marshy world. The Acadians and Indians used similar craft, such as the dugout canoe, pirogue, bateau and skiff.

To love wooden boats is to embrace the past, present and future as a circular presence. A part of the builder remains in wooden boats, as surely as the thumbprint of a sculptor in a shard of pottery. His blood certainly stained it somewhere, and even if he never shed a drop, the oils of his hands are in it, flakes of his skin, beads of his sweat. To stand at Martha's Vineyard or any other place where wooden boats still are abundant, looking out at graceful sailboats, sturdy working vessels and all other manner of craft, is no more uplifting than to step back in time here. To a time when fleets of shrimpers left, their cypress planked hulls and strong, graceful lines cutting through early morning fog. When fishermen and trappers returned with skiffs and bateaus and barges full of furs and catfish. It beckons to the same past longingly, a past where oyster skiffs, lobster boats and catboats flanked the coasts of America, spartan and utilitarian perhaps, but wholesome and beautiful in their very rugged ways.

Though raised in a bateau, a capable and earnest craft, the skiff is perhaps the most useful—and lovely—of American work boats in the Deep South especially. The high, sharp stem of a skiff moving through black swamps, surrounded by the very cypress trees from which it was made, conjures the sense of integrity lurking beneath the beauty.

To build a wooden boat is to find creation in the details. Details not revealed in vats of fiberglass connected to spray guns, not apparent behind the welder's mask. Few power tools are useful in the building of a wooden boat, and the craftsman must become intimate with the wood by necessity of the use of his hand tools. The boat builder's shop, even if he is also a furniture maker, for example, also includes the tools of his first love. The builder's bevel, the draw knives and spiling battens. The table saw might see use in ripping plywood or planks to rough fit, or the miter saw for cutting sheers and chines to length, even the router for trimming edges. But in the end, the boat builder relies on the vital tools of hand, eye and inspiration to make a wooden boat more than just a floating hull. If he is using modern tools to create an aberration in the modern world, he is only doing so to thumb his nose at the notion of disposability.

Builder Ross Gannon once questioned author Michael Ruhlman into what the he held dear. Is it the boat that is to be treasured, or the notion given a child concerning the caring for things, the disposability of our lives? In fact, it is both. To fashion a boat, or merely to own one, made of wood is to practice fundamental values sadly lacking in today's stop-and-go world. A world where little is held sacred and the idea of taking care of treasured things is obsolete because there is little left to be treasured.

What my father passed down to me was not merely a love of wooden boats. Within those gunwales, he taught me to take care of things that mean enough to be taken care of. I care for his little bateau not only because it is of his making, but also because it is a thing that deserves to be cherished. Had I never known the builder, perhaps I would not feel as strongly emotional about it. But still the treasure of it would be evident.

Wooden boats are not invulnerable. They will not last forever. They do not need to. It is enough that they serve a generation or several generations, solidly and with devotion, and fade back to the elements from which they came. That is something no other material in a boat can do. Return to the details of creation when its time is done.

Even if all the John Gardner-designed Whitehall boats are gone, left to rot, sunk in disaster, meet whatever end they are destined, they persevere. They exist in his lines and in his offsets, rolled in crisp white sheets, ready for the next builder in search of the details of creation. That is the epiphany of wooden boats: like the world around us, they are constantly renewed, born again to be cherished and cared for.

What the wooden boat captures for me is the same thing that enchants the angler, particularly the fly angler. There is, in the boat and the rod, a conduit between ourselves and the things we most desperately seek. To glide across still lake water in a wooden boat is to feel a closer presence of the water, just as to hook into a trout or a bluegill with a fly rod, particularly if bamboo, is to become more intimate with the fish. The graphite rod and the composite boat do not resonate with the same connection. When I am in need of the deepest entrenchment into home waters and fish, only the wooden boat and bamboo rod satisfy me. In a different life, a life lived the way I would have preferred

I might have been a boat builder. A man who fashions vessels as a search for divinity.

My father built many boats in his day. In fact, people came from all over Louisiana and adjacent states to have my father build and repair boats for them. He did it for the extra money, for school clothes and Christmas gifts.

"He had an eye for boat building," our family minister told me once. "He just knew by instinct what was right and what wasn't, what would work and what would not." No small feat for a born landlubber, raised on the streets of Depression-era Ft. Worth, Texas. But he was *Siti imaxa*, thus water and the things of and within it were part of his spirit.

He was, in 1962, working for the local granite and marble works, carving tombstones. When I was born, he found better work, though marginally, at a carbon black plant. But that year, he built a little twelve-foot bateau out of cypress, oak and plywood, mostly scraps. With quarter-inch fir plywood all the way around and a little three-horse engine, he could lift it easily into the back of his pickup by hand. He couldn't afford a trailer.

Later, after I was born and old enough to sit upright there in my bulky, bright orange life vest, when I could hold a rod in my hands, I was his constant sidekick. He was not a sports fan. Though I'm sure at some point he threw a ball to me, I don't remember it. Any spare moment he had from working three jobs, we were in that little wooden bateau on Lake Fausse Point.

My grandfather was with us one day. I don't remember this, but Dad told the story so many times I know it by heart. Somehow it came up in conversation that the boat was constructed with quarter-inch plywood.

Pa Biz, as my grandfather was known, was furious.

"You brought that baby out here in a boat with a quarter-inch bottom?" he raged. "*Dammit*, boy, this lake *eats* boats!"

Properly chagrined, my father laminated another half-inch piece of plywood over the bottom, fiber-glassed the entire bottom and four inches of the sides, and robbed the piggy bank to buy a trailer since it was then too heavy to lift into the bed of his pickup.

Certainly my grandfather was right, because my father himself preached it to me many, many times when he finally set me free with my own boat to poke and prod with my fishing rod around Lake Fausse Point. And many times, indeed, did I see that lake get up on its hind legs, or like a coiled serpent, ready to strike, raging, tossing itself about in the bowl of its lair.

I was in my twenties before Dad let me take his boat to the lake. It was his pride. He built many boats, but that one was the best, he always said. Everything about it was right. It possessed, he implied, that magical conjunction of chine and sheer, that elusive intersection of form and function, that made it stand apart from any other. Trusting me with it was a mark of manhood, in essence. A rite of passage.

He left it in my care when he departed this earth to sing at the feet of his grandfathers. I have tended it as he taught me: never put it up wet. Never let dirt or leaves collect in the bilge. Take care of it, and it'll always get you home. It always has. The well-regarded lie is that wooden boats are fragile—they are finite and do not last, and worst of all, expendable.

It began to experience minor issues. A leak, high on the sheer line, at the transom, that I couldn't locate. He built the sides low, to reach down for all those thrashing fish without a gun'l in the armpit, so he installed a wide spray rail and subdeck aft to prevent swamping. Also, when I knelt on the foredeck I felt it give more than it used to. I thought it was just because I was heavier than I used to be, but no, not even my expanding midsection could explain it away.

Susan and I were heading across Lake Fausse Point on a spring foray, turning westward near Eagle Point, when we struck something. Something solid and huge that had once been far below the surface, but with *Siti's* thinning now reached skyward and found the little boat. At three-quarter throttle on my fifteen horsepower engine, the impact catapulted the boat airborne, and cracked the upper tumblehome of the transom. We idled it home, which took hours, and I repaired the transom with thickened marine epoxy and long lag bolts. But with the issues that materialized later, I feared the impact had weakened the structure.

So with a mustering of resolve and courage I cannot even begin to describe, I decided I simply had to remove the deck of the boat and see what was amiss.

I cannot find the words for the monumental force of will it

took to set a pry bar to the layer of plywood and begin to work it free. It was *his* boat, by thunder. His pride and joy. I've always said, only half-joking, that if some ruffian had ever accosted us on the lake with a gun and said, "Either the boat goes or the boy does," I'd have surely drowned. Just a year or so before Dad left us, my cousin and I were struggling to get the old Mercury on the transom started, without success. Tired and in terrible health, Dad came outside to show us what to do to make the old Merc fire and hum contentedly at idle. It was his Mercury, after all, his boat, and that it would for any reason at all not run, not do what it had always done so well, was unthinkable.

And there I was, about to take a pry bar and mallet to Nick Stouff's boat, two years older than me, truly my cradle in life, my schoolhouse, my sanctuary. Yet I managed to make the first blow with the mallet against the bar, and another, and when I finally peeled back the layer of plywood laid more than four decades ago, I was sure he had given me the strength to begin.

Dad used Weldwood glue to put it together. All the frames and the chines seem to be solid and do not give when stressed. But the topside of the old girl gets the full heat of the Louisiana sun on her planking, and over the years, that old Weldwood glue crystallized and turned to powder. The deck beams were in place but no longer steadfast, and the old copper nails were pulling out as the hull flexed. There was, at the transom, a very slight bit of rot in the sheer strake, and the joints connecting that aft subdeck with the gun'ls had broken loose, the glue again turned into powdery, brown uselessness.

Credit must be given, though: that old Weldwood glue held firm for forty years. I spent a week loosening all the topside joints that seemed even slightly questionable and have refastened them with marine epoxy adhesive and screws. I added extra bracing in some areas just to reinforce the transom, deck and rails. New plywood replaced the old and the old girl came through nearly whole again.

Perhaps she'll last another forty years. Perhaps my own son will one day poke and prod the shallow, black waters of Lake Fausse Point with a fly rod and a boatload of legacies. My life has been defined by that little boat, in a way. The lessons learned in it. The moments gathered and held close because of it. Take care of her, and she'll always get you home.

Wisdom

Mid-winter. The lake is not ready. It has grown so thin the slightest wind churns the black water to brown, laden with silt. But at the south side of one of my favorite ponds, the edges of it converge into a point, an arrow pointing the way to four-lane highways and, later still, the marsh and the Gulf of Mexico.

Near this convergence there are reeds and cattails, brown and withered though winter still has not reared its head enough to really have any impact. When I stand at the tip of the point, I can cast to both sides easily.

To my left, on the west side of the pond, a peninsula of thin, dense marsh grass juts from the bank like an exclamation. Over the nearly two years I've been fishing this pond, I have always found a fish or two there.

Just before dusk one night during a spat of that dubiously-titled phenomenon of nature, Indian Summer, I tied on my favorite just-before-dusk bug, the Accardo "Spook" in black and red. Manufactured in Baton Rouge, the Spook is just the thing to drive big bass nuts. Though the air had chilled, the water still retained some heat from the sun. In my hand, my Granger Victory bamboo fly rod glinted warmly.

The Spook landed near the marsh grass point, and at once, the water blasts skyward as if leaping away in terror. I felt the weight of a fish when I snapped back the rod tip, but then it was just as suddenly gone, and the Spook flew behind me.

Cursing, the time-honored wisdom chanted in my head: *If they feel the hook, they won't bite again.* But, I reasoned, perhaps he didn't really feel it at all, just caught the body of the popper.

I placed the Spook there again, but nothing happened. The conventional wisdom must be correct. That's why it's called wisdom. A few jerking pops of the Spook drew the attention of a few small bluegill that slapped at it with their tails. Disgruntled, I reached into my pocket for a smoke, lit it, and just as I put the pack back into my pocket, the water leapt skyward again.

The rod was tucked under my arm, of course, but it didn't matter. The fish near the marsh grass didn't strike; it knocked the Spook into the air. Without even a failed hook set, the popper sailed fifteen feet away, landing within a jumbled pile of leader and line.

I gathered the slack out of the line and cast back, but the Spook sat there, as the ripples of its landing expanded outward, fading like lost opportunity. I gave it little twitches, then a healthy pop.

Kapow! I lifted the rod, the tip bent over, then like a catapult ungirdled, flipped away from the reeds, and the Spook followed, landing at my feet.

Strike three.

Again that little voice whispered to me: *Fish won't strike again if they feel the hook.* He had to feel the hook that time. Probably felt it the first time, too, that's why he blasted the Spook out of the water. He was pure-dee hacked off at it. The third appearance of the popper resulted in a more enraged, vengeful strike. That I missed again.

It took four bad casts to finally make it good. Back in its spot near the point of that marsh grass. I'm not great at false-casting even with a tiny dry; with a big Spook at the end of the leader, I tend to flail the water like a mad dog until I get the fly where I want it. It's a good thing I'm not a trout fisherman.

No way he'll bite a fourth time. Wisdom says it can't happen. There are rules in the world, and there are rules in fishing—

An eruption like a geyser scared me so badly I nearly jumped out of my boots. The Granger bent over again, line zipped through the guides—

And *poof!* He was gone.

It was all I could do not to throw the rod down, run about madly, thrashing through the mud and water, kicking at red ant-hills and flailing my fists at the heavens in fury. Four! The same stinking fish hit four times, and I didn't get a hook into him!

I sat down on my tackle bag to brood. Perhaps there was a school of fish there? That was the only explanation, but why couldn't I hook one? I inspected the point of the Spook. It was sharp and sound. Grumbling about wisdom, I cast to the east side of the pond until I got enough line out, then moved the Spook over to the marsh grass again.

With a soft slurp, so gentle I almost didn't see it, the Spook slid away below the surface. Only a few small swirls marked its vanishing.

I struck the fish like there was no tomorrow.

This time, the rod bent, and stayed bent. The fish took off for the grass, but I put pressure on him, and he panicked, moving toward the center of the pond now, taking my line with him. That was fine, go boy, go! All the while I'm saying loudly to myself, "Fifth time! Fifth *stinking* time!"

We danced for a few minutes, until finally, he breached the surface of the pond and I saw the bass wasn't nearly as large as I thought he would be. Perhaps three pounds? Surely no more. But this largemouth had the heart of a lion.

When I lipped him out of the water at last, he writhed in what I am sure was not fear, but rage. If he had significant teeth, I probably would have lost my thumb. The Spook had found its mark in bone, and it took forceps to remove it.

I held the bass up under the rapidly fading sun, and said, "I hope that was as much fun for you as it was for me," then laid him back into the water. Leisurely, as if nothing extraordinary had just happened, he twisted away, back to his spot in the marsh grass. Just to make sure, I cast to the same place several times, and received no hits. There was only that one fish there. One really arrogant, determined bass.

There's a lot of room for time-honored wisdom. It doesn't become wisdom for no reason. But there are times when laws don't work. Four times that fish hit before I hooked him, and on the fifth time, he just took it slowly down like a debutante sipping tea from fine china. Time-honored wisdom sometimes must fall to the wayside in lieu of the mood of the prey.

I broke down my rod in the last moments of daylight. There were bullfrogs croaking in a chorus of deep hollows, echoes from the depths of caverns. With the tube safely in my backpack, I walked slowly along the eastern edge of the pond. Frogs jumped away startled by my passing, and with each splash of escape, its comrades croaked more loudly, as if raising the alarm. Off toward the center of the pond, fish were rising, but the light was too dim for me to make out more than subtle expansions of silver, like gently sprinkled fairy dust on polished glass. I probably could have caught a few more by feel and hearing, but my day had already been made by one arrogant, ill-tempered bass and the determination to not let wisdom stand in the way of trying.

The origin of the fly rod traces back to Scotland. Those first rods were made of wood and used to cast—more like pitch, really—lines made of horsehair.

Later, as fly fishing moved to the rest of Europe and America especially, new woods were found that made the rods more like casting instruments, and Chinese silk became the preferred choice of fly line composition.

Eventually, someone discovered what used to be called Calcutta cane, from India. First they used sections of this to make tips for the rods. Eventually again, someone discovered Tonkin cane, which only grows in a remote cove of a bay in China. Like Cuban seed cigars, this particular variety of bamboo will grow nowhere else in the world, and in a century of searching, no other bamboo has been found that is even remotely as suitable for rod building as Tonkin cane.

If you've ever cut a piece of bamboo, you'll know it's hard as heck. Bamboo from Tonkin Bay is shipped to America. A bamboo fly rod is made by drying the two-to-three-inch diameter culms, then splitting them lengthwise into thin strips, and flattening them to smoothness. The builder places those strips on a mold that is set to taper from the thick butt section of the rod to the fine tip, sometimes fine as a pencil lead. Six of these are planed into equilateral sixty degree triangles, glued together, to form a hexagon shaped fly rod. There are no bumps or nodes from the joints of the cane like Huck Finn used. Bamboo fly rods are flat, straight, tapered and glued into precision instruments of incredible delicacy, surprising power and amazing grace.

Bamboo rods were largely replaced by fiberglass in the late 1950s after a good run. By the end of the 1970s or so, graphite became the material of choice. There are a couple hundred modern bamboo rod builders, so the art is still thriving.

About this whole fly fishing business. It's rare here, in my part of Louisiana especially. Most folks don't get it, think it's at best weird and at worse illegal.

While there are many variations in spinning and bait fishing rods, there are ten times as many in fly rods. By the way, do not ever call a fly fisherman's fly rod a "pole." A pole is something you hang electrical lines from, or a basketball goal. Fly rods are precision instruments. They are not "poles."

The difference being, in general fishing, you cast a weighted lure tied to a thin monofilament line. You are casting the weight of the lure, then. In fly fishing, you are casting a diminutive fly on a slightly heavier PVC line. You are, you see, casting the weight of the line, and the fly just goes along for the ride.

Therein lies the rub. Two or three different length and action traditional fishing rods might do you fine for your whole life. Fly fishing ain't like that. If you are a fanatical fisherman, you need rods ranging from six to nine feet, in varying degrees of action, the stiffness and where it bends in the length of the rod.

So you wiggle out about twenty-five feet of this fly line, that comes in all kinds of nice colors. Once it's in the water and lying semi-straight in front of you, you lower your rod tip to the surface of the water, lift slowly but accelerating, and pull the line up with you over your shoulder, until the tip of your rod reaches about the one o'clock position. Maybe one-thirty, but two o'clock is too far! Your line will whiz over your head, stretch out behind you, and when it just starts to stretch out again behind you, you snap the rod forward again to about eleven o'clock.

If you've said your prayers every night before bed, washed and bathed regularly, gone to church at least annually, followed the Ten Commandments and never sacrificed Pacific Island virgins to pagan gods, the line will then shoot forward, taking some of the excess lying at your feet with it, and land straight as an arrow in front of you as you lower the rod tip to about 9 o'clock, and your leader and fly will gently land within at least a three-foot circle of where you wanted it.

This is the essence of fly fishing: prayer. Fly fishermen are the most religious of fishermen, because it takes divine intervention to make all this work.

But if you've lived a life of decadence and debauchery, you'll put too much power into the back-stroke, especially if you are a reformed bait-caster, and your line will jerk like a coiled serpent striking. You'll stop the rod too far back, like at three o'clock, then slam it forward like you're Mickey Mantle going for a homer.

In this case, your line will, if you're lucky, end up in a messy little pile right at your toes, all three dozen feet of it. If you're not lucky, you'll look like a kitten who got into the yarn.

There's the attraction of it all, you see. It's not so much about the fish. I could catch way more fish with a glob of squirming earthworms impaled on a gold Eagle Claw hook.

And there's the crux of it. It's the learning curve. It's the challenge. It's—especially, to me at least—the abandonment of coarseness and the refinement of skill. Three years ago I was doing good if I could get thirty feet of line out. Today I'm doing sixty feet pretty easy and with decent accuracy, but by no means does that make me more than average with a fly rod. Many of my friends can cast the entire fly line, roughly one hundred feet.

Louisiana's southern areas, particularly those within the Atchafalaya River basin, are at the mercy of wind, rain and flow. Months of high winds, constantly shifting like restless spirits unsure of the direction they wish to take beyond, will fury from the north for a time, pushing basin water levels out to the bay. Then the wind, like a hapless vagabond, will shift south, and the onslaught of tide pushes into the basin again.

Water hyacinth, that Asian invader that has so plagued Louisiana waterways, had been browned and withered by the Christmas freeze. During the 1884 New Orleans World's Fair, Japanese exhibitors at the horticultural pavilion gave away packages of water hyacinth seeds to all their visitors. They were told to just throw them in ponds and waterways, wait until they grew and bloomed beautiful, orchid-like flowers.

They did, and the plant soon overtook most of Louisiana's waterways. By 1897, the Corps of Engineers was summoned for help. They enlisted hundreds of men using pitchforks, who would throw the lilies out onto the bank. There they would dry out and die. But this just provided more space for still-floating hyacinth; they reproduced faster and more abundantly. In 1900, a stern wheeler with a conveyor-rigged system set out to scoop up the hyacinth, and grind it to a pulp. Later they tried dynamite. Then flame-throwers. According to an article by Buddy Stall in the *Clarion Herald*, "A full cone of fire, hot enough to melt a block of steel, was squirted on a hyacinth raft. When the fuel was exhausted, a frog emerged from the blackened mat and began sunning itself. The scientist using the flame-thrower was even more astounded later during the next growing season. The burned plants were not only the first to sprout, but also averaged nine inches taller than surrounding plants. The next attempt was in the form of arsenic. Some of this got into the food of the workers at the site and resulted in the death of one man and critical illness to thirteen others. The hyacinths grew on."

But winter will help keep the water hyacinth at bay, and I was glad to see its weathered, scarred condition. In the 1940s, the nutria was introduced as a control measure for water hyacinth, having already escaped captivity due to a hurricane earlier in the decade. The nutria however eats more than water hyacinth, and has become a dangerous pest in its own right in Louisiana.

Sometimes when I am drifting along the scarred, ravaged banks of *Co'ktangi*, broils of small bubbles reach the surface of the water and burst there, and I fear these are the breaths of ancestors, gasping for air down deep in the silty mud. When the water is clear and the sun strikes it at an angle and plane of refraction, shadows below the surface seem like fingers, spindly and crooked, reaching out for me, pleading.

That's how all of my waters appear to me, most especially Lake Fausse Point and *Co'ktangi,* like graveyards for restless souls. There is joy here, make no mistake: peace, solitude and food for the spirit. But it is also a watery expanse of burial plot. Only the European unease with graveyards and cemeteries disquiets me. Fear of the dead was unknown to my people, for they are always with us. To say that these waters are haunted is to imply something frightening, something unnatural. It is merely as it always has been, and should be.

Co'ktangi grows old with me, though it is far more ancient. As silt raises the bottom, thins the water, my own life recedes with it.

I never heard of Mardi Gras until I was in ninth grade at Franklin Junior High School. I think that if my father had the day off from the carbon black plant, and the weather was reasonable, we were in the boat. Though in later years he mellowed in his resolve, he abhorred crowds and felt oddly out of place among throngs of strangers, thus he avoided them with great zeal. I am the same way, when I can help it. I am sure someone mentioned the words "Mardi Gras" before ninth grade, but I don't remember it at all, and I certainly don't remember a parade until I began my career full-time in the newspaper business.

Scott, my best friend and soul-brother, and I would chase fish between cypress and tupelo and red maple stands in a little wooden bateau my grandfather built decades before. My grandfather was a general contractor who built many things for many people, and though the little bateau floated and did not leak, it was evident that my grandfather was not the boat builder my father was. It had a decided twist lengthwise which caused it to pull to one side when under power. "Power" is a precarious term to apply to the seven-and-a-half horsepower 1957 Wizard outboard, its compression so bad it might have actually produced about five horsepower at best. It took us nearly an hour to get to the lake from the Rez.

Scott and I first met at junior high school, and in 1980 or so he arrived unannounced on my doorstep in July. He threw me a pack of chewing tobacco—a habit I indulged back then—and said, "Let's go fishing." It would be a friendship that evolved into a brotherhood linked and flowing through water.

That particular Mardi Gras, I had no thought of parades or beads or purple and gold costumes, and apparently, at least then, my brother did not either. We made the long ride to the lake and fished most of the day, filling the live well of the boat with thrashing, frantic hand-sized bluegill and the occasional bass that would, in the evening, be fried into a delectable supper by my mother, served with French fries cut from whole potatoes, catsup and Ritz crackers.

It was near enough to dusk that we knew we should be pulling the crank rope of the old Wizard and pointing the slightly-askew-of-horizontal bow toward home, but the "one more cast" mentality had firmly imbedded itself within these two fishermen. If I remember correctly, we were somewhere near Peach Coulee, back before that side of the lake got so shallow and the cypress trees submerged off the shoreline still held nests of big bream, before someone dared put up signs and fences, trying to claim the natural world for themselves under the guise of so-called "hunting clubs."

The sun was sinking toward the line of cypress to the west, shadows of old gnarled cypress stretching long and their branches made dark fingers on the water's surface. I was just about to take my turn saying it was time to head home (we had traded uttering that phrase several times already) when a cry erupted from the darkness of the woodland on the bank.

There's no easy way to describe what we heard. It was like surgical steel, razor sharp, slicing not through my flesh but through my heart and mind and soul. If I imagined a woman in the most horrendous agony, that is how I think she would sound.

We sat there, lines slack in the water, mouths agape I'm sure. I wanted to crank the little Wizard and flee, but I was petrified into inaction, awaiting, dreading another screech from the shore.

Then, through a sun-dappled patch between two huge cypress trunks right there on the bank, the big cat stalked.

I don't know what was ahead of him, but he didn't look at us at all, instead moved methodically, softly, toward something in the brush. In all, he might have been in our sight for no more than ten seconds. Though he didn't look directly at us I thought I saw the suggestion of yellow in his eyes. He was easily big as, perhaps larger, than a healthy and robust Labrador retriever.

Then he was gone. Gone, like the night passes from one meridian to the next. We made our way home, feeling at once terrified and privileged.

It was not until a week later that I told my grandmother the story. We sat at the kitchen table sipping coffee, and she turned to stare out the window somewhere far, far off that I could not see, for long moments.

"The old folks said we were panther clan, but there's no way to prove it. Maybe," she said with a lift of her chin and fire in her eyes that reminded me of the yellow I saw on the lake shore, "you just did."

I don't know. According to the experts, Louisiana's big cats are a variant of the Florida panther. Nonetheless, reports of large cats in Louisiana and much of the south have been recorded for centuries. Maybe what the brother of my soul and I saw that day was not a flesh-and-blood animal at all, but a linkage, a reaching out from a distant past I didn't even suspect. I know that I have never seen another. Yet, I also know that the woods and marshes here are full of black bears, and in my entire life I have only seen one, dead on the highway after being hit by a truck. Who's to know?

I'll always remember it, to be sure. I'll always remember the stealth and mystery of it, the way its cry raked across my bones like a rasp, rattled my spirit. Flesh and blood survivor of a wilderness largely vanished, or spirit guide, in either case it was a small miracle I feel blessed to have received.

Three: Precipice

Old-woman-boat-lender wind came blowing. The old woman said, "If I had known that, I would not have lent my boat to my children. Now they are gathering wood on the sand bar, just playing. Sometimes they come and borrow my boat. They fooled me indeed. It happened to me because I felt cold. If I knew it would get warm like that, I would not have lent my boat. I needed wood myself, but I felt cold and did not go. Therefore, I lent my boat.

Today Old-woman-boat-lender-wind is blowing. However, I think it is not Old-woman-boat-lender-wind. It is too cold today. I think the Old-man-boat-lender-wind is blowing.

The wind between north and east we call Old-woman-boat-lender-wind. In the morning it makes it cold. Later it warms up. Very early in the morning that old woman feels cold and does not go to the woods to look for wood. Therefore, she lends her boat to the children. Later it gets warm, but it is too late to go when the children return.

In the winter, that wind is too cold and buzzards and everything die. Therefore, they call that wind Buzzard-die-wind in the winter. That is all now.

(Benjamin Paul, Chitimacha, American Philosophical Society recordings)

Glimpses

Almost daily, banshee winds howl from dawn to dusk, knocking over garbage cans, rattling street signs, tossing around debris. I could not recall a spring like that. Even the windy spring of 2001 wasn't so bad. I made one scouting trip to the lake, only to find water levels extraordinarily low from the westerly and north-westerly winds. Everything was muddy, too, like well-milked coffee. It was good to be there again, but useless to attempt to fish.

Other parts of Louisiana were reporting wonderful catches, but those areas affected by the Atchafalaya River remained hit-and-miss, even for those brave enough to fight the winds. I could maybe do it with spinning tackle, but boat control was a frustrating consideration at best, and the condition of the water in my immediate area proved not very promising.

So I was still pretty much grounded. I sat at home and tried to involve myself in worthwhile projects, but just didn't have the heart. There was something else, too. Something missing from spring besides lake water, fly rods and fish.

My father's people had many sacred and revered animals in our culture. Among them was *kich* (pronounced "keesh"). This was a little mottled-brown bird, probably some variation of wren, that would speak to our people and we spoke back to it. *Kich* would warn Chitimacha of danger, friendly visitors, hostiles, if there would be rain. The old people knew exactly which sounds *kich* made to indicate each event.

My grandmother was the last one who could talk to the bird, even though she wasn't Chitimacha by blood. She was taught to understand it, to speak to it, by her mother-in-law, Delphine. Each spring, after the winter finally faded into memory, *kich* would come and speak to her. It would perch in the big fig tree in the back yard, and they'd converse there. I remember holding her hand as a small child, listening in wonder as the little bird would call to her, and she would answer in Chitimacha. Though not a fluent speaker in our language, she knew enough that the little bird would reply in return.

Kich also predicted death from time to time, but in my recollection such a prophecy was never made, or if it was, my grandmother kept it to herself.

When she passed from this world to join her Creator in 1997, I was already living in the old house where she had spent seven decades of her life. In that first year, *kich* came to me. I don't know how I recognized it among the sounds of all the other birds. Perhaps from my childhood memories the tenor of its call conjured recognition. But it perched in the fig tree every year since then, speaking to me, giving omens, promises and prophecies.

I do not understand it, because I was not taught Chitimacha. I believe that the language needed to speak to *kich* was not only Chitimacha, but a translation of the words necessary to converse with the bird into Chitimacha. That dialect likely died with my grandmother.

Yet the little bird came to me every spring, and I'd go sit with it, listen, at least give it company, at least let it know someone still believes. If everyone stops believing in something, it ceases to exist.

I still believe, but I have not heard *kich* in the fig tree this year, and I am growing concerned. I have come to rely on its presence each spring, look forward to it. In my perceptions of our visits, though I do not understand it, I like to think that in addition to whatever news it brought me, we shared memories of the old woman who for seventy years was its sole companion, its only confidant and solitary believer.

Has it grown frustrated with my inability to comprehend? Have I failed to recognize some warning, some promise? Or is the strength of belief from just one man not strong enough to sustain it? My faith is not as strong as hers, my will not so resolute.

So I sit and listen, longing for the sound of a little mottled-brown bird in the fig tree. Sometimes I curse myself for my indiscretions. For two-thirds of my life, I turned my back on my grandfathers, despising the boundaries, prejudices and pitfalls of being their heir. I am like Rabbit, who was ordered by the Creator to bring medicine to a very sick little girl. Rabbit was warned not to wander or stray from the signs, but Rabbit did and got lost. In his haste to make up time he fell and split his lip on a sharp rock, a mark he still carries today to remind him of his indiscretion. Though I eventually came back to my blood and embraced it, I am like Rabbit. My lip is split, and I have no strength to make things right.

If everyone stops believing in something, it ceases to exist. I have always felt this. I have also always felt that sometimes it doesn't matter if you believe in something or not, so long as something believes in *you*. The little bird believed in me for seven years, and now I wonder, have I failed its confidence somehow?

I am longing for lake water, for the back ends of dark canals, and for little mottled-brown birds this spring. They are my fulcrums. The pivots upon which my existence revolves. My grandmother, the last medicine woman of the tribe, cured herself of throat cancer in the 1970s. She did this by finding the roots of the plant she called *bahjootah*, which grew in my back yard. I was with her when she collected it, but it no longer grows there. I don't know it's taxonomical name, and barely remember what it looks like, but she drank the tea she made of the roots for six months, the six months she was given by doctors to live, and the cancer vanished. She lived twenty years more and died a natural death.

There is no *bahjootah* in the back yard anymore, and I fear there will be no *kich* in the fig tree this year. I am not strong enough to keep them extant. My lip is split, and no matter how I have hurried to make up the time I lost, perhaps I am too late after all.

People who do not fish shake their heads wearily. It is but a symptom of the modern age's inability to expand perceptions. Those who do not work with wood are perplexed by the time and energy involved in constructing a cypress porch swing, when such swings are available at big-box building material stores for forty bucks. Those who do not involve themselves in the pastime of another find difficulty in understanding.

Herein lies the malady of modern life: we have become so entangled in our own web of toils, challenges, difficulties and random successes, we can spare scant accord for the webs of others.

There are those who do not know the names of their grandparents, first or last. There are those who admit they do not even know if their parents are living or dead, and there was never a rift in anger between them—they have become estranged by the demands of living and the illusion of achievement. Such things are appalling. The truest definition of lost.

Here at the precipice of spring, I try to push winter aside by sheer will. When the air is warm enough I lurch through tall brown grass to get to a pond, flail the water for hours for a single midget bream. I am trying to rush things that cannot be coerced. I recognize the hypocrisy in my actions: I must slow down, practice what I preach, wait the seasons' turning of their own accord. Perhaps I am not longing for new cars or fine possessions, but my impatience for spring makes me no less improper. The absence of *kich* in my fig tree leaves me exhausted, as if the rest of the world throughout winter has not sustained me.

On one of those premature trips to a pond, I spend the last hour of the day casting an Accardo Spook with the Victory. Off near the edge of the pond, a large bass was so intent on nest-making that it ignored my popper even when I passed it right over its head. I even hit it in the tail with the Spook once. The bass didn't even panic and flee, sole-minded on its purpose. We are alike in that regard, at least: determined and rushing spring and all it promises.

This little pond I first discovered two years earlier, and for that entire first season no one else fished it. That was a great year, just me, a fly rod and a pond full of uninitiated bass eager to strike whatever was offered. Inevitably, enough people saw me while jogging on the nearby road or riding four-wheelers through adjacent fields that, the second year, anglers overran the pond. Now, the third season is here, and whereas I never caught a single bream in the first two years, that's all I catch now. The large predators have been taken out, it's clear. Susan, my fiance, and I spent an entire evening and received nary a rise, though an approaching cool front may have been responsible. Still, it's clear this little pond has been ravaged. Whereas I could have fished it forever without distress, in one season the bucket-haulers have mauled it into an unproductive, half-dead body of water.

The rain returned the next day. I awoke that morning to the sound of it. Half-expecting it from the forecast, the disappointment set in anyway. So many things I wanted to get done, fishing not the least of them.

Rolling over, I glanced out the window. Gray skies dropped rain, the roof line streamed it before the window. Groaning, I collapsed back to the pillow. Temperatures have been mild, reaching the high seventies with no banshee wind. With no reason to get up, I just lay there and listened to the rain, and the house responding to the changes in temperature and humidity. It moves, this old house, creaking and groaning, and sometimes when pressures build up over time between frames, joists or crown molding, it will snap loudly, startling me. It is awakening to spring, this old house, flexing and stretching its muscles and bones.

But the rain didn't let up. I got up and made strong coffee, taking a cup to the piddling room and opening all the blinds. I sat there at my piddling desk, noticing a half-finished Jitterbee in the vise, but ignored it. Sipping coffee, watching the rain outside, I was still comforted. Surrounded by things cherished and familiar to me in that room. Staring out the window at the front yard, the rain seemed to distort the present, open glimpses to other times between the falling curtain of drops.

The coffee was black and unsweetened, the way I like it, thick and strong Cajun brew. The smell of freshly ground coffee beans used to permeate this old house when my grandmother set up the antique grinder. She always added eggshells to her coffee when she brewed it, said it calmed the bitterness. I was but a child when we ground coffee together in this house and sometimes the smell of it brewing reminds me of her.

Out there in the front yard, dimmed by the rain, shadows moved between the two sago palms planted by my great-grandmother to memorialize the death of Constance Stouff, her daughter, who died of a fever before she was a teen. Those palms are nearly a hundred years old now. Off past the palms, nearer the road, the rain drops thin veils through which I can almost see a horse-drawn wagon approaching the house. It carried the bruised, cut and bleeding body of a young Indian man who needed my great-grandmother's care as medicine woman. There had been a dispute off the reservation over a white man's wife, I was told, and as I watched in my mind's eye the wagon bringing the boy up to the door, I recalled how it wouldn't be long before the sheriff and a deputy would arrive, demanding the surrender of the boy.

The truth remains indistinct, like the veils of rain falling outside, like the scent of my coffee conjuring grinders from the past. What caused the mob to fall on him remains unclear. But the sheriff arrived, demanding the boy turn himself in. My great-grandmother, Delphine, went out to meet them. She refused them steadfastly.

But terrified, the boy found the strength to flee out the back door. The sheriff drew his pistol, took aim and shot the boy in the back of the head, dropping him dead there on the spot, on the same ground I sat and looked out at this morning, drinking coffee and watching rain.

Delphine shrieked and threw herself at the sheriff's throat, but he beat her down with the pistol. As she lay there at his feet, stunned by the blows, he pointed the gun at her head and cocked the hammer. Yet the deputy dissuaded him. "There's been enough bloodshed," he told the rage-maddened sheriff. "You can explain the boy, how are you going to explain *this*?"

I get more coffee, go and open the door to let fresh air into the house. The yard is almost a shadow under the rain. The next day, the rain reminds me, a mob from the local community drove through the reservation, a gang of thugs, shooting at anything that moved. No injuries were reported, but an entire day of terror dragged on into eternity, gunfire snapping, women and children huddling in their homes, crying out at the sound of blasts and breaking window glass, at bullets hitting cypress planks and doors. Eventually the mob dispersed, and an uneasy truce again persisted between the Indians and those nearby.

They took a door down from inside the house and placed it on sawhorses. The boy's body lay here, as the women cried and the children wailed, and the men sang songs eight thousand years old. This old house soaked their tears into its floors, saturated its ceilings with their sobs. It holds all of these still. Later, the boy was buried in a Christian cemetery just across the street from where he was cut and beaten.

The Indians filed charges, and a grand jury returned no true bill. The incident was quickly brushed aside. Justice remains unserved to this day, but both the perpetrator and the victim lie in the same ground, and face the same Creator to answer for their lives.

The rain continues to fall. The coffee is steaming in my hand. I feel selfish for bemoaning the rain, because I can't go fishing, or cut my mom's grass like I promised, or piddle with building a boat. Though ninety years ago a murder played out right here at my doorstep, I stand here safely, unafraid. I am well-known and well-respected in my community, a journalist who may not always be liked, but always above reproach. Some weeknights I go to wine tastings at a friend's restaurant, though I am not much of a wine drinker. I trade jokes with doctors, lawyers, businessmen and city council members. I fish with good, upstanding people who take me for what I am, no more, no less.

But sometimes I forget that I come from murder. Murder and oppression. When I begin to lose sight of who I am and where I have come from, the rain reminds me, the house jogs my memory, and both humble me. I am not bitter. I am not one of those indigenous persons who believe we are owed anything except this: never forget. That's all. Don't brush it aside, don't alter the history books, don't mince the words. Just never forget.

There'll be no fishing that day, yet again. But I let the irritation fade, and count myself among those descended of incredible bravery, monumental resolve. Perhaps I won't be able to take a fine bamboo fly rod in a nice boat out to the lake today, but I can rest easy here knowing that my freedom and my place in the community was earned in part by my own accomplishments, and also by the sacrifices of those who came before me. Their blood still rests in the soil outside where rain is tempering the past with soothing grace. Their voices still rest in the ceiling joists here, the floors and the door frames. I finish tying the Jitterbee and put it in my fly box. I clean house a little. I sit down under a warm lamp and read for a couple hours.

Just after noon, I surprise myself with a yawn. I lay on the sofa and let the sound of the rain on the metal roof sing lullabies. The cat comes, nuzzles her head against my cheek for a moment, then settles in beside me and closes her eyes, a calico ball of contentment. I drift off to sleep, and think of legacy. Perhaps it was better to not go fishing today after all. There'll be other days. Perhaps today was a good day to remember things I never lived. A good day to open my ears and heart to hear, and to not rush things that should not be rushed.

Rain fell all day.

The Pinou

The spring would come, but I was not only stricken with the "winter has been too dadgum long and if I don't get out and catch copious numbers of fish soon I'm going to turn into a quivering bowl of guacamole-flavored Jello" syndrome, but I also had a hankering for a canoe.

I warned my friends that the first person that holds up their hand palm-out and says, "How, Chief Bayouwater" or something equally cute would get slapped with a lawsuit.

Not a pirogue, mind you. A pirogue is something that we, as Louisianians in general and Louisiana Indians in particular, have somehow been bred out of. I mean, the pirogue gains its origins from the dugout, which my ancestors made by felling a good tree then hollowing it out to form a canoe using fire and mud to control the burn. I kid you not, that's absolute truth. The Cajuns came along and started making dugouts out of cypress planks, then later plywood.

But somewhere along the line, we have evolved away from the use of the pirogue. Our ancestors just fifty or sixty years ago could stand in a pirogue about the width of a two-by-four and use a push pole for propulsion. These flying trapeze artists obviously possessed some gene for this ability, which has not been passed along to their descendants.

Back many years ago, my fishing buddy and I decided we wanted to fish some of the ponds we couldn't get to with the boat and trailer, so we loaded dad's homemade pirogue into the truck and went and dropped it into an appealing pond.

I've told this story before, but it bears repeating, I think. Entering a pirogue is the first step in a series of harrowing experiences. The first person has to board and make their way to the far seat, crawling in this vessel which, despite the fact that you know it is fourteen feet long and twenty-eight inches across, has just taken on all the characteristics of a rabid alligator in a river. It rolls and bucks, threatening to plunge you into the pond, until all you can do is drop on your face and pray for your life, which amazingly, stabilizes the pirogue so you crawl to the back seat as carefully as you can.

Then the second person has to enter, but now your weight in the stern has further destabilized the pirogue and watching him get to the front seat, turn around and sit down is rather like watching someone in slow-motion. At last you're all settled in, and you realize you left the tackle box on the bank, and have to decide whether to go back for it or just fish with whatever tackle is already on the rod.

We decided to use what we had. However, the beer had made its way to the middle of the pirogue. It's important to note that my friend remembered the beer, but forgot the tackle box. Go figure. A man's gotta have his priorities. I do not drink beer if I am boating, but I don't preach at those who do, if they remain responsible. But whoever said, "Beer and boating don't mix," undoubtedly had a nightmarish experience with a pirogue.

It wasn't so much the drinking of the beer that caused the problems; it was the reaching back to the middle of the vessel to open the ice chest, retrieve a beer, close the ice chest and return to a semi-upright position without causing a major maritime disaster.

The first cast was mine. I reared back and pitched my lure (I wasn't a regular fly fisherman yet) as I normally would, which sent the pirogue into spasms of rolling and lurching so much that water spilled in over the side, ruining the ham sandwiches and chips. My pal's cast was a little better, having learned from my misfortune. So along we fished, and finally, my friend's cork suddenly shot off across the surface of the water.

He looked at me. I looked at him.

"What should I do?" he asked.

"I dunno," I admitted.

"Should I jerk?"

"Don't you dare," I warned. Just talking about it was making the pirogue start to roll.

"But we're here to fish," he protested.

"I know that, but if you jerk, what's gonna happen?"

He jerked anyway, and the pirogue rolled, water slopped in, and my shoes were soaked.

"I thought you weren't going to jerk?" I yelled.

"It's okay," he said. "I missed him, anyway."

"Jerk," I said, but he thought I was still complaining about his fishing-in-a-pirogue technique. "You ready to go home?"

"Yeah."

"I got some fish in the freezer," I noted.

"Sounds good to me."

That's pretty much the last time I tried to use a pirogue, and even though I still have that old vessel of Dad's, it's not the boat I want. I wanted a canoe.

See, I've gotten tired of spending all that money on gas for boats, all the maintenance costs, all the rest of it. If I had a good canoe to fish ponds or hidden canals that few people get to, man, I just know I could mop up on the fish. The grass, you see, isn't the only thing that's always greener.

I think my southern Indian ancestors, who invented the dugout that eventually became the pirogue, were hampered by the fact that water here is usually still. However, my northern Indian ancestor kin, who made birch bark and deer hide canoes that were wide and beamy and more stable, had it going on in fast-moving water. The modern pirogue is a manifestation of one, the modern canoe a result of the other. We've lost the genes for operating a pirogue with six-inch-high sides, but a canoe is wider and the sides twelve inches higher.

It's like thumbing my nose at the man, at big oil companies, OPEC and Osama bin Laden all at once. All I gotta do is drive to a place in the truck, and put my canoe over for a relaxing day of fishing with the fly rod.

First I started looking for a canoe online, and the money involved put me off. Canoe sticker shock is a dreadful thing. There is a line where sticking it to the man is meaningless if you're going to pay all that money to do it. Like setting up $50,000 worth of solar cells to quit paying the power company, you see?

Since I could not decide whether I wanted to buy or build, I decided I'd try to build. What the hey, I figured, I've got two boats under my belt; I can do a canoe. I wanted to do a crossbreed, though. A hybrid, so to speak, of the canoe and the pirogue. I decided I would call this a pinou, pronounced "pee-noo" since it is a little of both.

So I gave it a whirl one weekend, and remember, I'm designing this as I go: short and wide. Sorta like myself, right? No problemo, although I suppose it can be argued that while I am short and wide, I'm not very stable.

I broke the first pinou under construction Saturday and one on Sunday, each when bending the bottom chines or, as we say in Looziana, the "stringers." I've bent stringers for three boats so far with no problems. Okay, I broke one side of the first one I ever did, on my runabout, but that was it. A little marine epoxy will cure many ills. The pirogue is traditionally built narrow, and I think I was pushing my luck widening it more like a canoe. Either that or I'm just a klutz.

Every boat shop must be fitted with an essential item: the Moaning Chair. This is the place you sit and moan when you have done something really stupid in your construction project. So after I spent all day on the second pinou and broke the chine, I went inside and got me a beer, went back outside and sat in my Moaning Chair and moaned for a good half-hour. Then I tore the whole thing down and threw it away.

I was telling my fiance this, and bemoaning that I might have to actually break down and get a set of plans to build a water craft of this type, and she said, "Oh, well, God forbid that you should tap into the collective wisdom of dozens of generations of boat builders who make that sort of craft and have perfected the art."

Not a bad point, really, but it would have been cooler to say, "Yup. This here's me pinou. I designed and built it myself." Now, instead, I have to say, "Yup, this is my canoe. I bought a set of plans from some outfit in New York and built it myself." It's just not quite as satisfying, somehow.

But I broke down and ordered a set of plans for a plywood canoe. As it turns out, the plans were just not to my liking at all. So much for collective wisdom and I stuck them in a corner with the rest of the plans. I have lots of boat plans I acquired and never built: "Elly," a Norwegian *kosterbat* some one-hundred-and-fifty years old, "Marsh Cat" a fifteen-foot sailing catboat and a Riva "Aquarama" runabout. If I do build it, then I can only assume folks in New York know a lot about pirogues. I mean, canoes. I think *Last of the Mohicans* had canoes in it, and that was around New York, wasn't it? It'll be okay.

Though I don't plan on going exclusively canoe, if I indeed find that I can fish out-of-the-way, previously inaccessible waters around these parts in the absence of the big ugly bass boat crowd, not have to pay for gasoline in my boat, well, that's all the better. I still got my little boat that my dad built, and I'll finish my sixteen-foot skiff for when I got a fishing partner with me. Heck, I might just go native. Wait, I mean go...uhm...well, *native*, yeah, that's it!

The culprit in all this is satellite imagery readily available via the Internet. There are places on public property to fish that are only visible by satellite and only accessible by a small, easily carried vessel like a pinou. Canoe. Whatever.

I guess a lot of it boils down to the fact that a guy who wrote a book called *Native Waters: A Few Moments In A Small Wooden Boat* just has to accept the lot given to him and spend his days in wooden boats, not plastic ones. I don't mind. I feel most tranquil and at peace in a wooden boat with a bamboo fly rod floating along black-water canals like generations of ancestors before me. For me, anyway, that's about as close to heaven as you can get.

I finally got it going without breaking anything. It turned out bigger than I intended. I wanted something in the thirteen foot range, but I made the silly mistake of measuring out that at the bottom, forgetting that when I put the stems on each end, the forward and aft rake would be significant enough to make it just a hair under fifteen feet long. It is about thirty-five inches across the bottom, and both these measurements are within the realm of the manufactured fishing or hunting canoes I have studied on the market today.

I think I'm actually going to be classy and paint the name on the bow: *The Pinou.* Problem is, with a double-ended vessel, pointed on both ends, which is the bow? I guess it's pretty arbitrary, but such arbitrary things make me nervous. What if I'm wrong, and shame my ancestors and myself by paddling my pinou around backwards for the rest of my life? The cypress trees would shrink away in embarrassment, the finches chirp hysterically at my folly. I really need to make sure I get it right.

The notion of a canoe or a pirogue is kind of romantic, too. I was inquiring with a duck hunter the other day whether anyone still hunts out of a pirogue or canoe, and he said yes, but it's becoming a lost art. Sounds right up my alley, doesn't it? Wooden boats, bamboo fly rods and lost arts. What more can a relic like myself ask for?

I'm only just over forty-years-old and already an eccentric old curmudgeon. Can you imagine how I'll be in twenty years?

I finally launched it though it was not quite done but as far as I wished to go without knowing if I would be happy with it. I was. Oh, I have to get used to it; I'm not very experienced with such vessels. But I didn't tip it over and I got in and out without having a coronary, so that's a good sign. I like the way it paddles, and I think that will improve with some ballast. I was so uncertain I would like it, I didn't build the forward seat until later.

Yes, I like the notion of paddling through the swamp or down a small bayou, away from all the big ugly bass boats, just me and the gators and the belly-busting-with-laughter finches watching me paddle my pinou backwards. When I was a teenager great bright flocks of them use to be on Lake Fausse Point Once, my fishing pal and I were in my little bateau down Peach Coulee, and dozens of those little yellow finches with the black masks circled the boat for a couple of minutes or more, a spectacular maelstrom. Then, as if saying goodbye, they shot off over the trees and to this day, I've not seen a single one again. There's many such things. There used to be, now and then, a whacking, pounding sound in the cypress and tupelo stands, usually when I am alone but, now and then, with the brother of my soul in the boat. As if something enormous were coming through the trees, crashing through the saplings, trampling irises and reeds and deadfalls underfoot and then, just before it seemed we'd see it emerge, just as we just knew it was going to leap out of the woods, it would fall silent. *Neka sama* my father's people called it. An ancient spirit, a nefarious soul that sometimes came out of the fire to snatch young children from the hearth.

Ah, but there I go, rambling again. A relic and an eccentric, eh? I guess part of what appeals to me about a pinou is that I suspect the last surviving vestige of my father's people's legacy shrinks away from roaring outboards and noxious two-cycle smoke. Yellow finches and *Neka sama*. Peach Coulee and dancing lights in the still of the night. What a teeming, magical place the swamps and lakes and bayous must have been when there were only pirogues and dugouts, bateaus and small skiffs. Before the putt-putt even of the old one-lungers, the wonder and awe must have been...humbling.

I know I'll never be able to recapture that completely. But maybe, from behind the shadow of an old cypress tree, perhaps from under the shallows of a clear, green-black cove, there's still a hint of it out there. That's what I really go for. Fish are nice, fish are great, catching is always preferable to being skunked. But a glimpse of a world gone by, untouched by combustion fuels and rainbow-tinted slicks of petroleum, untainted by noise and churning props...that's the true rewards of an outdoor life, at least for me.

Transporting a fifteen-foot long vessel without a trailer is a challenge. I didn't want to spend a lot of money, mainly because I ain't got it. I also didn't want to burden my truck with a canoe rack until I'm sure I like this whole paddle-craft thing. So I did some investigating and found a thing called a truck bed extender. It fits into the trailer hitch receiver already on my truck, extends an iron bar about three feet, then comes straight up with a tee-shaped set of iron bars which can be adjusted for height. I used this to support the pinou, tied down securely and fitted with an orange warning flag.

The choice of where to go was difficult. I am not a paddler, yet. I had one harrowing experience with a traditional pirogue and gave it up for twenty-five years. So I wanted a place with no boat traffic to make a wake and tip me over. I settled on a secluded pond away from traffic and the public eye.

The pinou hauled very well with the truck bed extender, hardly wobbling or anything. I packed in a personal flotation device, or as we used to call 'em, life vest, ice chest with a bag of ice and two Diet Cokes, my tackle bag and one fly rod, two paddles and a net. Not thinking wisely I unloaded the pinou from the truck with all this inside and dragged it to the water before kicking myself in the behind. Reminder to me: put all the stuff in *after* you get it to the water, it's a lot easier!

It looked awful pretty there in the water, just the forward third of it on the bank, all hunter green with a black waterline and varnished wood inside. I actually had to sit and admire it for a minute, pardon my swelled head, and I thought about my dad in that minute. I remember being about twelve, thirteen maybe, and my parents got me a stereo system for Christmas, one of those all-in-one jobs that used to be so abundant with the turntable on top and the smoked plastic lid. I had no convenient place to put it so I begged dad for an additional twenty-five bucks to get a little pressboard stereo rack from the department store.

"Say, I've got some pretty nice plywood in the shop," he said. "We could build you something from that."

My adolescent mind conceived this as the most ridiculous thing I had ever heard. Why on earth would anyone spend a day or two in the shop making something like a stereo rack when they had plenty of them right down the road at the department store. He ended up giving me the money—it was never about the money, of course—but the lesson appeared to have gone unlearned.

Shaking off that memory, tasting its bitterness of shame, I got into the pinou and pushed away from the bank. I was surprised again at the ease with which it paddled and while I still need a lot of practice, it took virtually no effort to get the boat going at a good clip until I found a likely spot to fish. Casting my eight-foot fly rod was not hard at all from a sitting position and while I didn't exactly mop up on 'em, I caught two nice bream and lost two flies to two monsters of the deep that I never got a glimpse of but nearly gave me heart attacks when they struck.

My biggest problem is drift, and I'm unsure what to do about it. A one-mile-per-hour wind, just the merest exhalation of a babe, and that flat-bottomed girl is heading down the bayou *tout suite*. I like to fish quick at first until I locate some fish then slow down and fish every inch of a likely spot, but the breeze from aft kept me going when I didn't want to. I'm working with my paddling buddies on the 'Net on how to correct this.

Just to be sure I could, I stood in it to stretch my back a few times, and even fished from a standing position for a little while and yes, the boat is a little tippy, but at no time did I fear it was going over, just sloshed from side-to-side a bit. I walked from my aft seat to the ice chest secured to the front seat with bungee cords to get a Diet Coke and back to my seat again without incident.

I cast a boa yarn leech my friend Rick Zieger in Iowa sent me and got several strikes. One of the two fish that nearly gave me heart failure was on Rick's white boa yarn leech, the other on a red-and-black Jitterbee of my own tying. I imagine if I had been able to spend more time paying attention to my line and less paddling I would have done better. I may consider a small electric trolling motor eventually, but the sweetness of paddling along a quiet pond was really wonderful.

Not wanting to be on the road after dark on my initial maiden test fishing trip, I loaded the pinou back up with ample time to get home before dusk. But I took a little time, as has become a tradition with me, to spend a moment in quiet. Though I quit my two-pack-a-day cigarette habit a year ago, I do still enjoy a smoke on the water now and then, and keep a pack of short cigars in my pack. I lit one of these and stood near the pond, watching the sun throw lances of dragon fire over the cypress and willow trees to the west. Golden hour, and everything was amber or auburn or brilliant green and red and black. A long shadow stretched from my feet, narrow and skewed, with a fedora and a cigar and for a moment when I glanced at it I thought it might have been my dad's shadow as I had seen it so many times at the end of so many days, but of course, it was my own. Odd how they seem to look so much alike now.

Fish were rising to minnows or small insects I couldn't even see but I didn't reach for my rod. I stood there, smoke drifting around my head and thought of my father again. I wondered...no, scratch that. I was thankful that I did learn his lesson, after all, and I am sure he knows it.

Now and then, as the sun moved closer to the horizon, it would center in the space between tree limbs and cast a spot of radiance like heaven's gates opening to earth. I'd watch them glow and then fade slowly as the day continued to shorten. Microcosms of life, I thought. Emergence, swelling to glowing brilliance, fading, then gone. That little pressboard stereo rack didn't last a year before it sagged and delaminated and went to the trash, but the wooden bateau my father built two years before I was born still carries me safely to the lake and back when I ask it to. My little pirogue-canoe hybrid shows promise of being just as faithful.

There are lessons in all of it. I've said many times that the most important of them I learned growing up between the gunwales of a small wooden boat. Some things haven't changed, after all.

Several things happened that spring, some expected, some completely unforeseen. Perhaps the best of these was that my first book finally went to press, and *Native Waters* was especially well-received, though no landslide to be sure. Still, the kind words received from those who read it were touching and humbling.

Also as the spring waned and I waited for the moment when I could retreat to the water again, a writer and producer from the television series *Fly Fishing America* contacted me regarding a feature segment on the program. Stunned and not a little frightened out of my wits, I agreed to discuss the matter and awaited a phone call.

The price of gasoline also hit record highs, in excess of two bucks a gallon. Let me schedule a fishing vacation in the boat. That's all it takes to cause global economic collapse. Little did I know then how right I was.

What's a guy to do? There's no stream-side fishing here. It's boats or virtually nothing, save for a few small ponds that everybody who doesn't have a boat converged on in the spring. I'd be supporting oil-producing nations that vacation, like it or not.

I finally made it to the water in earnest near the end of April. It was mid-afternoon before we went out. A recent acquaintance, who goes by the name the Old Fella, and my son boarded the boat and we arrived at *Co'ktangi* about three o'clock. My compatriots were fishing bait. I rigged up my favorite bluegill fly, the Jitterbee, under an indicator on my eight-and-a-half foot Rapidan.

Water levels still were a little low, but much better than last time I had made a scouting trip to the lake. But I only motored the boat half as far into the cove as usual, and we began fishing a bit nearer the entrance than I usually like.

The bite was dismal at first, but we managed a few small bream. I usually throttle down and start fishing along the south side of the cove at Susan's Bayou, and sure enough, when we got there things improved remarkably.

My son, then thirteen, caught more fish on that trip than any previous one. I tried to negotiate down the canal, but the boat wouldn't make it in the shallows there, especially with three persons aboard. We found a couple spots where the chinquapins, or redears, were ganged up and the three of us took turns pulling them out. Of course, the Old Fella and I made sure we were busy checking our bait or Jitterbee so that the youngster would get in a few extra turns. The chinquapin were big and feisty, mixed in with a few goggle-eye and red-breasted bream thick as a Stephen King paperback.

The Jitterbee, originated by Louisiana's own Randy Leonpacher, is my favorite sub-surface warmwater fly of all. Tied with black and another color in chenille on a size eight or ten hook with a gold beadhead and two rubber legs aft, the Jitterbee is the finest panfish fly I know, and catches quite a few bass and catfish, too. I started off with red-and-black but the 'gills seemed less than enthused. I switched to chartreuse-black and this was welcomed with tip-bending vigor. We also landed two catfish, and about four small bass.

Oh, we had our share of toils, too. We laughed in bemused frustration at them. I laughed through grinding teeth when a missed strike brought leader, indicator, Jitterbee and a couple feet of line twirling around my rod tip, wrapping inside and outside of itself, in a convoluted mess that took me twenty minutes to disentangle. The Old Fella and boy laughed with heads shaking as they worked loose two snarled lines that kissed upon a mutual swing backward for the cast.

It was our first outing of the spring, and a fantastic one. When the sun was getting low in the sky, I found the only hole of deep water in the cove, at the mouth of Sawmill Bayou, throttled hard to get the boat on plane and departed. We bumped a log pretty hard on the way out, but there was no damage. That log had never been there before, but that's the way it is in the basin: always changing. We got home just before dark, satisfied and tired. It was a good trip. Despite the weariness, the recharge of the soul had begun.

I went back Monday and Wednesday, but the bite was much slower due to a storm front having passed through, with strong south winds that actually brought water levels higher.

Though the wind was still up the following weekend, I knew that a cold front would be dropping in Saturday night. Not about to miss any opportunity to get on the water again, I went out twice on Saturday.

The fish were extravagantly crashing at everything that touched the water. I fished a Jitterbee under an indicator the entire weekend. Within half an hour of arriving at the lake Saturday morning, I had landed four very nice bass. The rest of the two trips that day were filled with sun perch, redears, catfish and smaller bass.

It's not a comfortable boat. It has bench seats fore and aft. The bench seats are not comfortable, my knees are bent toward my chest, and my back ached badly by the time I got home. It still has an eight-pound thrust Minn Kota trolling motor on it. My father bought that motor in the early 1990s, a point where I knew he was feeling his age. Before that little trolling motor, he would paddle the little boat around the lake with his left hand and cast with his right, all day long. Even as light as the thrust is, it moves the little boat admirably.

I fished a few streamers, but the Jitterbee was still the preferred prey of everything I caught. I was deeply satisfied. There I was, on the lake my ancestors took as their namesake, in my father's wooden boat, fishing with bamboo fly rods. What man could have been happier? I had invited no one along Saturday. I needed that time alone with the lake, the boat, the rod and the eager, thrashing fish that came to my hand.

When I was very young, we'd fish from dawn to dusk. We always had oatmeal creme pies and soft drinks in the boat if I was along, but when dad went fishing alone he brought no food and no drink. We would spend the whole day, but eventually I would grow cranky and tired, and when we finally made our way home, it always seemed to me he was leaving something of himself behind on the lake. Today I know what it was. As the years converge behind me, I know what he felt as he throttled the engine up, the boat's nose lifted and she peacefully slid along the surface of *Siti*, lake of the Chitimachas. A little part of himself lived there, a little part of myself lives there also. Now, when I fish along the shores of the lake, sitting on the front bench seat and working the trolling motor, I am mournfully aware of the absence of him, but his spirit is strongest on this old lake. If the boat was my cradle, the lake was my playground and sanctuary.

I stumbled on a nest of redears. They attacked the Jitterbee with such ferocity as soon as it hit the water I missed several trying to get the slack fly line in my hand to make a hook set. They were big and dark and beautiful. I fished along the south fork of Sawmill Bayou until it converged in the rear, where a hunting club has put up cables and wire and a metal gate. The bile rose in my throat again, as it always does. For eight thousand years my grandfathers and grandmothers fished these waters, lived on these shores. For my entire life until that gate was erected I knew the twists and turns and canopies of cypress behind it. Now those who would barricade free-flowing waters and possess that which can never be possessed forbid me the right of my blood. The little boat pointed its bow at the back of Sawmill Bayou, drifting as I thought about the loss, and it floated just to the gate and slowed there, stopping inches from the metal bars. Together, we stared behind that abhorrence, wishing not for fish but for freedom.

I coaxed the boat away. It struggled with reluctance, but obeyed. We followed the right fork of the bayou out, catching more fish as we went, until we emerged on the open lake again. Following the north shore, I caught more big red-breasted sunfish over sunken timbers. Darkness threatened. It was time to go home. I trolled away from the sunken timbers, put up my rod and sat behind the engine. A single crank started it up. There were a dozen-and-a-half panfish in the live well under the front bench seat. I knew I needed to get home and get them cleaned and put up. But I took a leisurely cruise on my way out of the cove, letting the blazing oranges and ochers and silvers saturate my skin. The varnished topsides of the boat were like fire, like sacred fires, like the fire my grandfathers brought from Natchez to burn eternally until the great darkness settled over our nation and so very much was lost.

"This one's for you, pop," I said aloud to the lake, to the boat, to the old man who was with me, and to the brilliant sunset of sacred fires. "This one's for you."

Out of the lake, I turned the bow toward home, gave the engine about three-quarters throttle and the boat slid across my native waters quietly, purposefully, carrying me there and back safely once again. Just as it has always done. Just as I always depend upon it to do. Just as my father built it to do.

The attendant at the boat landing near my home called the next day.

"They're tearing 'em up right here!" he said. "Right off the landing, in the trees! Big goggle-eye and chinquapin!"

Of course, there was no need to say more. The words "goggle-eye" and "chinquapin" coupled with that most wonderful of adjectives, "big," were enough to set me into gear. I was already envisioning a fish fry, particularly for my mom.

The landing is less than two miles from home, and when I arrived there with the boat, I was dismayed to see that water lilies had covered it for yards and yards out over the lake, except for one spot just big enough to launch two boats side by side.

I paid my three dollars, and dropped the boat into the lake. But upon trying to pull the trailer out of the water, it refused to budge.

The truck was spinning wheels. It's not a huge truck, but it's a full-size Chevy with a six-cylinder power plant. Still, the trailer wouldn't come out. Another angler came by to help, jumping on the back bumper to help gain traction, but still no-go.

"It's probably stuck on a drop off," he said. "May have to pick up the back of the trailer to get the tires rolling."

I waded out to the back of the trailer while he got behind the wheel of my truck. I mean, I couldn't ask him to wade out there, could I? He gunned it, spinning up white smoke from my tires, and I picked up on the trailer. No cigar.

Finally, the attendant came with his four-wheel-drive truck, we hooked up a chain to mine, and he pulled, I picked up on the trailer and it emerged from the water at last, then stopped midway. There was a length of one-inch pipe under the frame and out, then around the axle, disappearing somewhere in the water behind the trailer. Me and the kind person who was helping me both had to use a lot of muscle to bend it enough to get the trailer to slip out.

The attendant promised he'd have it removed. I figured I was done with the whole sordid business and took off in the boat, soaked up to the waist, but determined to go fishing.

Sure enough, just along the lilies near the southwest bank of Grand Lake, the goggle-eye and the chinquapin were simply falling head-over-heels in love with a chartreuse-and-black Jitterbee under a VOSI, the venerable Vertically Oriented Strike Indicator. My four-weight Diamondback rod made the experience even more wonderful.

Until I touched the foot control of the trolling motor.

Already there were five nice fish in the live well, and I could see my mom's grinning face at supper over a platter of golden-brown fried goggle-eye. But then I touched the foot control of the trolling motor to move the boat a bit farther down the line of lilies, and *WHACK!*

The motor began dancing a jig, gyrating and jumping all over. I knew what that meant, but I had to lift the motor up just to be sure. I was sure. One blade was completely broken off.

The fish came out of the live well, back in the water. Back to the landing. This time, I back the trailer down on the opposite side of the narrow slot between the lilies, then bring the boat on.

Of course, the trailer refused to come out of the water.

I am beyond annoyed now. I am rapidly approaching ballistic.

The attendant comes with his truck and chain again, but this time, with the weight of the boat on the trailer, she ain't budging.

He's a good fellow, the attendant. We talk a lot, tell jokes, discuss woodworking with antique cypress. But he's confused and embarrassed, as I am.

"We pulled that pipe out of the water while you left," he said. "I'll be durned if I know what's got you now. Nobody ever gets stuck here. I've never seen it."

Figures. Leave it to me to break a record.

So he gets his big farm tractor, and we try pulling the truck, boat and trailer out with that. Nope, ain't happening.

"What will you give me to leave it here?" I asked. "Make it kind of a landmark. Something to remember me by. Years from now, when I'm rich and famous you can tell people this was where I got my truck stuck and said the hell with it. Threw my hands in the air and moved to Missoula. How about it?"

About that time, another fisherman comes by and offers to try pulling me out with his four-wheel drive truck. I agree, sure it won't work, but we give it a shot. This does the trick, and I am at last safely on the hard surface.

I look at the trailer, and the axle is covered with clam shell, the material the boat landing is surfaced from. There is, apparently, a ledge out there that the axle of the trailer fell over, and it took quite a bit of effort to pull it up.

I thank the folks who helped me and head home, then spend an hour hosing down the truck and the boat, which are covered with a gooey mess comprised of mud, clam shell fragments, sodden water lilies and other debris. Then I go take a nap.

Monday I ordered two new props for the trolling motor, one as a spare to keep in the boat along with a nine-sixteenths wrench. Meanwhile, I'm hearing folks all over talking about fishing last weekend.

"The basin is hot!" they say. "It's smoking! Just throw a line out, the fish are everywhere! They're jumping in the boat! They're throwing themselves on the fillet table!"

My new props would not come in until Friday. The way my luck had been going, I was doubtful. Even after they did arrive, I awaited the next calamity with a sense of dread.

Murphy was a fisherman. I guarantee it.

It turned out to be perhaps the best spring I've had in years. I would almost say it was worth the wait but, well, it really *was* a miserable wait.

The fish were exuberant, daring and feisty, and the extraordinary bite went on for weeks, abundant with slab-sized bluegill, redears, goggle-eye and the like, and for the first time, I never picked up a spinning rod all spring. The fly of choice remarkably remained the Jitterbee, which outperformed all others throughout.

But best of all was the return. May, and I was nearly a hundred pages into my first mainstream novel and the winter was finally done. One evening, twilight diffused by threatening rain clouds, I coaxed the boat along Sawmill Bayou and the wind suddenly dropped away. When the roar of the engine dies and the boat settles to her haunches, her nose coming to rest seconds later, silence becomes absolute.

There are moments. Moments when everything is magical. They arrive without warning, unexpected. This was one of them, I knew it as soon as the engine fell silent and the boat settled into a quiet drift. The last hour before dusk, and the setting sun turned everything golden, saturated the greens, browns, reds and blacks of the lake nearly to the point of exaggeration, unreal. There had been a slight breeze earlier, before I moved from one spot to this one, but now the wind was gone and the surface of the water was still as glass. Shad, fleeing a predator, undulated their backs under the shimmering plane of it, rings of rising fish expanded outward like the universe unfolding.

Damselflies swarmed, joined in mating, and they touched the water so slightly they left not even a swirl in their passing. They were so slight, so diminutive and their lives so brief they hardly seemed to exist at all, but there in the last hour of the day their paths seemed to sparkle with star fire, tiny pinpricks against the green-black water. Frogs bellowed to each other, speaking across great distances, but the sudden screech of an owl startled them into silence.

One of those moments. I let the boat drift along the little canal's mouth unguided. Everything seemed made of gold: green-gold, brown-gold, red-gold, all shades of the rainbow augmented and uplifted by gold. Sunlight peeked over the cypresses, throwing lances of gossamer light, fanning. A large, black and hairy spider scurried around the back side of a tree, disturbed at the near passing of the boat. It, too, seemed to be fringed by gold, a halo of shipwrecked sunbeams. The whole lake seemed to immerse itself in those last few moments of the day, and I had the distinct and powerful conviction that I would behold some great moving of heaven and earth, some momentous revelation, if I only knew where to look.

These are the moments that sustain me. This, in all its golden glory and liquid majesty, is my cathedral, temple and choir. It has been said that before we are born we knew the secrets of all time, but an angel came along just at the moment of birth and touched his finger to our lip—creating the small indention just under the nose—and sealed that knowledge away from us forever. Out here, in these moments, all those secrets are like the words of a song just on the tip of the tongue but not quite remembered, like a name in the back of the mind not quite recalled. Struggle for it, try to conjure it up, coax it out, but it remains elusive and unreachable.

These are the moments when it all makes sense to me. There is no concrete here, no cold steel, no drone of machinery or ringing phones. Clouds drift in, for there is a promise of rain tonight, and I almost look forward to it, the scent and sound and feel of it on my skin. The sunbeams are dappled now, piercing clouds and hiding behind them. A small circle opens in the billows, and the rays stream out brilliantly, and I wonder if I might see the Lorax lift himself by the seat of the pants through it. He understood, the Lorax did. That there is no erudition between concrete and steel, in mahogany halls or windowed towers.

It all makes sense to me in this place, these moments. How life is not nearly so important as living. How watching is not so necessary as seeing and hearing not so vital as listening. Away from this place, there's too much noise to hear, too much static to see. When I retreat from where I must spent most of my waking hours my eyes ache from powerful electromagnetic fields, cheerily planting tumors in my brain. My joints protest, stiff and sore, when I move away from the hours trapped by the ticking dictator on the wall. My shirttail is tucked neatly under my belt, hair combed, my shoelaces tied, but my heart is dry as old pecan branches, brittle as old window glass. The Lorax understood this. What would be left without damselflies touching the surface of lake water invisibly, owls startling booming frogs into silence and, there at the back end of dark canals, voices whispering secrets thousands of years old?

Along that north shore, the boat drifted again upon that canal I always pass and seldom reach into, but it draws me, calls out to me in a voice both soothing and menacing. I let the boat point her nose into it, and softly we moved in, a narrow, shallow and short canal, the back end of which is canopied by embraced limbs. As always, the nape of my neck tingled, and power surged around me, making the hair on my arms stand. One of the thin places, the back end of that canal. A screeching, perhaps a bird, raises gooseflesh again. I shred a cigar and let the tobacco drift over the canal, touch the water as slightly as the little dragonflies on the cove. Sudden, startling, an owl swoops over the back end of the canal, darting upward, vanished. Here the canal forks and I go no further, let the bow rest. Farther along that northern shore of the cove is a short, straight canal with no fork, also canopied in trees, where the hair on the back of my neck also stands up and the gooseflesh rises on my arms. But that canal was man-made, this one I believe to be natural, probably here with my ancestors were here, and I suspect in both places they still are here, in the back ends of those dark canals. The little electric trolling motor kicks up mud, and I am reminded again of the thinning. The steady march into the way of memory.

Not for the first time, I wonder if adjectives, verbs and nouns can ever describe the truth of what I find down the end of those shallow canals. I look out at it, as owls dart overhead and unidentifiable shrieks, calls and warnings sound from the trees, and wonder if it's really possible to describe magic such as this. It humbles me. In forty years, I know, none of this will likely be here, filled up with silt, grown over with marsh grass and small trash trees. I know that in just a month there'll be no more frantic, voracious bream here, when the temperatures rise and the shallow, thin water grows too hot for them to tolerate. The magic may still persist down the dark end of shallow canals, but when the canals are gone, when the cove and the lake are gone, will the absence of water from the recipe, from the concoction of the brew, diminish the magic? Like casting a spell without the right words, perhaps the loss of water will end it all.

From time to time, when other fishermen are here, in the lake, in the basin, they tend to speak loudly to each other, as if the distance from forward of the boat to aft requires a great shouting to be heard. I wonder if they are ill at ease with the silence, with the magic. Seekers, unsettled by what they seek. Now and then I meet another type of fisherman, quiet, contemplative, and we pass each other in our boats and our eyes meet and perhaps there is a whispered greeting but no more. These and I understand each other. We understand the magic found at the back end of dark canals, and the fear lurking within going the way of memory. Shouting destroys what can be found here. Yelling and loud laughter betrays the silence, magic shrinks away from it. Stay in your factories, plants, offices and cars to shout. We have no need of it here, where the slightest rumble can destroy a doorway, collapse a gate.

It has been six years since my father left this world, left this place. Sometimes, when I am here, I think that when his soul left his body there in the bedroom of the little house on the reservation, it passed through the moonlit night, following water. He could have gone straight west, but he followed water, as he had throughout his life, along Bayou Teche, up the borrow pit near the levee and at last to *Co'ktangi*, where perhaps some of the happiest moments of his life were spent. I imagine he hovered there for a time, above it, within it, throughout it. Then the slightest exhalation from the back end of a dark canal lifted him to his grandfathers. No better place to depart the world than *Co'ktangi*. No more fitting end to a life spent on water.

Six years, but I still speak to him, particularly here, here along the flow to memory. I speak to all of them here. They are like radio stations, sometimes clear, sometimes static-filled; some are stronger than others, modulate more forcefully, punch through atmospheric interference with greater strength of will. Some are like a barely-recognized favorite song but no matter how much fiddling with the knob it never quite becomes clear, tangible. White noise obscures them, but I speak anyway.

Yet it is time. There is never enough of it for peace. The sun is sinking dangerously low, and my ride home is long. I crank the engine and the golden rays, damselflies, clouds, dark ends of canals, all shrink away, appalled at the roar of the engine, leaving only purple patches of memory, dancing, dancing across my vision.

The boat returns me to concrete, steel, noise and chaos. Down a tunnel, and the light at the end is fluorescent, the mouth of it brickwork. I don't know when I'll be able to steal away again to damselflies and gossamer twilight, but I am longing for it already.

Miraculous weather settled through most of the spring until late June. Dry, tolerable winds for the most part. It was, as mentioned, the best spring I can remember.

Word came to me that the Beach, the former village of *Ama'tpan na'mu* but now used as a boat landing in part, was afire with bull bream. Anxious to get into more hot fishing action, I put over the boat and took the short jaunt away from the boat landing proper to the more undisturbed areas of the Beach where, I knew from past experience, the big panfish tend to group in the spring and fall.

There were plenty of fish there. I caught two on my first two casts, thick and feisty. There were also more fishermen than you could shake a stick at. I know this, because after catching my second slab bream, two of them suddenly appeared as if from nothingness to my port and starboard.

Both were tackle fishermen, jigging with long poles, bobbers and grubs. I was, of course, fishing my venerable Jitterbee under an indicator.

"Uh, fellas, ya mind?"

Both ignored me.

"It's kinda hard to cast with ya'll so close," I said cheerily.

Again, complete silence.

Frustrated but unwilling to get into a pissing contest with two hardware-chunkers, I backed my boat away and found another likely spot. Soon the big sunfish were coming to hand again and, again, two boats appeared from thin air.

This time when they ignored my requests, I kept fishing. And the simple act of slinging forty feet of fly line tipped with a sharp-hooked fly convinced the intruders there were better places to fish. But then more came, and the lesson had to be repeated. And yet again.

I packed up and went home.

I don't understand it. I really don't. I was taught to respect another fisherman's territory. If a fisherman sees another angler, he starts his fishing far away, far enough to belay even the notion of elbowing in. When two people are fishing in a boat, lines should never be near each other. If the man in the bow catches a few fish in a spot, you do *not* cast into his spot until you are invited. If he moves on, then he loses his spot by forfeiture, but you stay the hell out of it until then.

Makes no sense to me why there can't be more common courtesy on the water. There's plenty fish for all, or is it that shouldering-in fisherman just aren't good enough to find them on their own? That must be the reason. The unskilled angler must depend on muscling in on other fishermen to receive any satisfaction from the sport, since he is unqualified to study the variables of weather, water levels and quality, to locate fish on his own. I suspect that the tackle fisherman will never admit it, but when he sees a fly fisherman, he recognizes a superior angler that *must* know where the fish are. There's a remark sure to be taken as fighting words, eh?

Truth be known, I do not shun tackle as if it is the diseased carcass of a dead carp. One of my greatest relaxing pleasures is to rig up a sinker and treble hook with a glob of earthworms and sit behind the house catching small catfish out of Bayou Teche. I take the dogs with me, let them frolic and play along the water's edge. I do not have to cast, mend line, and pick up slack from my feet. I don't have to strip or snap or pop. I just sit there and wait, watching the sunset, smelling the twilight, until Mr. Whiskers decides to bite. If I catch, fine. If I don't, well, that's fine too. I have spent no money on gas or oil, on ice or drinks (other than grabbing something from the fridge on my way out the door.) The dogs love the outing and so do I. Sometimes I think we fishermen forget such simple pleasures. We almost let the world— this incessant, roaring beast coercing achievement, advancement and ladder-climbing—convince us that we *must* fish our high-tech high-modulus rods and hand-tied flies, we must don our neoprene and fedoras and chest-packs, to really be fishermen. Oh, but in a calm breeze over Bayou Teche at dusk, with a bait caster in my lap propped up on my knee. Then the sudden *snip-snip-snip* at the end of the tight line, the dogs perking their ears up in anticipation as I ready my hands on the rod handle...these are the simple joys our fathers and grandfathers knew. Like that old black magic, it's good enough for me.

To me, traditionalism doesn't end with bamboo fly rods and wooden boats. An evening on Bayou Teche catfishing is but an extension of the same spirit. I fished just this way as a kid, like my parents did, on these same shores. I even delight in not having a dedicated catfishing rod. I use my old high-tech bass rod, a medium-action Shimano rod with low-profile bait casting reel. Gimme a break, I'm a Luddite, not a Neanderthal.

Summer Days

So yes, there's still a bit of bait in my life. I have to admit it. I have been known to indulge myself in the time-honored, highly cultured and enviable pastime of catfishin'.

I know what some of you are thinking: catfishing? You? Here you are, the pontificator of high esteem, who espouses the use of wooden boats and bamboo fly rods, shunning all things otherwise, have lowered himself to the practice of catfishing? You, who once said you'd just as soon retire from the whole sport before you stooped to the lowest level of fishing with tackle and live bait again?

Yes, and I'm enjoying the heck out of it, thank you very much.

It's not a serious pursuit, mind you. It's something relaxing to do. With a box of worms, I can easily grab my bait rod, tackle bag and a folding chair, walk down to the bayou behind the house, taking the dogs with me, and fish until dark. I catch "little," you understand. Meaning, I catch a lot of them, but they're mostly "little," and that's fine, because who wants to clean fish anyway?

The best part of it is the dogs, really, but we'll get back to that. I buy worms from the store. You can't get worms like I used to get when I was a kid. The *real* earthworms, husky and solid, the ones that turn up in your garden. No, the stores sell Canadian Night Crawlers now, and they keep them in the refrigerator next to the cheese and salami. This is because they're from Canada, of course, where it's always winter except the second week in July, when Canadians enjoy spring from Sunday to Tuesday, summer from Wednesday to Friday then fall until Sunday again, and then winter comes back. So they have to keep the worms cool down here in Louisiana by keeping them in the refrigerator next to the cheese and salami, sometimes the wieners, and hope the little kids don't make a boo-boo.

Canadian Night Crawlers are humungous and 99.8 percent water. How they accomplish this without disintegrating is a mystery, but I firmly believe that less than two-tenths of a percent of their bodies is solid matter. Yet catfish down here love them, even though I think they make fish burp, like watermelon does people. I believe this because, when I am fishing with Canadian Night Crawlers, I see lots and lots of rising bubbles in the water.

I have started using my high-tech bass rod and open-faced bait casting reel for catfishing. It's the rod I used to chunk plastic worms and spinner baits with before I was reformed and converted to fly fishing. Now I have a high-tech catfishin' pole, you see. I sit in my chair down by the bayou behind my house, throw out a rigged weight and hook stuffed with a glob of Canadian Night Crawlers, and relax. I tried all those fancy-dancy catfish baits on the market. The dip baits, the stink baits, the blood, liver, cheese and shad baits you shoot into a tube on the hook, roll into a ball and put on the hook, you name it, and have not caught a single catfish. I think they may work for catfish north of I-10, but our catfish down here are too smart. Most of them stink so badly, I wanted to throw myself overboard to get away from it.

As mentioned, I always take the dogs with me, Mocha and Daisy. Daisy is a new addition to the family, my girl's black lab of advancing years. You realize that black labs are extraordinarily intelligent dogs but Mocha, my English springer spaniel, has roughly the intelligence quotient of a bowl of grits, so you can imagine the team I have in my company.

Though the bayou is only a few hundred feet from the house, it takes the three of us nearly half an hour to get there since Mocha and Daisy must investigate every scent closely, roll in it vigorously, and move on to the next one; then they must wander into the neighbor's yard every time, going suddenly deaf and turning me into a crazy man screaming, "*DAISY! MOCHA! GET YOUR BUTTS BACK OVER HERE RIGHT NOW! RIGHT THIS MINUTE! AIN'T YOU HERE YET? GET OUT OF THEM PEOPLE'S YARDS THEY EAT DOGS RAW OVER THERE AND HANG THE SKINS OUT TO DRY ON THE PECAN TREES!!!*" This usually gets their attention and they run back to me in terror of such horrible people, meanwhile, the neighbors are on the phone calling the cops.

Finally I get set up to fish, and do so relatively unbothered for an hour or so while the dogs investigate all the smells down by the bayouside, roll in them happily, then find another smell to repeat the process. Most of these smells are something that met an untimely demise. Then they have to splash through the water for a time, which is good, because it gets some of the smell of the things they rolled in off them. Mocha does not like the water to touch her belly or her chest, so the deepest she'll go is leg-level. Daisy, on the other hand, was an Olympic swimmer in a previous life and is happy as a coffee bean bug in the water.

So happy, in fact, that when I cast my Canadian Night Crawler and weight out, Daisy jumps into the bayou in hot pursuit. I must find a nice stick to throw for Daisy to distract her while I cast my line in the other direction. Daisy never brings the stick back to me. She retrieves it and then hides it in the weeds, though I haven't the faintest idea why. Then she sits by me and waits for me to throw her another one, which she also hides in the weeds. I would wonder if she's crazy or something, but we all know Labs are mega-intelligent so it must be something I'm just not getting, dim-witted as I am.

Mocha, meanwhile, is watching all this swimming and fetching and hiding of sticks business with complete astonishment. She watches Daisy swim way out to the middle of the bayou, looks at me and whines, then looks at Daisy, then looks at me and whines again, and repeats this process until Daisy returns safely to shore. If I am not sure what Daisy is doing when she hides the sticks in the weeds, I'm sure I'll never figure out what Mocha is thinking. I tried to throw a stick just for her to fetch, and she looked at me and whined. Daisy went to get Mocha's stick, and hid it in the weeds. I wonder if she's made a deal with a pair of beavers?

I have to watch it when I catch a little catfish, too, because after I unhook it if I don't throw it far enough into the water to swim away at once, Daisy will grab it up and go hide it in the weeds. Then I have to go dig it out and try again to release it.

We go on like this til nearly dark, then I pack up my gear and head back to the house. It takes another half hour to get back because all the scents in the yard apparently smell different moving south than they did when we were moving north, and the dogs must carefully sniff them and vigorously roll in them yet again. Finally we make it back to the house and I put my gear up in the shop. The dogs come in with me. I have faked Daisy out, because she has a "hot spot" on her back right above her tail where the hair falls out if she gets stressed. When she moved to live with me and Mocha, she stressed out pretty bad (wouldn't you?) and lost a lot of hair on her back and tail. I have been applying a cream and it's growing back nicely, but Daisy hates the cream.

So I have to fool her, and while I'm picking up my tackle, I catch her by the collar and hold her there in the shop while I put the lotion on her skin. She suffers this indignation with head lifted high, stone-still, until I'm done. I *oooh* and *ahhh* over her, saying things like, "Oh, that's such a good baby puppy dog, snoogums, oogums, what a sweet little Daisy!" I have to pick up the bottle of lotion quick, otherwise she tries to grab it away from me with her teeth, presumably to go hide it in the weeds with the sticks and little catfish

Then it's back to the yard for the dogs, and inside to get cleaned up for me. Another catfishin' trip done.

The yardstick by which all dogs are measured has long been my beloved Shadow.

An English springer spaniel of estimable character, boundless energy and daredevil bravery, Shadow came from a pet store in Lafayette. He was a bundle of liver-and-white fur, so sad and lonely in the display window, he had to come home with me. He just had to.

Shadow grew into an amazing dog. Cunning and clever, he was everything the canine breed strives to be. Regrettably, he met his demise at age four to a mama copperhead snake when he got into her nest of young 'uns, that insatiable curiosity his undoing.

I wasn't home when it happened. She must have struck him multiple times. I belatedly found the nest and dispatched the whole family. I was heartbroken beyond words. My friend and ally, my faithful companion, had died there in the yard, alone, pumped full of agonizing venom. I probably could not have saved him even if I had been there, even if had I rushed him to medical help, but at least he wouldn't have faced death alone.

When I'd take him out to the pasture, and while Chance—his buddy, a Cocker spaniel—would bound here and there, stopping to smell everything, Shadow would run.

That dog could fly. He would wait, impatient but still, until I gave him leave: "Run, Shadow."

Then he'd leap into motion, belly low, legs pumping and ears flapping behind him, and he'd run like lightning across the pasture. I have never had a dog that fast, don't think I'll ever see a dog that fast again. Perhaps it's just affectionate bias, but I'd have put Shadow up against any Greyhound around.

He had accompanied me through a divorce; relocated with me twice until I finally settled into the home I'm in now, the old family place. It was odd: he'd always walk without being taught, on my left side. That's my bad eye, the one that never really worked much since I was born, and I have very limited vision in it. It was like Shadow knew this, somehow, and took up sentry there on that side as we strolled down path and trail.

I never knew if anything I had done had made him such a good dog, or if he was just born with the spirit. These many years later, I think it was both.

But I guess there was something else haunting me about Shadow's death. Not just that I felt I had failed him, somehow, in his battle with the copperhead and his lonely death. It's that there was nothing there to fill that vast emptiness, and I didn't want anything to. I waded through his sudden absence like self-flagellation.

I dug a grave in the back yard. Over so many decades, the number of pets that have been buried in that yard totals dozens. I dug, and I cried, and when it was done, I lowered Shadow into it, and just before I covered him up, I noticed that he was curled up in a ball, legs tucked under him, nose hidden under his front leg. Almost exactly the way he was when the store attendant handed him to me four years before.

It may not have been appropriate. I don't know the ways of my ancestors well enough for so much has been lost. But I placed tobacco and cedar in the grave with Shadow, and a small feather. I also placed a dog snack there to sustain him on the journey. This is the way of my people, and perhaps it wasn't done that way for a dog, but it was done that way for *my* dog.

I still think of Shadow, talk of him often, and there'll always be a part of my heart reserved just for him. Still, sometimes, when Daisy and I are out in the fields, walking trails and she's searching happily for bugs or insects or birds, I detect the slightest movement on the peripheral of my vision, out the corner of my bad eye, the side he always walked with me on.

The rational part of me claims it's only the wind, but I whisper softly, just to be sure: "*Run*, Shadow."

And in those times, I think of a verse by Beulah Ferguson Smith, and wish my old friend a happy journey wherever he was

bound as he brushed by my side:
   We have a secret you and I,
   That no one else shall know,
   For who but I can see you lie,
   Each night, in fireglow?
   And who but I can reach my hand
   Before I go to bed,
   And feel the living warmth of you,
   And touch your silken head?
   And only I walk woodland paths,
   And see ahead of me,
   Your small form racing with the wind,
   So young again, and free!
   And only I can see you swim,
   In every brook I pass. . .
   And, when I call, no one but I
   Can see the bending grass...

Things Stirring Noisily

It all started when I published my first book, and *Native Waters* became available in early spring. Never could I have guessed that my life as a reclusive hermit was ending quickly.

Now, I didn't want to make too much of this, because I am always of the opinion, "I'll believe it when I see it," a philosophy that comes quite easily to a person who has chased many a rainbow down more than one dead-end street. My first book signing was a grand success, though, thanks to Franklin's good folks. "That's it, nice ride, time to get back down to earth." That's what I thought.

In late March I was contacted by a gentleman from Barrett Productions, who produce the television program *Fly Fishing America*, and they said they'd like to do an episode about me, my heritage, my fishing, and my native waters.

"Moi?" I thought, astounded. "Lil' ol' me?"

I almost accused him of being any one of several friends whom I thought were playing a practical joke on me. I admit I did go on the Internet to find out if there really were such a production company and a man by his name who worked for them, I agreed reluctantly.

Yes, reluctantly. Remember that I wanted to be a reclusive hermit author, shunning all fame and publicity, like Harper Lee. Now I got these folks wanting to come make film of me fishing, for Pete's sake. How do people ever get used to fishing on camera? There's a serious trust relationship that has to be established first, I imagine. You just trust the camera operators, editors, everyone involved to *not* show, under any circumstances whatsoever, you hooking yourself in the seat of the pants; your hat flying off along with the most God-awful tailing loop in the history of fly fishing; the blackbird you hooked; and most importantly of all, all filming must *cease and desist* when I say, "Tinkle break!"

But you know, it occurred to me that all my life I have been complaining that, "If I could only get a break," I'd make something of my writing. I mean, I tried publishing for years. I sent out manuscripts, waited eight months and got them back with rejection slips. I started taking a razor knife to cut a tiny sliver of clear tape that I put along the edge of the sheets of my manuscripts, mailed them, waited eight months, got it back with the usual rejection slip and, sure enough, there was my sliver of clear tape, undisturbed. They had not even looked at my work. That's when I realized it really didn't matter if I had any talent at all... getting published is all a crap shoot. A roll of the dice. So I bit the bullet, grumbled about vanity, and published *Native Waters* myself.

So here are these people offering me a chance to be on national television. Here's the "break" I've always pined for, staring me in the eye and challenging me to be man enough to take it. I took it. It interested me that *Fly Fishing America* is not a "how-to" type show so much as it is a "character-driven" show about people who fly fish. It features people in their environs, doing what they love, what makes them who they are. It is about characters who interact with each other and the natural world, characters who are, in the end, aren't that unlike you and I.

But I'm a "character" now. Jeesh.

What would my father say? I come from a long line of characters, you know. My grandfather was quite a character. My father was a rather famous character. Reporters, television documentarians, anthropologists and historians came from all over the nation and world to meet him, that's how much of a character my dad was. I guess I'm expected to be a character too. It's my torch to bear. I just haven't had a lot of practice at it.

Then a couple months later, the film company called back. I really expected them to say that they had discovered, despite my best efforts to conceal the truth, that I was in fact a catfishin', bait castin' Neanderthal. They'd explain that the show would not happen, leaving me with no star at Grauman's Chinese Theater and more than a little egg on my face for having told my friends about my upcoming spotlight.

But it turns out they were doing a show on the Blackfeet reservation with an Indian there who's a professional trout fishing guide. I thought, "Well, that's it, they found some other Indian to do a show on" and resigned myself to a life of obscurity. But no. They decided it would be kinda cool if I fished with him in Montana, and he came down here and fished with me, and they'd do two shows on Indians fly fishing on their native waters.

I hate flying. Terrified of it, completely paranoid about it. I have flown six times in my life, therefore I am not imagining anything and my fears are not groundless (pardon the pun.) I know I am terrified of flying because I did it six times. Now, that was only two trips, but each required a layover going and coming back. So since I actually changed airplanes and pilots, left the ground and returned six times, I maintain that I have flown six times. Makes perfect sense to me: that's six different chances for something to be wrong with an airplane or a pilot. This logic may seem strange, but it keeps me down to earth.

But I agreed and I ended up in Montana! Montana is the Shangri-la of fly fishermen, you know. It's where *A River Runs Through It* was set. It's like, fly fishing nirvana. Fishing on the Blackfeet reservation for trout. Trout! Trout that are not speckled and do not live in saltwater, thank you very much. We're talking real trout here, also something regarded as a fictional beast down here in the south. Dragons, unicorns, jackalopes and freshwater trout, all make believe animals.

I even wrote a little diddy about my upcoming adventure, to the tune of *Oh, Susanna*! and it goes like this:

I come from Looziana
With my fly rod on my knee;
I'm goin' to Montana
Where the trout-fish wait for me.

I cried all day when I left,
that airplane went so high;
I'm scared I'll fall right to my death,
Montana don't you cry.
Oh! Montana, don't you cry for me;
Cuz' I come from Looziana,
with my fly rod on my knee.
I had a dream the other night,
When everything was still;
I thought I was in Montana, dear,
I was fishing just o'er that hill.
The little fly was in his mouth,
That trout-fish caught my eye,
Said I, I'm coming from deep down south,
Where the cat-fish we do fry.
Oh! Montana, don't you cry for me;
I come from Looziana,
with my fly rod on my knee.
I'll then touch down in Lah-fah-yette,
And then I'll look all 'round,
And when I find my Chevy truck,
I'll drop and kiss the ground.
But if I do not find it,
This Injun'll surely die,
And on Surrey Street I'll be buried,
Montana don't you cry.
Oh! Montana, don't you cry for me;
I come from Looziana,
with my fly rod on my knee.

Okay, so it needs a little work. Gimme a break, I'm a columnist, not Rodgers and Hammerstein.

I still think Harper Lee had the right idea.

Four: Montana

The day cold and fair with a high easterly wind: we were visited
by two Indians who gave us an account of the country and people
near the Rocky Mountains where they had been.
– Meriwether Lewis

I had a few email contacts with Joe Kipp, the Blackfeet Indian who would be my host and fishing guide. His initial question to me, "Can swamp NDNs fish?" was followed by the notation that he hoped I was afraid of grizzly bears because he was afraid of snakes and alligators. This would become quite a prolific banter between us later on.

The first time I ever joined an Internet chat room was also the last. It was a Native American chat and nearly every participant's screen name was some variation of NDN. It was SweetNDNLegs or NDNDaddy or even NDN 4EVER. I admit it took me a few minutes to figure out what NDN stood for, and I only realized it when I spoke it out loud:

"What the devil does N-D-N mean, anyway?" I blurted in frustration and, of course, having done so, finally understood. Swamp NDNs are apparently not clever chat room participants.

I did my best to get around flying. I looked at driving it but thirty-six hours in the truck just seemed debilitating and I'd probably burn more fuel than the stupid airplanes. In my younger days I didn't mind driving far and wide, but as I've grown older I just don't weather it well. Part of the problem may be that my truck is pretty plain Jane, and it is just not comfortable for long treks. So the plans that I have to fish every state in the union before I die may be difficult, but I'm thinking a little more comfortable truck will help considerably.

That *is* my plan, you know. To retire young enough and do what my dad wanted to do: take off and see the country. I don't know if dad intended to fish it all or not, but knowing him, I'm sure there would have been a rod handy at all times. I am not quite sure why I didn't listen to him when I was very young and he said to me, "Boy, I don't give a damn what you do for a living, just as long as you get rich." This was something of an overstatement, of course, as I'm sure he'd have objected strongly to a career in illegal narcotics or something.

I toyed with the idea of train or bus, but both of those are prone to accidents as well. I figured if I was gonna go out, I might as well go out with a bang. Grumbling about the price of fame and the logistics of flapping my arms fast enough, I set about getting ready to go. The night before, I packed my roll-on and carry-on bags. I was told by those who know such things to pack a couple changes of clothes and toiletries and bring them with me in case Continental Airlines lost my luggage. This was fine and dandy, but my fly rod and tackle was in my luggage, so if Continental Airlines lost it, I'd be quite well-dressed to stand around looking nice in Montana when I'm supposed to be fishing. Nobody told me I could bring rods as carry-ons.

I was flying out of Lafayette, with layovers in Houston and Seattle before I reached Kalispell, Montana, which is west of Glacier National Park. I needed to be east of the park, across the mountain range, so somebody from the film company would be there to get me. I also looked up the types of planes I would be flying. This is a peculiar kind of morbidity for people who are terrified of flying. It's kinda like, if you're afraid of heights you look at pictures of skyscrapers, or if you're afraid of dogs you look up pictures of pit bulls, that sort of thing. I was flying a 737 to Houston, a 757 to Seattle and sadly enough, a prop-job from Seattle to Kalispell. At this point I began to wonder again if I had taken leave of my senses. I read a lot about it, changed my mind about a dozen times, and finally the day came and with a little help from my friends, got on that big ol' jet airliner in Lafayette to ride the friendly skies.

First, however, I had to go through security, where I was forced to empty my pockets, take off my alligator tooth necklace (a matter of great curiosity to the security employees, who had difficulty believing it was an NDN thing, since I don't look very NDN, but then, if I had dark hair and skin they'd probably profile me as an Arab, so what do you do?) belt and shoes, all of which passed through security devices. Meanwhile, the loudspeakers in the airport—every airport, for that matter—are announcing that it's not funny to joke about bombs, guns or nuclear weapons (no mention of tomahawks) and not to leave your baggage unintended as it could be confiscated and destroyed. I was careful not to let this happen, because then I'd be standing around with no rods, tackle *or* clean clothes when I am supposed to be getting filmed fishing. Then, once through security, I had to return all my personal belongings to my person and proceed to the plane.

White knuckles does not begin to describe the flight to Houston, which took less than an hour but seemed to end somewhere near my reaching social security age. I was also extraordinarily motion sick, despite the medicine I had taken. I always get motion sick, even in cars, unless I'm driving. I don't get motion sick when I'm driving, but somehow I doubted the pilot would let me behind the wheel of the 737, so I just sat there with my stomach churning, gripping the seat arms, staring at the back of the seat ahead of me and reading how, if we crashed into water, I could use the cushion as a flotation device. Comforting, very comforting.

"Ladies and gentleman," the pilot announced, "we have now reached our cruising altitude of twenty-one thousand feet and I have turned off the seat belt light."

This, you can imagine, was more information than I needed to know and I promptly passed out for the rest of the flight. Or at least until the pilot started descending. "Stair-stepping" they call it, dropping a little at a time. Each time the plane dropped my stomach remained at the previous altitude and the pilot refused to go back and get it for me. The guy sitting next to me handed me a bag and I wasn't even offended. By the time we hit the tarmac, I was well but ready to belt the pilot.

Then it was on to Seattle, and on that flight they had a movie but I didn't want to pay five bucks for the headphones because I was afraid I'd need the cash for copious amounts of nausea medication. The nice attendant offered me a chicken sandwich that looked similar to a bagel that had been run over by a herd of buffalo and smelled suspiciously similar to something buffalo herds leave behind, so I declined, got a Diet Coke and concentrated on keeping my stomach somewhere below my heart.

From Seattle it was time to get aboard this narrow prop-job airplane to get to Kalispell, Montana. I have nothing against prop-job airplanes, and I'm sure they're quite reliable, but I could not help glancing out of the window now and then to make sure those puppies were still spinning. That's the bad thing about jet engines, you can't look outside to see if they're still spinning. I could also look down and see Glacier National Park passing far below, and despite the vertigo and terror, it was absolutely stunning to see.

But at last the plane was on the ground in Kalispell and the props were spinning down to a standstill and I got off the plane and you know, Montana could have been Baghdad and I still would have been thankful to be there.

I looked around, expecting to see someone holding a handwritten sign reading "STOUFF" or "ROGER" or "CHITIMACHA BOY" or even "HEY, SCAREDY-CAT YOU MADE IT TO MONTANA!" That's what they do at airports in the movies when the people meeting there don't know each other, right? I did get excited when I saw a guy holding a handwritten sign with a name that started with "S" but when I looked back it was "Schwitzelgruber" or something like that, not me.

So I'm standing there waiting for my luggage—still fearful that I'll be without my clothes and fly rod—looking around, wondering if they forgot to send someone, or if they called the office right before I left canceling the whole thing and nobody let me know. Then I see this guy walking with a buncha papers and a book under his arm. I looked away, then glanced back, and noticed that the book was *Native Waters* by yours truly.

At first I thought, "Wow, what's the chances of that? Someone flying into or out of Kalispell, Montana brought *my* book along to read on the flight!"

Then I realized the chances of that were actually infinitely improbable and that I *was* getting a sign, after all.

So then I was in Montana, shaking hands with Mick, the show's writer and my transportation across the Rocky Mountains to Browning, Montana and the Blackfeet Reservation to fly fish for trout. Oh, and yeah, my luggage made it, by the way, though it was at least half a day before my stomach caught up with me.

The Rocky Mountains were created between fifty and one hundred million years ago, one of the major geologic events of the North American continent. Stretching from New Mexico into Canada, these jagged peaks include Glacier National Park in northwest Montana. An ocean once lay here, and its marks can be found in the rocks that formed the mountains. From the airport in Kalispell I had to cross the park to reach Browning, Montana, where I needed to be.

The Blackfeet Indians call these mountains "the Backbone of the World." As usual, Indians describe things best. Geologic uplifting and ancient oceanography is good science and fascinating stuff, of course, and knowing the incredible age of the Rockies is valuable information...but once I was into them, I knew that no phrase could be more fitting: Backbone of the World. Like a gargantuan fossil, the Rockies were vertebrae, and we traversed them as infinitesimal beings.

For a flat-lander and a swamp rat, the jagged peaks, boulder-strewn slopes and white-capped summits were stunningly beautiful. I understood that I was not in the more lush part of Montana near Missoula, but I was not disappointed. Many years before, I spent a summer in Arizona, near Flagstaff, and experienced the mountains there. But the Rockies...they humbled and excited me beyond measure.

Mick was kind enough to drive me right across the backbone, high into the Rockies and the most spectacular country yours truly has ever laid eyes on. It was also the most harrowing. Of course, someone who does not like to fly is generally someone who suffers from acrophobia, fear of heights, and I certainly do.

Often people tell me, "But Indians aren't supposed to be afraid of heights, that's why so many Indians work building sky-scrapers and suspension bridges." What a gross generalization. Let's straighten the record up right here: those were mostly Navajos or the like, Indians who lived on top of mesas in Arizona, who played along the edge of rock cliffs as babes. South Louisiana Indians get dizzy when they get north of Alexandria. In fact, there is a hilly area along U.S. 90 just the Rez-side of Lafayette that was in historic Chitimacha territory and we used to vacation there and return home to tell our friends about the time we spent on the peaks.

Montanans are accustomed to driving through mountains on roads that sometimes have a metal or stone guardrail separating their vehicle from a drop thousands of feet down. Louisianians are not accustomed to this. While Mick was driving across the park it was all I could do to look out the passenger window and see hundred-foot-tall fir trees down there looking like toothpicks. Instead I kept my eyes up and to the left, watching our climb far along the Backbone of the World.

"See that speck of white up there?" Mick pointed. I did, and it looked like a patch of late snow. He explained it was ice, probably five miles across. I was beginning to feel like I was at the center of something enormous, something wide and reaching, something far distant from anything I had ever known before. Now and then, between mountain peaks, I could see almost into eternity, great expanses of earth, nearly into forever.

We stopped at the interpretive center and Mick told me that now and then they close it down when there are too many grizzly bears around. This whole grizzly bear thing was starting to raise my hackles, but I kept my peace. We did get to see a bighorn sheep right next to the parking lot, a beautiful creature that I hoped was coming by to welcome the Chitimacha to the Backbone of the World.

Cutting those mountain roads and making the stone guardrails along them was a WPA project of the Depression era. They have weathered well all these decades since, but in many places major repairs were under construction. I was pleased to see this. Now and then we'd pass spots where trickles of glacial melt-off splattered into the road. Many hundreds or thousands of these would eventually form the streams, creeks and rivers I'd be fishing over the next few days.

Higher and higher we went and at some point I began to discern our descent. We stopped at another visitor's area the park service built where a rushing, green-blue river chortled and grumbled at the tourists standing on the wooden decking overlooking it. Here I had my first meeting with wild water. We had seen numerous little trickles down the rock face along the Going to the Sun Road, but I was not prepared for what I was about to see.

It was a fast beast, this river, growling as it went, crashing between and over gray boulders, exploding itself into a thousand sputtering droplets then reforming an instant later to continue its frantic, single-minded advance southward. Its determination humbled me, its power startling. Deafened nearly, I listened hard to its words, trying to understand the meaning in its roar.

Here was a world my father always wanted to visit. He spoke

of it often. He practiced visiting it, really. He would venture farther and father afield on his travels before he retired, giving his "talks" to school kids and other groups about the Chitimacha and southeastern Indian peoples. He talked about the Black Hills in South Dakota, about Montana and Wyoming, the places he saved pennies all his adult life to one day visit. He never quite made it far enough afield before the carbon black, sawdust, shell dust and years of inhaling them to make and save those pennies caught up with him. I carried him with me though, along those mountain roads, into the valleys and along gin-clear streams. He had been to Europe in the Second World War, grew up in Ft. Worth, Texas, and traveled at least once that I remember to Georgia. But he longed for the Black Hills and Great Plains, of wild horses and running water. Just once. Only once.

Everywhere I looked, nearly, there was water. Creeks no more than a trickle, like a cup or canteen overturned; streams like small veins, capillaries, tendrils of a larger whole. Streams surging, streams rolling over rocks of every color, shape and size, streams whispering, muttering, speaking and shouting; streams singing, chanting and weeping; streams and rivers, meandering, tranquil or hysterical. I was told you could live a lifetime and not fish a fraction of all the waters in Montana. These were Blackfeet rivers, long, long before Norman Maclean touched and fished them, but if there was anything that could possibly bridge the dichotomy of those so different cultures, it was the love of these clear, speaking rivers.

At last we emerged from Glacier National Park and descended from the Backbone of the World into the plains and foothills of the Blackfeet reservation. The earth unfurled here, still full of billows and surges, but when I craned my neck around I could nearly see forever in all directions. I thought, perhaps, if I looked hard enough I might see to back when there was no concrete highway beneath Mick's vehicle, no mobile homes or cattle fences, only Blackfeet and grizzly bears and spring wildflowers.

We stopped at a convenience store to make a phone call to Mick's friend, Darren Kipp, cousin to Joe. I was glad for the rest and reprieve from the vehicle, letting the motion sickness fade and my stomach settle.

Darren is the man behind a very successful film production

company on the reservation and has garnered many accolades. Darren directed us on out of Browning to the long road that led to Joe Kipp's ranch. Meeting Joe for the first time was equally rewarding: here was a man with a quick and surgical sense of humor, generous and enthusiastic, yet with a no-nonsense air about him that exhaled confidence. The proprietor of Morning Star Troutfitters grinned as he shook my hand and asked if I was ready to catch some trout.

Joe and his wife, Kathy, served up a great supper of beef they raised themselves and, after a long experience with airplanes, motion sickness, mountain roads and the sheer exhilaration of Montana, I crashed into a deep slumber in the bunkhouse Joe keeps for his trout fishing clients. Coffee, I was told, would be at seven. I dreamed that night of dancers, but they were not mine. Blackfeet, perhaps? I couldn't know, but they were fast and furious and it might have been the Ghost Dance.

It was chilly when I woke up, and I reminded myself that it was still spring in Montana. In a state where non-winter months are few, I was experiencing but a small sample of the harsh cold Montanans are born into intimacy with. The coffee chased most of the chill away, though, and not much later Mick returned with his crew of two videographers and one audio technician, respectively, Bill, Jake and Julie. A long discussion ensued which concluded with the plan that we would get my Blackfeet fishing permit first, then we would head to Cutbank Creek, a very fine stream on the reservation for an introductory interview on camera and start fishing from there.

But first I had to understand about grizzly bears.

It was really pretty simple, when you get right down to it: while in grizzly country, the worst thing to do is startle a grizzly, especially a sow and cubs.

But if a meeting does happen, the next worst thing to do is run, they told me. I was advised not to look a grizzly in the eye and to speak to it in a low, calm voice, "Whoa, bear, easy, grizzly," was the recommended mantra, while sidling away.

Now, they tell me, if none of this works and a grizzly charges me, I am not to run or scream or try to fight (as if I would try to fight a grizzly bear!) In fact, the only chance of survival one has if a grizzly does charge is to roll up in a ball, interlace the fingers behind the neck to protect the spinal connection at the base of the brain, and let him bat you around until he figures you're dead and goes about his business.

It's not a subject to take lightly, of course. There are, I was told, about six hundred grizzlies on the Blackfeet reservation, which is about a million and a half acres.

"That's not bad," I said, comforted.

"Yeah," Joe said, "but most of 'em are where we're going to fish."

All of a sudden alligators and water moccasin snakes seemed like cuddly pets.

But it's easy to see why Morning Star Troutfitters has been a success under Joe Kipp's guiding hand: he knows his ancestral waters and he knows where the fish are and how to catch them. He knows how to put just the right amount of fear and respect of the true nature of Montana and all its joys and pitfalls into a client then slap him happily on the back and say, "Now, let's go get some trout!"

There were some things I had to figure out first, though. All this trout fishing business. Not the least among these were putting on a pair of waders (we don't wade in south Louisiana, we sink three feet into mud if we try) and how to walk through a rushing stream with water trying its very best to take your legs out from under you. The waders were at least one size too big for me and made for a man at least ten inches taller, so they bunched up around my midsection like a neoprene tummy roll. I felt like the Stay Puft Marshmallow Man lumbering through Manhattan.

Joe set out a canvas on the ground and some folding chairs for us to struggle into our waders. He eyed me with typical Indian mischievousness and pointed to a red stain on the canvas.

"Know what that is?"

I said I didn't.

"That's the last son of a bitch who ripped a pair of my waders," he said and turned back to his tackle. I was about to go sit in the truck when I saw his shoulders heave with laughter.

We sat by Cutbank Creek and did our first interview, then made a few casts without any takers before deciding to move on to another section of the waterway. It was a wider, slower stream that I had seen yet, flanked by small groves of trees and expansive grasslands.

Here I was confronted with wind unlike I had ever experienced before, and Joe told me, "It's all in your head," and I tried to believe him, but I think it's like grizzlies. Montanans are used to wind and grizzlies, respect them, think about them, but they're second nature now. In the stillwater bayous and swamps of my world, casts are seldom more than forty feet and if the wind is blowing too hard we stay home and find something else to do. Not so in Montana. You'd never get to fish. Dealing with wind became a skill I had to learn fast. I had to learn to cast into, through, broadside of and with wind that sometimes was at thirty miles per hour. Though with Joe's help I got the hang of it, I snapped off a fly first time out on my back cast. I must commend the film crew: when I did this, everyone went through great pains to act like they hadn't seen a thing, suddenly fascinated by a wildflower or distracted by a grasshopper, whistling in painfully contrived distraction.

Then I realized I had left my accessory gear in the truck and had to walk back for it, mumbling all the way about the idiocy of taking a swamp NDN into the mountains and expecting him to throw a five-weight into a thirty mile per hour wind some fifty feet. I fussed to myself as I tied on a new leader that it was pure nonsense, they'd send me back on a bus, or make me hitch, because I'd already wasted too much of their money. Then I realized my wireless microphone was still on, and I shut up.

When I stepped off the Montana ground into Cutbank Creek, little did I know that it was my first foray into a fascination—an obsession—with wild, fast water that would follow me for the rest of my life. What did I know of rivers growing up? Big, hulking beasts like the Mississippi, the Atchafalaya, the Sabine. Though I admit a Twain-esque devotion to them, it was not until I stepped into Cutbank Creek that I really understood rivers.

Though I didn't know it at the time, eventually rivers and streams and creeks—moving, laughing water of any kind—would rush through my dreams at night, behind my eyes as I gazed out the barricaded windows of the concrete bunker I spend my daytime hours within. It's one thing, as A.A. Milne said, to "watch the river slipping slowly away beneath you and you will suddenly know everything there is to be known." It is quite another to walk into it, let it course and envelope. It is electric. It is powerful yet gentle. It may, even at normal flows, suggest that it could sweep you away on a whim, crack your skull on rocks, break your bones and fill your lungs with itself. Like any deity, it offers love but demands respect, and the price of carelessness is high.

I learned about fishing pools. When water rushes along, hurriedly on its way south to eventually join the Mississippi River drainage system and finally end up in the Gulf of Mexico, perhaps via our own Atchafalaya River, it will carry a fly from one point to the next very quickly. We were fishing Elk Hair Caddis, a dry fly, and within moments Joe had hooked into a trout that put a nice bend to his rod but then broke off. Meanwhile, I was still struggling with wind, back casts and rushing water when the magic moment happened.

Joe had patiently explained to me about pools, areas where water rushes around a rock or log and leaves a small area of relatively calm motion. He explained to me about seams, the margins between rushing water and slower or nearly motionless water. He directed me to put my fly into one of these pools behind a small boulder and let it drift into the seam to be tugged downstream. Mending was another thing I had to learn, and I was starting to feel overwhelmed. We had four days of filming ahead of us, and I figured it would take me six just to learn all I needed to know about fishing the Backbone of the World.

The fly fishing I do in south Louisiana is very different. Water doesn't move much, if at all. I mean, I can cast, put down my rod, get a Diet Coke out the ice chest, comb my hair, read the newspaper, and my fly will still be pretty much where I put it. We usually don't have to cast very far, and our largemouth bass and bream are not nearly so spooky as trout so presentation is not so critical. Mending? Never heard of it until then.

Not so when fishing trout in fast streams. It took me some time to learn to mend the line, get the slack out to maintain something called a "dead drift" and if a fish struck I would not lose the hook set. All this while two cameras are focused on me, recording my every mistake and fouled cast.

Then it happened. I saw the slightest flash of silver, the littlest gurgling bubble and I lifted the rod tip. Instinct, at least, still worked. A strike is a strike is a strike, after all!

Oh, he wasn't much of a trout, by any measure, maybe four or five inches, but feisty.

"You sure these trout don't have a little bass in them?" I asked Joe.

I brought him to hand and carefully removed the hook from his jaw, and beamed up at Joe gratefully. My first trout, a sparkling rainbow. I let him slide away, his soft belly wriggling out from my palm. A creature surviving on the edge, living in cold water from glacial melting from those high mountains above me, a survivor of the finest kind, beautiful and delicate but at the same time hardy and hale. Many times I have read trout fishermen herald the virtues of these creatures, but at last I truly understood the affection I might nurture for them.

I forgot the television cameras, the show, the grizzly bears and the wind. I had caught my first trout, and right then, all I could think of was doing it again.

"Let's see if we can find another one," Joe smiled after a handshake.

And so we did. Boy, did we.

Chief Mountain stands near the eastern edge of the Rockies where the range turns to the northwest near Canada. A solitary and juggernaut feature, Chief Mountain is like a sentinel guarding the way across the divide. Though I was only in Montana for a few days, its presence each morning when I looked up into the Backbone of the World was a comfort. I dreamed of dancers every night.

Cutbank Creek turned up a bunch of trout for me, ethereal, beautiful rainbows. In the first day alone I managed to learn to cast in relation to the wind (some of the time), walk across streams without losing my footing (most of the time) and caught many trout, as well as something they called a Rocky Mountain Bonefish, or whitefish. Looked like a trout to me, what do I know? There wasn't a bluegill to be found, not even a catfish.

It had been decided that day we would head up to a very special creek north of Browning near Glacier National Park. To get there would be a two-hour ride and then a trek down a road that Joe described as "brutal." I was to learn later that he was in fact being polite.

Joe's son Max joined us that day and I rode with him for the trek. The rest of the crew followed in two other vehicles. Once we left the main road, the short trail to the creek was brutal.

More than once I hit my head on the top of the truck cab, and was jarred and jumbled, but I never I wondered if we'd make it through. Max knew his business—he had guided his first fishing client when he was six—and though I arrived bruised and shaken, we got there safely and none the worse for wear. We did, however, see grizzly tracks on the way in, but Joe said it was a small one and not to worry about it. Easy for him to say.

From a ridge overlooking the creek, I listened as it chanted and sang below us. The ravine edge was lower than the one on the other side of the stream, and bighorn sheep, mere specks, gazed down at us as we geared up, a process that took up to half an hour or more. I observed that trout fishing was pretty "worky" when you get right down to it. I mean, back home we throw our tackle in a boat, put the boat in the water, drive to where we want to fish, fish until we've had enough, then come home.

We ambled down the ridge slowly, finding ourselves at last on the banks of the creek. I learned I had to sidestep to get down the ridge, as wading shoes with felt soles are great for maintaining a foothold on slippery rocks, but slide like a wet penguin on dry vegetation. The creek bank was incredibly beautiful, smooth stones drying in the sun, resplendent in the water's flow. There was a downed tree nearby and water rushed between its dangling branches, swaying them like fingers dipping into the creek. We assembled and strung up our rods and Joe sang something in Blackfeet and I don't know what it was exactly but it felt like it was perfect for that magical place.

At that point I realized I had left my hat in the truck, and Bill, one of the videographers, was kind enough to go back and get it for me. He surely realized that a Montanan would be able to do so in about ten minutes, whereas a Louisianan might take an hour or never return at all. I was very grateful. The canyon that hid the creek was deep, its sides steep and forbidding. We would fish our way down a good ways, Joe said, to a point where we could climb out and join the trail back to our vehicles. Regardless, this was most wonderful place I had experienced since arriving in Montana, and that's saying a lot. The creek was gorgeous, secluded and pristine. Few anglers reach this place, and fewer still that aren't guided by Joe Kipp.

"You-know-who would have given anything to fish here,"

Mick whispered to me as we made our way along the creek. He was speaking of Norman Maclean, of course, the consummate Montana fly fisherman. I was certain Mick was right. The creek was untouched, a wild place with wild trout and possibly grizzly bears. But the risk was worth it. The rewards were remarkable. Through the day we passed shale banks and black, high vertical ridges on both sides, boulders big as trucks. Exhilaration was palatable. Joe would later tell the producers that while the Blackfeet reservation is regarded for its trophy lake trout, and Joe himself is the premiere guide to put anglers on them, he wanted me to experience the deeper immersion. The rare places.

In my entire time in Montana I saw not a single scrap of litter. I mentioned this to Mick who said he wasn't sure if that was because Montanans are so much more noble, or if it all just blows into Wyoming. Casting a fly rod into the wind for four days, I was sure the latter answer was correct.

Once again, our guide showed he knew his business and his waters and he put me onto many wonderful trout on the creek, all cutthroat. Joe would move ahead of us, survey likely pools and wait for us to catch up. While individual anglers can fish Blackfeet Nation waters with a proper permit, they can only fish the headwaters of many areas with a guide because of the bull trout. Listed as a threatened species, the Blackfeet authorize headwaters fishing only with a guide to help assure these fish remain viable. It is illegal to intentionally target these fish, and if one is caught while fishing other species it must be released at once.

We caught plenty of cutthroat, though. Joe knew the best pools and the best ways to fish them, and by the end of the day I had caught plenty. There was one particular pool that we fished subsurface and coaxed out a couple of especially nice trout. We even chanced upon a couple of bull trout which we handled carefully and released quickly. It was pretty cool because both Joe and I stood upstream of where water was raging over this dropoff, hurtling itself below, and the trout were in the pools behind big boulders or at the seems between the quieter water and the moving flow. I think my best trout on the creek was about sixteen inches, but I'm still a rank amateur, don't forget.

The hike back to the vehicles was excruciating, and I learned an odd thing: the smokers in the group just went along like nobody's business, while I, at the time nine weeks into my cessation, wheezed like a dilapidated Hoover. At the end of the trail was the same ridge we had gone down to fish in the beginning, and now we had to go back up. That ridge nearly licked me, I admit, and I had to take two breaks on the ascent to catch my breath. If a grizzly had come by right then I wouldn't have had to remind myself not to run...I didn't have the wind to try anyway. In fact, I got to looking at that ridge, all full of wildflowers, looking over the chortling creek, and thought, "Put me up a marker right here, and I'll just stay for eternity." But then I remembered I had not had any fry bread in Montana yet so I got up and made it the rest of the way.

After taking the brutal road back, we took the highway again. There was still plenty of time to fish since full dark doesn't come until about 10:30 in Montana that time of year, so we were off to Goose Lake. This was quite a piece away, but finally we turned off the highway again and began climbing into the foothills of the Backbone of the World. There were three vehicles, often separated by a quarter mile, and the folks in the lead vehicle that evening got to see a grizzly.

It was just a few dozen yards away from them, and at first they thought it was a cow. There's cattle everywhere you look in Montana, but then this creature took off in a way only a grizzly can run, they said, and there was no mistaking the awesome size, gait and profile of it.

Some of the crew wanted to turn back then, since the bear was heading right toward Goose Lake, but Joe just shrugged and said, "It's my land, too," and so we pushed on.

All the time we were gearing up - inflating float tubes and pontoon boats, putting on waders, assembling rods - we heard cattle raising hell in the distance. They mooed and fussed and groaned, obviously irate and uneasy. Someone asked Joe what the cattle were so upset about, and he laughed and said, "Because there's a grizzly out there, man!"

Learning to use a float tube wasn't hard, really. Just sit in it like an easy chair and paddle with the flippers on your feet. Since I have considerable expertise with easy chairs, I adapted quickly. Goose Lake is cold, of course, but there is heavy vegetation in it. Joe instructed us to fish along the edge of these by drifting or paddling and trolling subsurface flies—wooly buggers and the like

—along the weed line. This resulted in my two best trout of the entire trip, both in the twenty-inch range, just before sundown. These were cutthroat trout, characterized by the slashes of orange-red below their jaws, gorgeous creatures, soft and strong. Again, the expertise of Morning Star Troutfitters had allowed a south Louisiana newbie to fish trout and to exceed all his wildest expectations.

We finished up right at dark, made the long trek back to the Kipp ranch, tired and satisfied. The following day would be wrap-up filming, final interviews and a few more moments on the water.

The last day of actual fishing in Montana was the day before I headed home to Louisiana. We had been closely watching the news channels: Hurricane Cindy had eyed the shores of St. Mary Parish hard before heading into the New Orleans area, a minor storm but a premonition nonetheless. We would do the final interviews on Cutbank Creek just behind the Kipp Ranch. The area of Cutbank Creek behind the ranch was as fine a jewel as any I had seen in Montana, save for the high-altitude creek. A precious gem of a stream, it meandered in tight coils where we last fished, and as Joe and the camera crew found a comfortable spot to talk, I cast along the creek searching for a few more trout. It's the typical fisherman's malaise: just one more cast. Just one more cast...

In fact, I had not intended to fish so seriously that I'd need waders so I didn't wear them. At one point though I wanted to cross the creek. I decided I would "wet wade" as they call it in Montana, cross without waders and just get wet. Well, getting wet is fine and dandy, but I was not prepared for the temperature of that water. Waders keep you nice and warm, almost too warm sometimes, but when I stepped into knee-deep water at about forty degrees, I understood what cold water was. Completely. Boy, *howdy*.

I missed several half-hearted strikes and so managed no trout that day. Soon they were calling me over to do my interview, which I dispatched with as much dignity as I could. Then it was off to the ranch again where I put my rods up for the last time.

North American Indian Days was holding its fifty-fourth annual event in Browning and we went on down to the fairgrounds to get some footage there. We were just in time for Grand Entry, too, the moment when all the dancers in all their regalia enter the arena. It was a sight I hadn't seen in a long, long time and missed greatly. When I was a kid my parents and grandparents regularly made the pow-wow trail. We'd set up a booth and sell crafts my elders made all over the Southeast. We also had a teepee my grandfather made that we took with us and erected for several years, though he always had to explain that Chitimachas did not live in teepees, we lived in palmetto huts.

"Then why do you have a teepee?" the folks would ask him, perplexed.

"It makes the tourists happy," he'd say with a wink, and the folks—all tourists themselves—would nod knowingly and wink back.

I hadn't seen a Grand Entry probably since I was twelve years old, and I was glad to be there in Montana to see it again.

We broke for supper and I headed for the first booth I could find that had big black letters reading "FRY BREAD".

If you don't know what fry bread is, you have not lived. It's unleavened bread made by Native people, similar to Mexican sopapillas but something on the order of a zillion times better. I had not had real fry bread since I was in Arizona in 1980. I have tried cooking it here, but there's something about the altitude difference that just doesn't work unless you know how to compensate for it.

The booth-bought fry bread was amazing. I also had an Indian Taco, which is simply a taco on fry bread, and let me tell you something, *cher*, that was *some* good, yeah! At the trading post in Browning I saw a tee shirt that read "Will Work For Fry Bread" and I almost bought it, but opted instead for a tee shirt with a beautiful embroidered fishing fly and the legend "Here, fishy, fishy" on it. Hee-hee. Spinner baits, *phooey*!

Sunday was pretty much a resting day. We'd leave around three in the afternoon to make the long trek back to Kalispell to catch the flight to Seattle, then Houston and finally to Lafayette, a red-eye trip if I ever heard of one. This time Mick would drive south of Glacier National Park for a whole different view of Montana.

With Indian Days going on, Joe had lots of people coming vis-it and staying on the ranch so we said our goodbyes early. I understand how it is with all your people coming in, and the pressure of tending to our camera shoot to boot. We stopped long enough at Indian Days to watch part of the rodeo, but had to leave before Joe's daughters rode.

Then I was on that same prop-job airplane and leaving Kalispell behind, having shook hands with Mick and vowed to do my best to be as hospitable when they would visit Louisiana in the fall. I was exhausted, had a much easier attitude about flying on the way home, really. For instance, when I got on the plane in Seattle to go to Houston, I swear I sat down, buckled up and the pilot said right away, "We'll be setting down at George Bush International in about fifteen minutes." Just that fast. I slept the whole time, didn't even remember taking off.

A dozen hours of traveling later and weary as a dog, I finally found myself in Lafayette, looking for my truck in the parking lot, turning from Surrey Street onto U.S. 90 and pointing the front bumper happily toward the Rez.

Patches spun circles and crawled up one side of me and down the other when I got in the door. She had been in the care of friends who had come over to feed her daily, and there had been no bloodshed, remarkably. Her loud meowing sounded like, "Hey where you been all this time this guy he came every day and gave me food and then he was gone but he drank all the beer out of the fridge and then there was this day when the lights went out because it was storming outside and you know how much I *hate* that and another day there was this bird sitting on the porch and I thought I could jump on it but I bruised my nose on the window pane *and WHERE HAVE YOU BEEN?*"

I was still exhausted and slept most of the day. In my dreams were wild cutthroat trout and clear, rushing water. Chief Mountain loomed over them all, and cattle fussed nervously about grizzlies in their proximity.

I came home content, looking forward to having Joe and the film crew here in the fall, and hopefully catch some bass, big redears or whatever. Perhaps even some trout of the speckled variety on Louisiana's famous coast. My native waters, like his, are wide and varied. I believe what struck me most about the trip, besides the beautiful terrain, the awesome trout, and wonderful people, were the people. Remember that the Blackfeet people had saturated European contact only some one hundred and thirty years ago, whereas that same level of contact for Chitim-acha was some three hundred and fifty years ago. His people are not as far removed from pre-contact days as mine.

There are voices in his mountain streams as surely as in my lakes and bayous. I could not hear them as clearly as he, son of those lands and mountains, but their whispers were there. Perhaps he will hear the voices here, too, the words at the base of cypress trunks with soaked waterlines, along shell reefs and at the back end of dark canals. Even three-and-a-half centuries have not silenced them.

That's the power of native waters and native earth. They whisper and sing. They refuse denial. Wild trout and wild blue-gill, cutthroat or bass, it's all the same. The heart of the land and the waters is beating like powerful drums signaling from afar.

But I had seen more than that. I had seen where my home waters began life. On the east slope of the Rockies, the snow would melt. The rains would come. And it would carry those far away lands to me a particle at a time. Here, it would fall out of suspension and settle into the muck.

I had seen beauty and grace. I had seen trout and cold, clear water. But I had also seen the origin of the death of *Siti*. Joe Kipp's rivers didn't cause it. The meddling of man on the natural world brought about the death of my home waters.

Five: Dog Days

*A little boy named U'stapu was lying in a bunk close to the
shore of a lake. His people had come here from the prairies in order
to cross, but the wind was too high. As he lay there U'stapu discovered a boy fanning with a fan of turkey feathers. This was the
boy that makes the west wind. Then U'stapu said to his people: "I
can break the arm of the boy that makes the west wind."*
*All laughed at him, but he took up a shell, threw it at the boy
who was making the wind, and broke his left arm. Therefore, when
the west wind was high, the Indians used to say this boy was using
his good arm, and if it was gentle, they said he was using his broken
arm. Before that time the west wind used to be very bad, because
the west-wind maker could change hands, but since then it has been
much gentler. It is possible that this boy made the other winds also.*
(Documented by John R. Swanton)

I fish where thirty-foot dugout canoes carried the *na'ta*
named Long Panther and twenty-five warriors to make peace
with the French territorial governor after a years-long war;
where drums once thrummed massacre, famine and suffering.
Sometimes, at dusk, I return from a fishing trip to *Ama'tpan
na'mu* when the light is angled just so, and the hue of it so close
to amber, I think I might see him: the *na'ta*. That brave chief,
long ago, who stood with the butt of his spear planted firmly
into the shell reef. Massive sail-adorned masts tower above him,
glowering, bearded strangers a terrifying spectacle staring down
from their decks. Then they are gone, and I point the bow
through twilight to the five-hundred acre reservation where
home is, all that remains in possession of that great chief's nation. By 1900 there were only thirty or forty people of the lake
left on the reservation where now there's a little house that's always been in the family, a loving woman, our dogs and my
sense of place.

August

Coming home to the dog days of summer was like falling

face-first into hot sand. Sure, Montana was great, it was an escape, but it was time to come back down to earth. Back home, breezeless in late July and early August. The bills were still there waiting to be paid, the water still too hot for good fishing that would otherwise make me feel better, the overwhelming pile of things to do steadfastly not getting done at all. It was amusing, really: Montana and back after publishing *Native Waters*, upcoming appearances in a television program, and still scraping along from paycheck to paycheck, counting the pennies at each scrape. Summer squalls pounded through with thunder and lightning each afternoon, kept me off the water in even the cooling late evening hours.

The novel was stalled, and the heat was so intense across the nation record numbers of associated deaths were reported in places like Phoenix. One night I dreamed I was fishing along a busy street in Franklin, but instead of the street there was a rushing stream and I was catching trout in pools behind sidewalks, utility poles and fire hydrants.

It took me a few weeks, really. After my wonderful but exhausting time in Montana, I feared I was burnt-out on fishing because I just couldn't get up the gumption to go. I'd look at my tackle sitting there in the corner, untouched since it was last used on Cutbank Creek, Montana. It kinda glowered at me, as if feeling neglected. But I would think about fishing and just get all tired and lethargic.

Now and then, I'd go grab a bait caster and some worms and go catfishing in Bayou Teche behind the house. I'd take along Daisy, the black lab my girl brought to live with me. Mocha had vanished months earlier, lost or stolen, and all efforts to locate her were in vain. But Daisy and I would a spend a leisurely couple of hours catching small catfish and the occasional half-decent one until nearly dark then call it a day.

"Well, old girl, it's a day," I'd say.

"*Woof!*" Daisy would agree.

But then I woke up one morning and said, "I need to go *fly fishing*," so I drank coffee, put on my fishing clothes and mud boots. I loaded tackle and dog into the back of the truck and went to a pond. Daisy has been learning how to get along with a fly fisherman. Like most south Louisiana inhabitants, be they dogs, fish, people or pelicans (who must learn about that hook flying through the air on the back cast) Daisy understands cat-fishing and bait casting quite well. She is quite content to prance up and down the bayou bank, then sit by me and together we watch my line waiting for Mr. Whiskers to bite.

But the dog is as mystified by fly fishing as most of the rest of St. Mary Parish's residents. Being a water dog, she loves to swim of course, and I have pretty much trained her to swim behind me. At this particular pond I like to put on my mud boots and walk just a few feet off the bank. That way I get away from the tall shrubbery that lines the edge and I can cast parallel to the bank as I walk. She understands fishing well enough, but this whole line-whipping, nine-foot rod-casting business just doesn't seem to qualify as fishing, so she constantly wants to swim in front of me, right where I'm trying to raise a fish. I have largely talked her into swimming behind me now just by saying, "Back!"

So I'm fishing along, picking up small bass with a hopper fly and enjoying myself tremendously when I notice my right foot is getting harder and harder to pick up. It finally occurs to me that this is because my right boot is full of water. I have sprung a leak, it seems. So I went buy a new pair of mud boots, and since the leaky pair had been a little tight anyway, I got a new pair a size larger.

The next day I am at another pond, standing just off the edge of the bank in the water. I had caught enough fish in that spot so I go to walk farther down and when I lift my right leg the suction of the mud holds the boot in place and my foot comes right out of it. I am then teetering on one leg, reluctant to put my socked foot down into the water and mud, trying to hold onto my bamboo fly rod, lean down and put my foot back into the boot, all of which is completely futile and there I go, butt first, into the eight-inch-deep water.

I am a muddy, soaked mess, but you shoulda seen me, you'd have been proud: this dazed figure, sitting in the water, one foot in a boot the other in just a sock, a look of resignation and at the same time pure fury on my face...but like a true fly fisherman, like the consummate angler, I am holding my bamboo fly rod high over my head and there ain't so much as a drop of sludgy mud on it, thank you very much.

Daisy, meanwhile, is watching all this from where she is standing chest-deep in the water—behind me, I might add—with her ears perked up and a look of complete astonishment on her face. I look at her and say, "Well, why don't you do something to *help* me?" and she woofs quietly at me, wades over and licks my face as if to say, "Poor wretched man. This fly fishing business will be the death of you!"

I get to my feet, retrieve my boot from the mud and slosh ashore like some creature emerging from a black lagoon in pursuit of Julie Adams. I put my fly rod down some place safe—forgetting that my line is still out in the pond. I walk back into the water to rinse mud off myself, launch into a non-traditional dance trying to get my boot back on, nearly fall again three times, and finally succeed in returning to a state of bipedalism. Daisy is watching all this with panting fascination.

Now that I'm out of the pond, soaked but upright, I am determined that a little fall is not going to ruin my trip. I pick up my rod and take the slack out of my line, only to find that during the debacle, a small bass has taken my hopper fly and has been swimming around the pond for the past few minutes doing everything he can to shake it out of his mouth, including wrapping the line around several clumps of weeds and six willow trees. I must break the leader to get my line back in and tie on another hopper.

We move down the bank a little, and I find a nice little spot opposite the other side on a corner. There is a small shrub overhanging the water here, and I put my hopper right under it. It was the kind of fly cast fly fishermen dream of, and the moment the little hopper landed, a swell of water moved toward it, a huge v-shaped hump of something coming after the fly with single-minded determination. Daisy and I stare at it in complete terror.

A black hole opened in the apex of the wake and sucked in the fly without much fanfare at all. If a volcano could erupt with all the excitement and hysteria of a drop falling from a leaky faucet, that's what the strike would have been like.

"Oh, *shit!*" I said.

"*Woof!*" Daisy agreed.

I lifted the rod tip firmly, and when the fish felt me on the other end of that hopper he intended to have for supper, he dove for deep water in resentment of my presence. My rod bent into a question mark—that tired old angling analogy nonetheless in this case highly appropriate, I can tell you—and I thought I had hooked a Russian submarine, then *poof!* The rod sprang back and my fly landed on my left shoulder.

"Oh, *shit,*" I said.

"*Woof!*" Daisy repeated, which I can't translate, but I'm sure was something akin to, "Smooth move, ace."

The interruptions in a dedicated life of fishing get under my skin. I'm fresh from Montana having caught a lot of trout for the first time. I am getting a few fish back home despite the dog days of summer. I come back inside from catfishin' and I have a friendly message on my answering machine. It's my cellular service company saying that they'd simply love for me to call them at my earliest opportunity or else it's quite possible they may have to go through the unpleasantness of pulling my plug.

Yeah, well, that's no new thing for me. I skirt the edge of financial ruin all the time. Writers are poor, unless they're John Grisham or Stephen King. I am neither. I don't know if I could be one. I am usually too busy fishing to write bestsellers.

I am the opposite of a Yuppie, I am the venerable Yuffie: *Young Urban Financial Failure,* though of course I'm rural and Yrffie doesn't work. Used to bother me, now I just know it's my lot in life and I am able to take a certain amount of bashful pride in it. There are two kinds of Indians, you know: the kind with looks, and the kind with money. Thus I'm always broke.

It keeps life interesting, and forces me to keep a sense of humor about things. So I call my friendly neighborhood cellular service provider to make payment arrangements on an overdue bill, then question the representative closely on exactly how I got an $82 bill when it's normally $37.

Well, it seems I went over my allotted minutes. I did know I had allotted minutes, but I tend to view such things in the Indian way, like we view life: we're all allotted a certain number of minutes and hours and weeks and months and years in life, why worry about how many? I did not understand how cellular phone minutes differed from this, so I checked my plan summary, and emerged even more confused. I have, it seems, "anytime minutes" and "nights and weekend minutes" but then there these brackets in there for "peak" and "off-peak." Sorta like spring is "peak" fishing and summer is "off-peak." I understood it once I translated it to the proper terms.

Now to me, nights and weekends means "after dark every day, and from Friday at four p.m. until Monday at seven a.m. when I get back to the office." How was I supposed to know that's not how they define it? Peak, then, is from four p.m. to bedtime, whenever that may be.

But my rep tells me that nights are defined as nine p.m. to seven a.m., Monday through Thursday. Oddly enough, "weekends" is defined as Friday from nine p.m. until Monday at seven a.m. and "peak" is seven a.m. to nine p.m. in all other zones. I explain to her that I am not only an Indian, but worse yet, a Cajun-Indian, and that neither of my people have been very good at keeping schedules.

Okay, here in a nutshell then is the malady of the modern world: your life is no longer your own, and you do not control a dadgum thing in it. Think you do? Ha! Your cellular phone company has told you when night starts and ends and when your weekend starts and ends, right? Yes, don't try to deny it. You cannot call them and say, "Listen, my night starts at roughly dusk, whenever that is depending on the time of year, and morning starts when the clock goes off. This means I may need my cellular phone at six p.m. in November or eight-thirty p.m. in July if my outboard motor breaks down in the middle of the lake and I need to call someone for a tow home. It also means that I might need to call my fishing buddy at five a.m. sometimes in the year or seven a.m. other times. Can you please adjust my plan accordingly?" Lotsa luck, bub.

It doesn't end there, of course. Forget even the obvious things, like your employer tells you when you have to get up and get to work and when you can go home. Or that the school tells you when you have to feed your kids breakfast and get them on the bus. That's the obvious stuff. Your health insurance company can tell you what doctors or hospitals you can go to. Your cable company tells you what channels you can watch.

Signs tell you where you can go and where you can't. "Do Not Enter" and "No Left Turn" and "No Parking." You want food, you have to go buy it from a grocery store and to add insult to injury stand in line for twenty minutes to pay outrageous prices for it, even though you're thoroughly hacked off that they didn't have the Hellmann's and you had to buy Miracle Whip, of all the disgusting things. Your life is not your own when you have to buy Miracle Whip instead of Hellmann's.

So I'm on the phone with my cellular representative, a nice lady who was very helpful if not very cooperative to my requests, the line "Hey, I just work here," being passe' by now, and I start thinking about money. Someone read something I wrote recently and said if they could write like me they'd "quit their day job." I responded that I haven't figured out how to do that yet. It's one of the few things that I feel I exercise control over in my life, complete and absolute control: being derelict. Complete worthlessness as a contributor to any banking institution's annual statements. I've been running from financial security all my life, so why stop now?

People ask me if I'll still know them when I get to be a rich and famous author. Well, you know, that's a ticklish question. My only good answer is, "If I know you now, I'll know you then. If I got no use for you now, me becoming rich and famous is not likely to improve my opinion of you." Brutal honesty, I know, but why mince words? It doesn't even really matter, since I might get famous but I probably won't get rich. Fishermen, particularly fly fishermen, seldom get rich. The best we can do is hope to support our habit, and like a true junkie, that only gets us to indulging more and requiring more support. The phrase "vicious circle" was invented by a fisherman.

By the time I was done with my cellular rep I had her laughing and she asked, "Is there anything else I can do for you today?"

"Yeah," I replied, "Tell me where they're biting."

This brought the conversation to an end with a good laugh on the rep's part, and you know, I still had to pay $82, which my checkbook laughed at *me* over, I still don't understand "peak," "off peak," and "nights and weekends" but it really doesn't matter. That was at eight a.m, first thing in the morning, and the poor lady's likely to be screamed at all day by intense, highstrung, aggravated, furious and irrational people who got money and don't give a jolly damn *where* they're biting...but at least I started her off with a laugh. Maybe it'll carry her through this day at least, kinda the way a laugh carries me through my days, despite what I may have walked away from in my life, and what I went out of my way for. Isn't that, in the end, really what it's all about? And if it ain't, shouldn't it be?

And when you get right down to it, we ain't getting out of this life alive, you know? That's the thing about schedules and deadlines and wrist-watches and alarm clocks and telephone service: it's all really a moot point and the very best thing that could happen to any of us is the thing we hope for least.

Sure, when some of us go to Happy Hunting Ground there are people who will say, "He/she was a successful man/woman," or proclaim that (dropping the dual gender attempt because it's irritating me already, the devil with political correctness), "He was a good man who worked hard," or worst of all, "He never shirked a day in his life."

But listen, I *want* to be known for shirking. Nobody sits on their deathbed, it's been said, and thinks, "Gee, I wish I had worked more in my life," do they? By the same token, it's still valid that even a bad day fishing is better than the best possible day at work. That's why I say, the best thing that could happen to any of us is the thing we hope for least, and that's to be known for accomplishing nothing at all, at least by modern standards.

Imagine the funeral parlor talk. "He was certainly lethargic," they say with sad shakes of their head. "Yep, ol' Rog, he sure didn't amount to much, did he?" and "Boy, did you ever know a more *ambitionless* human being?" or "I wonder who's paying for all this?"

All I can hope for at this point, as I lie there in my blue suit and white shirt wondering absently about local water tables, is that someone, *anyone* at the service will speak up and say, "Yeah, but he caught a *helluva* lot of fish!" And then I can go on to my just rewards, knowing that at least *someone* understood that I did accomplish something, even if that person was the sole fishing buddy who outlived me.

Because unfortunately that's the way the world's gotten: if you weren't born with a silver spoon stuck in your yap, you gotta work your buns off to get one, and that leaves no room left in the day, the week, the month, the rolling line of years and at last to finally be considered successful at anything else but working. Who wants an epithet like: *Here Lies John Doe: Ebeneezer Scrooge Would Have Been Proud* or something to the effect of *Here Lies Jane Dane, Taking Her First-Ever Vacation*. No, thank you, I'll pass, give me lethargic and ambitionless any day.

I mean, for me it's being a fishing bum, but relate it to anything you enjoy and wish you could give up all else to do exclusively. C'mon, there's got to be something you could happily run off and be completely absorbed in for the rest of your days, leaving all other cares aside? For me, if I had all the money in the world and could afford to do nothing but travel the country and fish all fifty states, I'd certainly be happy as a bug in a rug. But maybe it's just a little more exhilarating—a little more real—if as I'm landing twenty-inch cutthroat in Montana I am also wondering if the electricity is still on back home and if I'll have enough money to get back and find out. That's what Sterling Hayden meant when he said we are "brainwashed by our economic system until we end up in a tomb beneath a pyramid of time payments, mortgages, preposterous gadgetry, playthings that divert our attention for the sheer idiocy of the charade."

What a deal.

No doubt getting a windfall makes me happy, like anyone else. You know what a windfall is, when you get money out of thin air that you didn't expect, especially when you need it most. Getting a couple hundred bucks when you're balancing the electrical bill, truck note and beer budget (Hey, that's important too!) on a pinhead is like finding buried treasure. But you know what really makes me happy in a way that's so much more genuine, so much more real? When Patches jumps in my lap, climbs up my chest and nuzzles her head against my chin, purring so softly I don't really hear her at all, just feel the vibration of her jowls against my cheek; when the dog sits patiently in the bed of the truck, waiting for me to string up my rod and tie on a fly there at the tailgate until I say, "Okay, let's go," and she jolts forward like a bolt of lightning; when I see a hopper fly suddenly sink without much fanfare at all and I lift the tip of my rod to feel something pull back, like a certain goggle-eye in a cluster of cypress knees when I was but a lad; rain rolling off the brim of my hat; low-lying mist on Bayou Teche in the morning; little mottled-brown birds that have come visit my people for thousands of years and speak to us; tadpoles in darting schools, hiding under floating oak leaves; sunlight, golden and amber, in the final moments of the day, lancing through cypress trees, turning the world into gossamer twilight; drops of water on pond lilies, round and crystalline like gems.

The difference between those things and money is money just relieves some stress. It doesn't really create good feelings, it just clears bad feelings out of the way for a little while at best. On the other hand, Reg Baird was right when he observed that whoever coined the phrase "Money can't buy happiness" never bought himself a good fly rod.

Mostly, though, it was just too dagnabit hot to worry about money or anything else. It was the hottest summer I can remember, but then, I think I may have said the same thing last year, and possibly the year before that.

"It gets hotter every year," people say, but I really wonder if that's true, or we just forget how hot it was in previous years and start spouting off at the mouth by saying silly things like that. I mean, do we really have the ability to compare the way we felt on Aug. 24, 2004 and Aug. 24, 2005 to make that determination. Sorry, any judge worth his salt would throw it out as inadmissible.

But there's no doubt, it was hot as the dickens. There was hardly any air moving, and when there was, it was usually at the leading edge of one of those summer squalls we get nearly every day. It's the dangdest thing to look at the radar most afternoons: the map is full of these multi-colored specks, bazillions of 'em, all summer squalls. When I was a teen, a buddy of mine and I were out in my little bateau fishing on the lake and one of those summer squalls surprised us by coming up from behind the treeline we were fishing. We knew we couldn't beat the weather back across the lake so we tied off to a humungous cypress tree with a thick canopy and rode it out. Though the rain fell like hallelujah, brethren and the lake stood up on its hind legs raising tarnation, we remarkably got only a little wet. Within twenty minutes or so the whole thing was over and we discussed whether or not we should go home or risk another storm. Of course, we started fishing again.

It seems like I handled the heat better back then, but again, that was more than twenty years ago. I was younger, slimmer and had more hair. It was nothing for us to stay out fishing all day and come home ready to hit the town that night. These days it's all I can do to fish until noon before I gotta go home and recuperate on the sofa for a few hours. Now when I go outside to cut the grass, wash the truck (something I haven't done since June) or whatever, the sweat just inundates me. I'm an embarrassment to myself and to my ancestors, but that is why we all desperately cling to environmental destruction: global warming lets us off the hook, we don't feel like wimps if we can quote science to back up the notion that it is hotter now than when our ancestors were alive. When we think about our fathers and grandfathers rough-necking out in the Gulf sun, pulling seines on the lake, working around those carbon black furnaces, we feel like we're just whiners. And you girls, you can just see your mothers and grandmothers washing clothes on the washboard on the front porch, churning butter by hand, beating carpets with a stick as they hang on the clothesline and you wonder how the devil they kept their mascara from running.

When it gets this hot, you wonder why people live in the tropics. It's not like we're immobile or something, we could all get up and move some place cool anytime we wanted. Yet we stay here and complain about the heat, the hurricanes, the humidity, the rain...but the etouffee, fried shrimp, frog legs and boiled crawfish make it all worth it, of course. You can't get that in Bangor.

Year before last, I believe I fished three hundred and fifty days of the year, literally. After a long hiatus broken only by one or two trips a year, I got "hooked" again and went overboard (how's that for overuse of double entendres?). Last year, I cut back a little and this year I am not fishing near as much. I blame it on the heat, but I know it's not so much that as the extra poundage I'm carrying since I quit smoking. Still, I haven't been in the boat since spring, because the water's so low and it's too hot to even think about it. Heck, it's seventy-one degrees in Browning, Montana as I write this, and the high here is expected to be ninety-seven degrees with a heat index of a hundred and five! On the other hand, Browning has grizzly bears, St. Mary Parish does not so it all balances out in the end.

Something Wicked

What we do have here in Louisiana, though, is hurricanes. Until you have lived through a hurricane, you really can't understand it.

In the hours before a storm reaches land, even two hundred miles away, the air grows thick and heavy. Flocks of birds, frantic, flee northward. Animals of all kinds act strangely, and house pets whine and worry, wondering why we, their masters, do not flee as well.

The autumn arrival of two hurricanes will live in infamy. Two days when the face of Louisiana and the nation changed nearly as dramatically as it did that day in New York four years earlier. Except this time there would be no enemy to rage at, no face to post on television screens, and only a name to roll in distaste off the tongue: *Katrina.*

That Sunday morning I fished a pond under gray skies and the little bluegill and bass were frenzied, attacking hoppers with savage determination. It often happens that way in advance of a weather front, and hurricanes are no exception. I am told some of the best saltwater fishing in years was just before Hurricane Andrew in 1992. Upon returning home and watching the news I saw that the storm was heading straight for Louisiana, most likely the Mississippi coast, possibly New Orleans. I advised my mother to stand at ready. There are very few things a son can boss his mother around over, but hurricane evacuation is one of them. "When I say go, we go," I said and she didn't dispute my authority for once.

Outside, gray skies, barometer dropping. The atmosphere presses against the skin, the eyeballs compress and the limbs grow heavy. There's a scent in the air but it's hard to describe: somewhat like rain, somewhat like ozone, maybe a little electricity somewhere on the peripheral but hurricanes rarely carry lightning except sometimes on the edge of the rain bands where independent thunderstorms swirl into existence of their own volition. It's easy to see how the old people knew storms were nearing, how they could feel it in their bones, by the pressure on their eyeballs, the gray touch of it on their skin. Though today we have radar and satellite imagery and we can watch it from our homes, many centuries ago the collective input of our senses was enough to keep us safe.

Katrina came like a monster, a juggernaut of devastation. By late Saturday it was clear she would cast her wide eye over New Orleans. A half million people fled the city alone, another million in the surrounding parishes and Mississippi counties.

We expected winds of sixty miles per hour here. I secured things around the house and around my mom's residence. An exodus the likes of which is seldom seen fled west, east and north of the Big Easy. It would not be long before Katrina took a slight eastward jog and though her eye wall passed partially over New Orleans, she kicked up a swell of water that proved fatal to that great city on the river and all along the Louisiana-Mississippi coast.

Monday morning, I watched the storm come ashore and Bradbury's borrowing from Shakespeare thundered in my head like crashing waves: *By the pricking of my thumbs, something wicked this way comes.*

Residents of the Gulf Coast have made peace, a sort of tenuous bargain, with the weather. We are, in a way, always aware of borrowed time. Though it had been forty years since a storm had significantly impacted New Orleans, no one was oblivious to the threat. The horror of what unfolded in the New Orleans area cannot be equaled. Since at least 1965, when Hurricane Betsy flooded the city, we have been painfully aware of the vulnerability of that national treasure, the venerable old city of New Orleans. But when Sieur de Bienville founded it in 1718, his engineers strongly advised against building a community there. New Orleans has lived on the precipice of danger and disaster for nearly three hundred years.

It's all about that mightiest of rivers, the Mississippi. Perhaps the most important economic, cultural and strategic point on the entire continent, the city's position at the mouth of the Mississippi River makes New Orleans what it is. That precarious bargain with nature, a vow sometimes broken on both sides, has led to New Orleans' unique culture. People living on the brink of disaster foster and nurture a zest for life, for hard work and hard play. New Orleans epitomizes that manifestation.

A storm surge perhaps as high as thirty feet but no less than twenty inundated the city and all the unprotected parishes below it. The disaster area stretched from the Rez to Mobile, and Katrina continued to barrel ashore all the way until she fizzled out of existence near Maine. Entire towns on the Mississippi coast simply vanished and the death toll astounds the senses.

Have you ever watched a four-foot wave crash against a bulkhead? Noticed the weight of a gallon of drinking water? Imagine then a wave twenty or thirty feet tall, pushed ahead of the storm. It crashed through Port Fouchon and Grande Isle, across Plaquemines and St. Charles and St. Bernard parishes, areas rendered helpless and vulnerable by the loss of our coastal wetlands, marshes and barrier islands to the greed of politicians, oil executives and dredging firms. The surge swallowed New Orleans whole, ignoring the levees designed to handle a Category 3 storm. Katrina was at least a four, probably a five despite what the official measurements indicated. As the storm raged on and surged the water of Lake Pontchartrain into the Northshore, the counter-clockwise winds pushed water south of the lake back into New Orleans again. In some places a dozen or more feet of water was recorded.

We all know the rest. There's no sense rehashing it again. The horror of it cannot be retold without weeping.

Hurricane Katrina, the witch, conjured up disaster, the Gulf of Mexico her cauldron, one-hundred-and-eighty mile per hour winds her stirring spoon; she flung water at New Orleans and did, in the end, what nothing else had accomplished in three hundred years of the city's history. The music stopped. The laughter stopped. All that was left was water. And memory. Purple spots, floating in the vision, but the purple spots were corpses, and the water was putrid.

I never much enjoyed visiting New Orleans, being particularly disinterested in cities in general. They congest and confine me, make me paranoid. Lafayette is the largest urban area I can stand, and only barely. Yet I understand the appeal of New Orleans, the French Quarter, the history, the romance and the excitement. Perched there between the lake, the river and the Gulf of Mexico, New Orleanians live with that bargain all of us on the coast made, but to the fullest possible extent. Had New Orleans existed somewhere fifty miles northward, in a less precarious location, the city would never have developed such character. The bargain, the ominous existence there at the precipice of disaster, gave the city a zest for life, for hard work and hard play, unlike any other. That same zest will be what drives New Orleans to rise up again.

Kich

This year *kich* did not come. I have come to rely on its presence each spring, look forward to it. Usually, when the days warm and the bayou behind the house begins to clear from muddy brown to green-black, *kich* would come. Sometime I would hear it as I loaded fly rods into the boat for a spring morning of chasing redears, bluegill and largemouth. In my perception of our visits, though I could not understand its call, I hoped that in addition to whatever news it brought me, we shared memories of the old woman who for seventy years was its sole companion, its only confidant and solitary believer. Each spring, its visits confirmed for me that something magical and ancient still exists along these bayous and lake shores. That some things can survive against disbelief.

Yet this spring it did not come, and as spring became summer and summer became a hot, muggy fall, I feared my lack of comprehension—my tenuous grasp on belief—had failed to keep the little bird substantial, extant.

It was still daylight when the power went down. We were not sure if it would return soon and as it happens, it remained off for some twenty-eight hours. We had a battery-operated radio and knew that Hurricane Rita would make landfall somewhere between Galveston, Texas and Cameron, Louisiana. Only three weeks after Hurricane Katrina devastated New Orleans and surrounding parishes, the relentless approach of Rita was both dreadful and menacing.

My people knew many of these storms. *Siti imaxa*, "people of the many waters," have lived along the Gulf coast for eight thousand years. We were fishermen then too, nestled within a rich and fertile river basin that provided virtually all our needs. The only Louisiana nation still living on a parcel of its indigenous lands, we built flat-topped pyramid mounds and smaller earthworks, and a strong, complex culture. Over the millennia many hurricanes battered the huge territory the Chitimacha called home, once a third of the present-day State of Louisiana. We probably fled northward to higher ground until the storms subsided then returned home. "Home" today is a mere five hundred acres nestled along Bayou Teche, near *Siti*. It is now an emasculated series of channels, smaller lakes and ponds due to water diversion projects and levee construction after the great flood of 1927. The people of the lake now number just over a thousand. We were fishermen then, and I still am today, though I make my bread and butter by writing city council or police reports for the local newspaper and laying out pages for press, dressed in khaki slacks and dress shirts. I lunch with my betters and laugh over cocktails with those who do not feel green-black water lurking behind their temples, water deep as all time. But when the ticking overlord on the wall releases me, I flee to *Siti*, to ancestral water and chase bull bream or largemouth bass with the fly rod, as my father and I did. Powerful as the notion of home waters is among anglers, a lifeline of eight thousand years binds me here. I am lost away from them.

Before the power went out, Susan and I watched animated, morbidly colorful radar images of Rita the same way we watched Katrina approach a few weeks earlier. Now here was Rita, growing in intensity over hot Gulf of Mexico waters, and she came, a beast bent on razing all in her path. The power went out, and if not for a battery operated radio we might very well have been alone in the entire world. It might well have been a century earlier, or a thousand years. Spaniards might not yet have landed, to be beaten back soundly, might not have allied themselves with a neighboring hostile tribe, returned and started the first of several raging wars.

Night came too soon. The sound of generators rattled when the wind calmed between bands. Hurricanes usually seem to hit at night, a mysterious behavior of an obviously non-sentient natural phenomenon. We tend to think of them as reasoning or at least instinctive creatures the way they crawl toward the coast, jog here and there, turn suddenly and leap like jaguars at small prey. At us. We are the small prey. Individually, our homes, our skyscrapers, levees and bridges, are all small, and suddenly at night with the sound of growing winds and generators rattling, the storm at our doors, we know it so surely.

Howls, all night. Banshee wails, bending trees, flashing spirits. We were never concerned for our own safety, the eye wall landfall was a hundred and fifty miles away, but it was hot and uncomfortable. Rita raged all night, throwing gusts at us, drenching us with rain, screaming fury and mindless rage. Blind malice. Now and then, sleepless, edgy, I would go look through the big windows in the old breezeway. A faint glow lit the sky, though I could never quite discern where it came from. Ghastly shapes, skeletal and defrocked, my trees whipped and bent, wild dancers to Rita's snarling melody. Debris flashed through the sky, large dark shadows but some seemed to be winged, and I wondered if thunderbirds rode with her. Thunderbirds always ride the eye of the storm, black and massive.

Sleep was fitful. Rita gave us her worst and dawn came at last, but the storm didn't stop. Outer bands passed over us, violent and sometimes more ferocious than the interior of the storm it-self. When the worst subsided enough to venture out, winds still leaped up throughout the day, battering and unexpected. The yard was a mess, carpeted with downed tree limbs, but nothing on the house was damaged. We stayed muggy and hot until late that evening when the power was restored and slept under air conditioning again, exhausted, thankful, knowing that many were not nearly so fortunate.

There was saltwater intrusion miles inland. Someone saw dol-phins, or perhaps porpoises, in the bayou that runs through the reservation, far from the coast. When Hurricane Lili came ashore on this spot along the Louisiana coast three years earlier, yellow-fin tuna were found dead an incredible distance from the salt. Hurricane Andrew virtually destroyed the Atchafalaya Basin, forcing Louisiana Wildlife and Fisheries to embark on a massive stocking program to restore largemouth populations. Decades of coastal land loss have allowed such surges into places they never before touched. It is the legacy left to us, after all else we've suffered.

That morning weeks later, I made fresh coffee, strong and black. The aroma drifted through the old house, tinged with bit-terness. Earlier in the week, at Bayou Teche near my newspaper office, silver specks flashed in the sun, shad gone belly-up in black water. Closer inspection revealed crabs, shrimp and a few bream, all dead, sunken, pale. For two weeks Bayou Teche res-ted, motionless and salty behind the city of Franklin, saltwater trapped with no winds, no rain to flush it back out into Atchafalaya Bay. Hurricane Rita pushed six or more feet of Gulf water into the bayou and beyond, the surge and winds churning up decades of organic matter laying below. Then that matter began to decay, robbing the water of oxygen. The bait fish were the first to go. Canaries in a coal mine.

Near Sabine Pass, Hurricane Rita left rafts of dead fish, some so vast they seemed to stretch beyond a man's vision. Also along the mouth of the Mississippi, where Hurricane Katrina came ashore. Inland, along the basin, sporadic reports, mostly uncon-firmed, of freshwater fish kills had become all too common. My native waters lay nearly exactly between the two landfalls, where storm bands overlapped on the outer edges of both.

But I made fresh coffee, black, no sugar. Hot, strong coffee like my grandmother made. She would stand with a cup of hot, strong coffee in her hand, at the fig tree, listening to *kich* and an-swering it in a language she never taught me. Dawn stole in, stretching out over the sky first in a silver-gray glow. Like a specter, somehow, like a dingy white sheet tossed over the world.

Looking out at the approaching dawn, making up my mind, I recalled growing up in that little boat. That lake, and the little wooden bateau, were truly my cradles in life. I have been here, in essence, for eight thousand years. I still spend as much time as I possibly can there, on the lake and at the old places, though my father is gone to his grandfathers and *kich* did not come to me this spring. I search the lake shore and hidden shell mounds for words and songs as much as bluegill and bass.

I finished my coffee and loaded a couple of fly rods into the boat, then trailered it to the lake. Still hard to see, the dawn growing, but I thought the water looked dark. The outboard en-gine fired, though it had been months since I used it, and I sped across the channel into the cove.

And I thought of the coffee in my cup that morning. I thought of midnight, pulled down as the storm overtook it with a silver-gray glow. This is where midnight went. Here, in the place we called *Co'ktangi,* midnight reeked. Like a sewer plant, maybe. Like stagnation and lifelessness. I pulled the throttle back and the boat settled into the blackness, churning up a foul stench. Dead water is black as midnight. Midnight, pulled down.

Along the south shore of the spot where ancestors danced long ago and turkey-buzzard men tended the dead along mounds later ravaged by dredges for the value of their shell, I idled through pungent, black water. The stench surrounded me, stifled me and burned my nostrils. The sun peeked over the levee and threw golden lances at the cypress trees, revealing watermarks four or five feet up their trunks, only recently receded. White salt stains made the cypress knees seem anemic. Nothing moved. Nothing scattered, swirled, jumped or sped away in a vee-shaped wake. There were bubbles here and there, lots of them, and I thought they might be turtles, but I realized it was churned organic matter, letting loose methane as it rotted. Some of it was leaves, twigs, animals and fish, that may have rested in that anaerobic layer of muck at the bottom of most Louisiana waters for long years, maybe decades depending on how often hurricanes hit there.

A circumference of the cove and a diversion down Sawmill Bayou revealed no change. Just that spring I was pulling giant shellcrackers from beneath cypress canopies here with Jitterbees under an indicator and a bamboo fly rod. A nest of bedding bluegill attacked an Accardo popper so frantically by the time they tired of it the fly was a tattered mess.

Midnight, pulled down and spread, unfurling, over the waters. Purple spots on the eyes like cataracts. I could stand the stink no more and, when I found a deep spot in the bayou, I pushed the throttle hard and the boat leaped up, outward, fast. I turned left at the channel, went to the lake. Here a north wind was building and the water churned foamy, but little better. I turned away, beaten. Returned to the landing, returned home. The waters would renew, but not today. Months, maybe years. Midnight, slung low, pulled down. The smell followed me along the levee as I made my way home. All would renew, but not soon.

I looked up into the trees but there were no birds, no sounds. Nothing can exist forever. Nothing can suffer neglect and survive indefinitely. Not mottled-brown birds or old lakes. Not old worship places or dead languages. I thought of New Orleans and the surrounding areas, the horrors Katrina brought and the devastation Rita left behind weeks later. My little blackwater world was a minor tragedy in a land strewn with tragedies. But it is the tragedy that remains the most painful. When there were miles and miles of coastline here, stretching into the Gulf of Mexico, when there were shell reefs and barrier islands, no hurricane surged water this far inland. No floods could touch this little cove far from the coast unless the Mississippi overflowed her banks, spilling into the Atchafalaya. Hurricanes simply weakened and began to break apart over miles of marsh and shell reefs that over the decades have vanished.

At home I hosed down the boat and had to scrub at smelly black stains along the hull. Stains of decay. When done, the boat covered, the tackle put away, I retreated to the house and sat for a long, long time, longing for green-black water, for the sound of splashing around the next bend in the bayou. I ached for the scent of rain to cleanse my nostrils of the persistent reek still in my lungs, the smell of black, dead water.

Old Trees

St. Mary Parish sat right smack dab between the two storms. Katrina and Rita overlapped us lovingly. We had evacuees from both directions in Franklin by the first of October.

Our sleepy little parish became a beehive. Thousands of evacuees converged on us, and we welcomed them with open arms, though they weren't always the most gracious and appreciative of guests. We did our best. There's no better place to flee a hurricane than into the arms of people who have themselves fled a hurricane. Nobody else knows what it's like.

But there were other casualties.

The old tree was here before Christopher Columbus first glimpsed the coastline of the Taino homeland, which he would call Hispanolia. Probably no more than a single tree among many, maybe big around as my ankle or leg.

Natural selection must have favored it, for it survived and prospered, grew tall and wide. A live oak, like those Napoleon coveted and cut for his warships by the thousands. Like that which Evangeline wept beneath. They dot the landscape of the South. One, among many.

I played and explored and brushed down quarter horses beneath it, but that's recent history. If you consider its lifespan as minutes past midnight on a clock, I've only been around it since 12:59:20 or so. But when Desoto came, it was already a century old, and by the time Bienville made war with the Chitimachas, it was twice that age.

My grandfather spent a lot of time around it, but that was only natural. He was just the latest. Generations of my family had meals under it, napped beneath it. Old men and probably women smoked corncob pipes and let blue smoke waft into its green leaves and gray moss. Children climbed in it, maybe built tree houses in it from scrap lumber they found floating in Bayou Teche just a few dozen yards away.

Its canopy provided much-needed shade. In recent years, where two limbs met and sort of melded together, a hive of bees buzzed busily, far above my head. When I was a kid, I chased crickets to fish with around its roots and trunk.

It is, in short, a member of the family. It was here before my non-indigenous forebears. It burst the shell of an acorn, sent out a taproot and shoot, and my Chitimacha ancestors somehow never trampled it; no deer ate the tender first few inches of it. Somehow, it survived right there.

A month or two ago, I noticed a split. The tree divided asymmetrically about twelve feet up. A split began there, and I was worried. Two-thirds of its bulk is on one side, with long branches thick as the bed of my truck that reach out toward the road. I consulted sources on what to do to reinforce it.

It wouldn't have mattered. Its heart was gone. It had apparently suffered long and lost its memory, its will. My grandfather used to spend a lot of time around it, and he could step behind it and I couldn't find him again. I think I know where he went now. Into that great oak tree's heart. Into that space of darkness now exposed to the sun. When it was sealed and dark and believed in, it probably held entire valleys and rivers and mountain ranges.

Broken, most of its bulk lying now on the ground, the void in its heart could still have encapsulated a horse.

It is not so much for its beauty that the forest makes a claim upon men's hearts, as for that subtle something, that quality of air that emanates from old trees, that so wonderfully changes and renews a weary spirit. (Robert Louis Stevenson)

Five hundred years, maybe even six. I wonder when the decay began. A bit of water settling high above in a depression at the fork of its trunk, eating away at the wood over time? Decades? At least. Maybe a century. I wonder what magic existed in its grain, what spirits dwelt in that dark cavity within. Every year it made a growth ring. Throughout that year, as it formed, it took in sunlight and fingertip touches and the soft brush of a bird's feather and the scurry of insects. It took in resonance and vibration as it grew that ring and, as winter came, and the ring was complete, it was encapsulated by the one that grew next. Five hundred or more of them. It is a history book. A chronicle of a landscape.

It's just a tree.

Some of you are thinking that. I know you are. It's okay. I know that's what the modern world has made us think. It's just a tree. But I also know better. It was more than that. Its roots drank the blood of the earth—that potent power—its leaves inhaled the air and soaked in the glow of the sun. It is still alive, and maybe that part of it still standing will survive another century or more, but I doubt it. The decay in its heart went to its bones, I think. I was going to be married under it one day. I was going to be buried under it one day further along. But it's far more than just a tree. It's a family member. It's a legacy and a kindred spirit.

At some point soon, I'll have to go out and cut it back, but all I'll be able to do is cut the smallest branches away. Its massive bulk will, for a time at least, become part of the landscape, because there'll be no moving it. It will persist, at least for a time. It didn't grow so long and stand so tall and wide to simply fade away into memory so swiftly.

One night, feeling lonely, I went sit on the roots of my fallen oak tree, mourning it. A sort of wake, I guess. I watched the leaves begin to brown, wilt. Unlike at any other point in my life, touching it, there was just a whisper of fading magic, a distant cry, a shallow gasp.

It was hot out there but I stayed. I get intolerant of civilization—suffocated by it—when it's this hot. Makes me moody and irritable and depressed. The heat of the sun radiates back from all the concrete, reflects off all those glass windshields and windows, from metal car hoods and I can't help but think: global warming is true, but it isn't caused by carbon dioxide, it's caused by all this silly stuff we make and clutter around us that collects and emanates heat.

Even here, where the humidity is the real killer, it's cooler in the woods. Away from cement and steel and glass. Away from civilization. I've been thinking that's why my tree split lengthwise and most of it fell over. Even the Rez has grown too much, too many metal roofs and paved driveways, too many noisy tugs passing in the bayou, too many airplanes overhead. Oak trees, like trout I suppose, don't fare well with civilization. Maybe water oaks do, with their shallow, spreading roots and thin bark. But not live oaks. No, live oaks are too noble for it. Too deeply immersed in places away from concrete and metal.

My old house used to be cooler, when it was surrounded by trees. But Hurricane Andrew swept all those on the sunny side of the house away. I haven't planted more since I moved in, knowing it'll be a decade before I even begin to enjoy their shade. Fearing, as it were, they'll go belly-up before they mature, from too much civilization.

I scarcely get to the water, to the woods, anymore. I'm going belly-up, I'm afraid, sickened by too much civilization. Poisoned.

Think about it: we're living in furnaces, we really are. We're living atop all this artificial stone, but at least real stone and rock and boulders don't get as hot as concrete and asphalt; we've got window glass reflecting heat everywhere, back and forth, heat rays ricocheting like bullets in a gunfight; our air-conditioners expel the heat of their compressors into the air, our cars spew hot exhaust from blistering hot engines, and the sheet metal on their bodies, the shells and roofs of buildings are like elements in an oven.

Soil and trees and water don't pull heat in and throw it back all around at us. Wild places don't do that. Please, I don't mean it's not hot out in the middle of the forest...but at least it's not magnified by our addiction to concrete and steel.

Our little community here is not so bad as a city. I think I'd go stark raving mad in a city. Belly-up for sure. But there's still too much concrete and steel here. Too many exhausts and too much reflecting heat.

I light a cigar as I sit with my old fallen tree. There's been much tobacco around it. There has to be. Tobacco helps open the doors between worlds. As the smoke wafts around me, I look back over my life, the things I might have done differently if I had the chance. Remarkably, and true to my nature as a dubious no-account, none of them involve career or bank accounts. No, when my head's on the pillow at night and the air conditioner won't stopped running so I can hear the crickets singing by the thousands outside the window, the changes I would make, the do-overs and roads-less-traveled, have everything to do with wildness and nothing with civilization.

But I fell for the slick advertising. I was wooed by the siren's call of success. I think the lengthwise split in my own heart began when I stepped away from my father's wooden bateau and to the door of that first car I owned, headed for where I thought there was something better. Turns out, I couldn't see the forest for the concrete and steel.

Sometimes I catch myself kicking my own behind for things: not starting a retirement plan early in life, letting go some financial what-not or another when I shouldn't have, taking on debt, whatever.

But at other times I just wish I could be one or the other, civilized or free, and not this mutated hybrid of the two, this feeble interpretation of both. They don't mix. The one side goes belly-up in the presence of the other. Splits lengthwise and collapses. Civilization always conquers wildness. It's too powerful, hard and poisonous.

The split in me began a long time ago, and collected not water, like my oak tree, but longings for things that now, at the other end of the split, no longer seem to matter. Yet they decayed my heart and most of me fell away somewhere along the line. Like my old oak tree, I'm only half here now. Half real. If my grandparents were here, they might know the magic to restore me, but it's lost to me. Unreachable. Vanished.

Belly-up. It's inevitable. Guess it's too late for me. I've fallen for the slick advertising. You can only "get away from it all" when you're young and don't have anything or need anything. Once you're older, you have to have money to "get away from it all" or they come throw you in jail for not meeting your obligations. There's a lesson there, I think, that should be taught to children in grade school, but that of course would never happen. Grade schoolers in wooden school houses with gabled roofs and clapboard siding might have understood it, but students in concrete and steel schools, encased by gypsum and fluorescent light, won't even hear it.

My cousin in Ft. Worth and I discuss it sometimes, and we sense the eventide. An era is ending. The old line of the Family is ending with he and I, we suspect and fear. Civilization has claimed the rest, moved them out of the Circle. Old trees toppling are like omens, like foreboding. The basin and the cove are drying up. An end of an era. Going belly-up.

A month passed. It was cool out. A small front had moved through and squashed the mercury down into the low fifties. A light northerly wind would, I knew, also push some water out of the lakes into the bayous and eventually to the Gulf of Mexico.

Dawn was barely peeking over the trees, and I relished the smooth acceleration, the gentle restfulness of the little wooden bateau, as always. We spirited down Bayou Teche and into the canal linking the bayou with Lake Fausse Point and the cove nearby I love most.

Last time I passed this way, water black as midnight reeked of storm surges, saltwater and death. Now the water was largely copper-brown-black, but healthier. Still, I would suddenly pass through pockets of dead black water and the smell would assail me. I don't know if it is a matter of buoyancy, but it always seems the little boat carried me just a little quicker, as if trying to get out and away from those pools of dank stagnation.

We made a wide turn near the locks at the Atchafalaya Basin Protection Levee, the preeminent earthworks of the twentieth century inhabitants of these waters. While my father's people built great monuments to the Creator at Grand Village, and stepped pyramids along the coast, effigy mounds in the shape of thunderbirds with outstretched wings, the marauding herds of hydrologists and civil engineers that followed left behind levees and locks. Indicative of a vast difference in cultural paradigms, my father's people made peace with the water around us, their successors struggle in vain to subdue it.

Passing through pockets of dead water now and then under skies just being lit by an as yet unseen sun felt like journeying between netherworlds, but at last I reached the cove and turned the bow to it. The little boat, no more than twelve-foot long and narrow, sped across the water like a bird, winged, outstretched. True to the designs and inspirations of its builder, it flawlessly and devotedly returned to the cove yet again. I wish I knew how many of these journeys to the cove it had made. I am sure it numbers in the hundreds.

That north wind picked up again and I believed I would be safer in the back of Sawmill Bayou, so I pointed the bow to the northwest corner of the cove, careful to avoid the sunken row of pilings I knew were there. My father warned me about them each and every time that I said I was going to the cove.

"Watch out for that row of pilings from Sawmill Bayou to the other side of the cove," he'd say, every single time without fail. "That'll put a hole in the bottom of your boat."

One weekend evening he came limping home, paddling up Bayou Teche to pull the boat home on the trailer. The engine hung there on the transom but with no lower unit.

"What happened, pop?" I asked, incredulous with dismay.

"Hit one of them damn pilings back of the cove," he grumbled and refused to discuss it ever again.

There was calm water in Sawmill Bayou, and I lowered the electric trolling motor into copper-black cove, but when I touched the switch nothing happened. I spent ten minutes fiddling with it and gave up, resorting to my paddle.

A leggy Accardo Bream Killer was my choice: good visibility, slow, tempting sink and light enough to throw on a long leader with my little four-weight rod. Now and then a whiff of deadness swept over me by the slight breeze there in the back of the bayou, from some trapped stagnation in the swamp. I fished carefully, paddled when I needed to, and wished desperately for rain. Shotgun blasts not far away reminded me that squirrel season had started.

I noticed downed trees across one fork of Sawmill Bayou, hoped spring rises would wash them clear; also Susan's Bayou was blocked by a fall that was, remarkably, still green and lush. The Bream Killer worked hard for me, in dappled sunlight and in shade, but I noticed that even considering the low water levels overall, there was far less water under my paddle than before Katrina and Rita. This cove faces east, and I knew the counter-clockwise fury of the storm's winds had pushed tons of sediment and muck into the back of the cove where it had no way of flowing back out.

My arm ached from paddling. I grinned and cursed myself for getting too soft, too accustomed to electric trolling motors. My father paddled this little boat all over the lake with his right hand, casting with his left, from dawn to dusk, while I enjoyed the ride from the time I was old enough to sit upright and hold a rod. I knew my father was feeling his age when he bought his first electric trolling motor. He was quite a bit older than I am now, though.

The Bream Killer dropped without fanfare into a shadow jutting out from the base of a big cypress tree, cast by a huge limb not far off the surface. I saw it settle in slowly, those long white legs undulating upward nicely until it faded into the copper-black and beyond my vision. But then the tip of the line moved upstream and without thinking I lifted the rod tip.

The line moved upstream more quickly then, and the weight of a respectable fish was more like a treasure to me than any gold or silver. Catfish? Bowfin? No, for when he came out of the water and danced on his tail, the green and white of him was that spectacular and familiar reassurance of a largemouth.

Soon I took him to hand, and yeah, I admit it, I kissed him on the nose. Two hurricanes had passed, missing us with their full impact but their intense outer bands had both churned and blasted us. A month before I had found nothing but deadness here, stagnation and stink. Yeah, I kissed him on the nose, and lemme tell you, brothers and sisters, I ain't ashamed of it at all.

I didn't kiss the four redears I caught after that before the wind picked up too much and I retired for the morning, but I felt like kissing them. My little lake and cove are coming back to life. It was all I could have asked for, all I could have wanted, right then and right there.

I cranked up the engine as the cove was getting rough from the wind but I took a leisurely trip out to the canal that led home. Now and then black water would be foaming and reeking as I passed through it, but I knew the lake was purging itself, slowly, unflinchingly.

And I thought about circles, not for the first time and surely not the last. How I have always believed my father's people, those who didn't fight the water but lived with and within it, existed in circular time, time with no beginning, no end, no middle and no apex. I think that those who came later, those who built levees and locks and dams live in linear time, time that has finality, has an ending and a closure.

At what might otherwise be the end of all things, I know that instead everything comes back to where it began. At least for me, and for mine. Back to this little wooden boat and this wonderful old cove of cypress trees, sunken pilings and the way of memory.

Back, at least, to when there were no levees, no dams and no locks. There may come a day when it can hold no more sediment, no more mud, no thick sludge and dry out under the sun, become a marsh then a prairie maybe even a forest in time. I'll be long gone by then, singing with my father at the feet of our grandfathers.

That's all in a time to come. For now, at least, there is still life here, precious and rare, and within the confines of a small wooden boat, enough belief to keep it all in existence perhaps just a little while longer.

Six: Autumn

*They were either biting yesterday, or you should
come back tomorrow.*
—Nick Stouff

Saturation

Rain, soft as kitten paws, trotting across the roof, dull thuds rather than ringing drops, but morning is saturated with it, scented by it.

No rain since the last hurricane, it came now as a twinkling blessing, a sparkling wish come true. Rain intensifies the colors of the world, gives them depth again, as if they have been slowly washed out by the bleach of scurrying human beings trying to make sense of their lives, by pollution and disbelief. I woke to the saturation of antiquity.

Everything feels crisp, alive. I peek out the curtains and the greens were mossy, like lichens, the gray-brown bark of the trees moistly earthen, the silver sides of maple leaves star-like. There are squirrels on the lawn and they shake their tails and tiny paws of glistening droplets.

I let the curtain fall back and get out of bed to shower and make coffee. Out the door I have to pause for a moment and admire the restitution of the world. Everything is wet, and in the presence of water I am most at peace, most at liberty to feel as I wish to feel, speak to whom I choose. It rained like this—gentle, unassuming—a thousand years ago and ancestors looked out from palmetto huts, breathed it in deeply, stood outside for a moment before heading off to tend to the day's duties, just as I stood there this morning. Did I say a thousand years ago? Perhaps. Maybe two thousand, five thousand, eight thousand. Before the colors of trees and earth and squirrel tails were washed out by timepieces, bleached by fluorescence, stagnant from disuse.

If it were not for the dictate of modern maladies, I could take my cup of steaming coffee to the bayou and walk along the reeds there, watch frogs leap away and tadpoles by the dozens dart here and there like a composite individual. If it were not for schedules soon turned to sand and responsibilities destined for obsolescence, I could let the rain sting my face on a boat ride to the lake and sit in it under a cypress canopy, watching bluegill strike at bugs knocked into the water by the deluge. There's more reality out there, anyway, than here, than behind the wheel of the truck on the road to work, than the concrete gauntlets and the steel bridges. More color, to be certain, more vibrancy and belief, than any four walls and growling air conditioner could ever hope to conjure. My grandfathers and grandmothers knew this for eight thousand years, yet it only took a few hundred to undo all that saturation, to bleach and wash out millennia of accumulated color.

Drops fell from the corrugated roof, splashed at my feet. Kitten feet leaping from a forbidden cabinet, startled by the sun. I should have gone about my business, knew the time was wasting, but I quit wearing a watch the day we buried my father six years ago, recognizing that life is far too fleeting to worry about the passing of hours, minutes and seconds. Far too brief, fragile and precious to measure it by revolutions of the hands of a clock rather than paddings of kitten paws on the roof, leaping from cabinets to splash into infinite creations at my feet.

Do you remember being a kid, trapped in the house by the rain on a Saturday? It's funny how time changes perspectives. Now I'd love nothing better than to sit and watch rain through old window glass all the day, seeing colors revived and the sleepiness of the world start to stir. Instead, I get in the truck and rubber tires spin like clock hands, carrying me through puddles muddied by the passings of other vehicles carrying other harried passengers and drivers, rushing headlong toward a time punch, lunch bell and early grave. The colors are a blur of speed now. I am moving at the speed limit, hurtling toward a date with washings-out and bleachings.

Because when I look at myself in the morning as rain is spiriting kitten paws over the roof, I see my eyes aren't as dark as they once were. I see my skin is not as substantial. I am fading along with the colors of the world, perhaps? Going the way of memory. No longer believed in, a relic, revived only by the rain. My own kitten-paw-bearer, Patches, sits on the bathroom floor and watches me, and I think sometimes she can see more of me than people can. Kitten feet and kitten eyes are penetrating like that. More aware. Unbleached and unwashed out. Sometimes she sees things I can't see, shadows I can't fathom that move through the house and she follows them with her eyes until they fade through a doorway, into a ceiling, under a floor. One day I fear she will look through me completely, and I have become as shapeless and insubstantial as the shadows.

Sometimes I wish I could be revitalized and sustained by schedules and perforated edges, my soul fed and nourished by spinning hands and wailing phones. It would be much easier, to join in the game. Wear the mask. I imagine sometimes I actually see happiness on faces at business meetings, clinking silverware on porcelain plates, smiles above starched collars and straining neck muscles. I am jealous, I suppose, of such detachment. But out there, away from the saturation, the kittens become lions, devouring, ferocious.

Rain from gray billows follows me but here on the streets and in the overcast dullness of the cityscape it collapses rather than settles. Succumbs rather than surrenders, is blackmailed rather than bargained with. Nothing is revitalized here, because nothing ever knew life. Concrete and steel, but what few trees and flowers and water may be found are a mere afterthought, a speck of oasis in a vast desert. Like thyme struggling to survive in the zig-zagging crack of a concrete slab, it may persist but never flourish.

Blue-grays are thin here, whites skeletal. Beyond the city and into the wilds, there is emerging color. I turn away, beaten. In this place I cannot even hear the kitten feet on the roof. In this place, I cannot even see colors.

The time came when I would be entertaining the production crew of *Fly Fishing America* and my Blackfeet cousin Joe Kipp as we filmed the second episode of what was to be entitled "Native Waters" to air on the program the following year.

The crew and Joe arrived on a Sunday and we were to start fishing Monday. The shoot was originally supposed to happen in October, but Hurricane Rita fouled up the coast so badly we postponed it. Freshwater fishing remained slow but I was hopeful we'd be able to put our flies in front of a few largemouth, *sac-au-lait* or big chinquapins that might accommodate by taking it.

We were also scheduled to make one or more marsh trips for redfish and speckled trout.

Joe managed to keep me from being eaten by a grizzly, or even seeing one, and I promised I'd do the same for him in regards to alligators and water moccasin snakes, but I imagine it's pretty much too cool now for either.

I planned to show Joe some old Chitimacha archaeological sites I know of and keep jealously guarded, as well as talk a little about basin sedimentation and coastal land loss, important issues I hoped the producers would not edit out, especially in light of that year's hurricane season.

It was fun and nerve-wracking getting ready for the filming. Of course, the weatherman was getting a jolly good chuckle at my expense by predicting desert-like conditions one day and Noah-caliber deluges the next, leaving me to wonder if he'd be predicting snowstorms followed by a heat wave.

I stocked up on my favorite flies, particularly the Jitterbee, and I cleaned the store out of the Bream Getter, as well as their complete supply of Spooks. The company founder, Tony Accardo, would pass away the following spring, leaving a great void in the world of Louisiana fly fishing.

For the saltwater part, I stocked up on Clouser minnows, developed by fly fishing legend Bob Clouser, and other flies that I don't know a lot about but are guaranteed to be redfish-raisers and speckled trout-busters. I had read Pete Cooper Jr.'s *Fly Fishing the Louisiana Coast* repeatedly in the preceding two weeks.

Of course, no fisherman can have a special fishing event come up without buying something. He always has to have a justification, though. Not so much for anyone else as himself. A true fisherman doesn't need to explain himself to anyone else. John Gierach said every real fisherman is essentially an anarchist, and that's the truth.

So I ordered two new reels, four reel cases, four spools of leader material, two containers of split shot in various sizes, paste floatant to keep my leader floating...well, you get the idea. I tried to talk myself into a new rod, too. The spirit said, "Yes!" The checkbook said, "Are you *NUTS*?"

It was a remarkable experience for me in Montana. I'd never seen water like that. There were voices there, too. I think Joe hears them loudly, clearly, but they were whispers to me, just on the edge of perception. They're the same voices, though they speak different language and sing different songs than my waters hold, but maybe Joe will hear those whispers as well. Chief Seatl said the water's murmur is the voice of our father's father, and I know the chief was oh, so right. Beneath the cypress canopies, in the green-black stillwater of our world, there are voices of ancestry. They're not all Chitimacha voices, either. My mother's people were here, in bateaus and skiffs, setting hoop nets and pulling seines. This is the land of both sides of my blood. This is my native water.

Readying for such an event is mind-rattling. I have often fantasized of throwing all my cares away, abandoning my job as a newspaper reporter and becoming a fishing guide, leading wealthy clients into the basin to catch slab-sized bluegill and lunker largemouth bass. I had it all planned out: I wouldn't be just your basic three-hundred-dollar a day fishing guide, I'd be your basic *character*. The kind of guide you remember almost better than the trip. Full of funny witticisms, brimming with personality, I'd be a literal shock and awe campaign.

Really, I only gave up the idea because my fishing prowess was clearly not up to par. Fishing guides are required to do one thing, and do it well: put their clients on fish, lots of them, and preferably of significant size. There was the rub, and so I elected to stay with the newspaper and concentrate on writing books instead. There are many coastal fishing guides who can do it. But of all the areas in Louisiana I could live, this just happens to be the only active land-building river delta left on the gulf coast, and that ecological wonderland just makes for difficult—not bad, you understand, difficult—fly fishing for reds and speckled trout. Go figure.

It was a great dream. In that dream, I made three hundred bucks a day and didn't have to pay for fuel or tackle. Of course, that's the dream. Even if I paid out two hundred, I'd still make a hundred bucks a day, that's five hundred a week, right? And of course, I'd have clients every single day, never have to worry about that. Go figure.

My clients would never complain if the fishing was bad, understanding that's just the nature of fishing. They'd never spill beer in the bottom of the boat, or throw cellophane wrappers overboard. Anybody who hired me as a guide would understand that they need to hope for the best and expect for the worst. They'd regularly give hundred dollar tips.

Such dreams keep me going, you know? There's also the one where I find pirate's treasure. Yeah, that's a good one.

But that's all it is, a dream. In fact, I know now I couldn't handle it. With the approach of the film crew's arrival with Joe Kipp I had never felt so pressured to catch fish. I was losing sleep over it, tossing and turning and getting up to look bleary-eyed at the weather forecast, tide charts and pollen count, for no good reason except that it was there, along with the UV index. Then I'd go back to bed, toss and turn hour after hour until finally falling asleep about thirty minutes before my alarm went off.

The week of my second appearance as a fishing celebrity—har-har, hee-hee—started on a bit of a flat note, and despite the best efforts of all involved, improved little, although there were moments of resonance.

I spent the entire weekend preparing for the arrival of Joe and the film crew from *Fly Fishing America*. Friday's weather forecast was dismal at best: a cold front would push through the area late Tuesday or early Wednesday, bringing heavy rains and a temperature drop of twenty degrees. That left us only Monday and early Tuesday to get some fair-weather footage. What originally began as a four-day film shoot had been cut in half.

I spent Saturday working line onto new reels, getting the boat ready, organizing fly boxes. I found to my dismay that my trolling motor battery was mysteriously shorted out and had to be replaced, a tab I had not anticipated and would rather not have endured. I had collected a nice assortment of saltwater flies, as we intended to do one day of freshwater fishing for bass, sac-au-lait and bluegill, and a second day of marsh fishing for redfish and speckled trout.

Sunday morning Joe Kipp called from Great Falls, Montana to let me know there was no ticket for him at the airport. Joe was scheduled to arrive in Lafayette Sunday evening and I would have picked him up there. But the travel agent had apparently made a colossal error and, after quite a bit of wrangling by the production company, the best that could be done was to have Joe into Lafayette by nine p.m. on Monday. This effectively meant Joe and I lost one day of fishing.

But the crew arrived Sunday and we met for breakfast Monday morning to hammer out a plan. Bryant, Jake and Aaron were great, professional folks who, thankfully, have been at this game of filming outdoors programs long enough to know that sometimes the fish bite, sometimes they don't. That doesn't do much to make a film, of course, but the facts remain solid. Jake was the only familiar face: he was one of the videographers on my Blackfeet trip.

We decided that we'd go to the lake, me fishing without Joe, for the afternoon. First we spent some time in Franklin, though, so the crew could do what they call "B-roll" footage of the area, the back story, so to speak. They took lots of film of Franklin's antebellum homes and historic district, downtown, Sterling Sugars' mill and the like before we headed out to the Rez.

Chitimacha chairman Al LeBlanc gave a brief welcome to the crew on film, then we launched at the reservation boat landing. My pal Francis Todd generously volunteered to carry half the film crew in his boat while I had one guy with me in my boat. We fished the cove all afternoon and, as expected, it rained on us a little and the fish were slow to respond. I asked the crew several times if they had packed their rain gear before we left, and all, including the skipper of the camera boat, assured me they had. So when it started raining everybody donned rain gear, except the guy who made sure they all brought it, who had completely forgotten his in the truck, and I got a little wet.

Since Hurricane Rita, the cove's water levels have decreased six or eight inches, making an already shallow situation worse. I could tell by the various pilings, duck blinds or sunken logs that have been there for decades, by which I usually gauge the water level, that I had lost at least six inches of depth due to sediment pushed into the cove by the hurricane. The cove faces east, the direction of the storm's winds, and its back end goes nowhere, so all that sediment just churned into the cove and settled out there when the wind and water subsided.

We fished the cove from front to back and back up, and I managed one small bass and a perch so tiny I slung him over the bow of the boat when I set the hook. But the cove was beautiful, just turning its fall colors, and the guys were able to get some truly stunning video of my native waters before we called it quits and headed home. It did give me the opportunity to talk about the problems the hurricanes caused to the lake and the basin as a whole, a little plug for conservation practices and a better understanding of hurricane impact. Later, when we hit the marsh, I also had an opportunity to talk about coastal land loss and the importance of Louisiana's marshes and wetlands to the entire nation.

That night we had supper at Cafe Bayou at the tribe's Cypress Bayou Casino and I drove into Lafayette to pick up Joe Kipp at the airport. We had a pleasant ride back to town, stopping in New Iberia for a fishing license for my guest, a brief trip through the Rez and then to the motel. We'd meet up at six a.m. Tuesday to head for the marsh.

It was not quite dawn when I arrived to meet the film crew and Joe Kipp at the Forest Motel in town. From there I led them to a nearby service station and quick-mart to meet our guide and hosts for the day. It was kinda rough having come in late from picking Joe up at the airport and getting up early to head out for fishing, but my excitement kept me driven.

St. Mary Parish Sheriff David Naquin had kindly volunteered months earlier to guide us on a trip to the marshes below Houma, Louisiana, in search of redfish and speckled trout. With the generous help of local anglers Lamon Miller and Carlos Snellgrove we were hopeful that the weather would hold long enough to let us get a few fish on film. That massive cold front was predicted to arrive later in the day.

A few cups of coffee all around then we loaded up the vehicles and headed for Bayou Dularge.

We were all hopeful, but warily. The cold front would bring winds of up to thirty miles per hour with an eighty percent chance of rain. Remarkably, by the time dawn slipped in that morning, the chance of rain had diminished dramatically, the arrival of the cold front pushed back a few hours, and all that really remained was a brutal gusting wind all day long..

Joe Kipp and I rode to Dularge with the Sheriff and Miller, and everybody seemed to hit it off pretty quick. We talked a lot about redfish and speckled trout fishing, about hurricanes and coastal erosion, about the general health of the fishery here. Turns out Joe had done some redfishing in the past but, like me, had yet to hook into one. We were still cautiously hopeful we would do so that day.

Carlos provided a breakfast of biscuits when we got to the camp in Dularge while the boats were being loaded and readied, then we all headed out into a pounding surf and busting winds. Joe and I were in the sheriff's boat, and the crew in Snellgrove's with he and Miller. Before we departed, as our hosts were readying for the trip, Joe called me over dockside.

"What's this?" he asked, pointing at the water.

"That's water," I said. I knew Joe Kipp well enough then to suspect I was being ribbed.

"You can't catch fish in that," he said, pointing with his chin at the green-black marsh water behind Carlos' camp. "The fish won't be able to see the fly."

"Man," I said, "that's *pretty* water down here!"

I can't say how many hours we tried to catch, because it all became a blur, but I can tell you this: my father always claimed the most important truism about fishing is that they were either biting yesterday, or you should come back tomorrow. Those who were not supposed to be making a fly fishing television show were fishing artificial baits and fresh shrimp, but an entire day of fishing these only resulted in the landing of one small redfish, a decent speckled trout, a catfish, and two small black drum. I hooked into one fish and lost it, and Joe came close two or three times as well, but no cigar. You can't blame it on the fly fishing, though: the shrimp-anglers were not doing a whole lot better! Several times Joe had fish chase his fly to the boat then veer off without a take.

We ran all over creation looking for an elusive combination of criteria: spots with as little wind as possible, and with fish that would bite. It proved to be too tall an order, but as Naquin said —more than once—that's why it's called "fishing" and not called "catching." I thought of reminding him that it's not about the "catching" at all, it's about the outdoors, the air, the exercise, but then thought I'd better keep my mouth shut or I'd find myself walking home.

Despite the urgency of getting at least a few fish caught on film, it would be impossible to say that we didn't all have a great time. The "fishing experience" was excellent, with lots of good-natured ribbing, mostly at my expense, but hey, I don't mind being the catalyst of good cheer. We broke for a lunch of sandwiches and chips then chased fish around a little longer to no avail. Early in the afternoon we called it quits and decided to head for some freshwater ponds back in St. Mary Parish.

We hooked into a couple bass here, lost both at the boat, but decided it was worth going back for Wednesday. We knew the temperature would drop about twenty degrees overnight and the winds would continue to howl, but the crew was running out of time and we still hadn't enough footage of fishing to make the show work.

That night we all cleaned up and returned for supper at the local Forest Restaurant. Joe asked for suggestions and was recommended fried crawfish and etouffee with a stuffed potato, which he enjoyed thoroughly. We were all pretty whipped by then, and retired fairly early. The next day we would return to the freshwater ponds to try again, though conditions would be even more difficult than the day before.

We arrived at the pond in weather that would not exceed forty-five degrees and though the wind was only a breeze then, by the time we got the boat into the water and loaded was blustering at fifteen miles per hour or more.

Joe and I were in my boat and the crew in a small aluminum johnboat with an electric trolling motor. I wish I could say the last day of filming was the saving grace, but it wasn't. I missed two fish on short strikes, but thankfully, Joe managed four small bass and a green perch that morning. We worked the edges of one side of the pond over and over, back and forth, since it was the only portion out of the wind, to pick up those fish.

At some point during all this I commented to the crew, "You know, it suddenly occurs to me that if my father were here right now, he would ask me if I had lost my mind, fishing in a twenty-mile-per-hour wind in forty-five degree weather."

I thought about that for a few moments more and then added, after Joe had landed another small bass, "He'd also tell me that the reason I am not catching fish is that I'm 'not holding my mouth right.'" When I was a kid, this comment always led to some strange facial contortions.

Perhaps the most humorous moment of that whole day was when a water moccasin snake swam by near the bank. Joe's reaction? Let's just say that a man who has faced off thousand pound grizzly bears with only a pistol in his hand didn't find himself too comfortable with a three-foot water moccasin nearby. You see, there are no venomous snakes on the Blackfeet reservation, probably due to the altitude, so Joe's people haven't much experience with them. As I have had absolutely no experience with grizzly bears, I considered the score evened.

After noon we managed to get the boat trailer stuck at the boat landing and had to get pulled out then headed for Polito's Cafe in Franklin for lunch, where we met up with some folks from the newspaper.

Then we went back to the Rez for a tour of the Chitimacha museum, which really gave Joe a perspective of who we were as a people and the vast, impressive history of the Chitimacha Nation. Our museum is perhaps one of the finest in the state of Louisiana and we are very proud of it.

There was only one thing left to be done that day, and we tended to it in the last half hour before dark: I trailered my father's wooden bateau to Bayou Teche, where Joe and I fished along the bank for some filming. Of course, it was for television, we weren't expecting to catch anything, but it gave us the chance to close things out the right way, I think, and the dusk-goldened rays of the sun made the boat glow like amber. That little boat was, after all, the place where all this fishing stuff began for me.

I took Joe to meet my mom after that then we all went our separate ways to get cleaned up for supper. Lamon, his wife Pat and his father Bob Miller along with my friend John O'Niell welcomed our guests in the best possible way: a south Louisiana down-home cook-out, I guess you could call it. I'm not going to make you suffer with mouth-waterin' by reciting the whole menu, but let's just say nobody left hungry and everybody was mightily impressed with the selection and preparation!

Back on Tuesday when we were fishing south of Houma, the sheriff said something that was important to the whole experience, I think: he said the catching of fish is good, it's always nice, but really it's about being with friends and family and spending time outdoors. Wednesday night at supper Lamon finished that tale by noting to our guests that the cooking and camaraderie was the same thing. It's our way, it's our lifestyle, he said. The crew, suitably impressed and rarely treated to such extravagance, took it all in appreciatively.

On Thursday the lot of them took off for the friendly skies

again and we said our good-byes, with the mutual promises that should I ever wish to return to Montana or Joe and the crew to Louisiana they'd have a roof and a pot of something good to eat ready for them. And that was the end of the shoot and a rough, rough week of fishing. I spent the rest of the day sleeping on the sofa with the National Geographic Channel on the television. I awoke a few times during the day and, though hazy, half-asleep snippets of programming, firmly believed someone was mating iguanas with king cobras and producing offspring of bats.

Both episodes of the show would air in the spring. The crew assured me that, while they wished we had caught more fish, they had enough material to make a show. It was quite an experience. Back in the spring I had no idea what was in store for me until that first email from Montana came in. Before I knew it I was on an airplane to the Blackfeet reservation, catching trout in the Rocky Mountains with Joe. It's been quite a ride.

Let me tell you, though, I was a nervous wreck about it. Like many people, I hate the way I look on camera, and we all know the camera adds ten pounds to you, that in addition to the *mumbley-mumble* I gained since I quit smoking that May. Plus, the oversized waders added even more bulk, I was afraid viewers who didn't know me would have the following conversation upon seeing the show:

"What's that?"

"I don't know. Looks like a beached whale."

"Well, whatever it is, it's fly fishing!"

"Yeah. Real *smart* beached whale, ain't it?"

Or something like that. I was thinking about having a few very close friends over to watch the show with me in a private gathering...okay, to tell the truth, I was thinking of renting the local movie theater and inviting all of them. But I decided that if I did, indeed, come off looking like the remnants of a shipwreck, I'd rather not be seen sobbing uncontrollably.

I didn't even know the show was coming up in February until I was watching what I thought were reruns of last season's show and say a familiar face. "Hey, that's Dave," I said, my friend and fellow writer Dave Micus, and realized it was the new season I wasn't expecting until April. My heart leaped into my throat and it was all I could do not to sell the house, load up the truck just like the Clampetts, and head for Bever-lee. Hills, that is. I looked on the Internet and found the schedule with my two shows on it and just stared at it for long, long moments, thinking, "Well, there's a fatal hemorrhage waiting to happen."

I then started worrying about the people that know a little something about fly fishing, who'd be sending me emails saying things like, "Hey, was that a fly rod you were fishing with or a baseball bat?" and even "Give it up and get a Zebco, ya bum."

I never expected all this. I know that no one is going to be beating my door down for a *Native Waters: The Sequel* subtitled *How I Got Caught Catfishing Like A Philistine.*

I believe in signs and omens. At first I was pretty pumped up, because I made it to Montana and back without a plane crashing or getting ate by a grizzly. Then, as I was awaiting the Louisiana shoot, two hurricanes rolled through and fouled things up pretty badly for everyone.

But we made it through that, and at first the show was on the network's schedule twice on Friday night, a double showing! Then, all of a sudden, as my debut neared, they cut it back to once that evening. This is, in my book, a bad omen.

"Hey, is that Stouff show coming up?" I could hear some executive in charge of scheduling at OLN ask.

"Yup, two weeks," an underling replies.

"Hmm," the exec says. "I dunno about all this. I mean, do you think the world can take him *twice* in one night?"

"He wasn't that bad," the underling says in my defense.

"Bad?" the exec wonders. "No, not bad. But he's no Brad Pitt."

Brad Pitt was the star of *A River Runs Through It*, the story of author Norman Maclean's early years with his family fly fishing on the Big Blackfoot River in Montana. I do know I am no Brad Pitt, don't worry. Tom Skerritt, who played Pitt's dad, is more like it. A quiet dignity of intellect. Yeah, that's me.

This may or may not have come through during the Montana filming when, on my first cast, I snagged a weed with my back cast trying to push fly line through a thirty mile per hour wind. Or as I was learning to walk through a rushing stream without my knees popping out from underneath me; or climbing back up a ravine, huffing and puffing with recovering-smoker's lungs and wondering if they'd let me be buried right there, or at the very least, anytime anyone mentioned the word "bear" jumping completely out of my oversized waders in terror.

Waders were a whole 'nuther story. I never wore waders until I got to Montana. Putting waders on must be similar to how medieval knights put on suits of armor. It was quite an adventure. Then I had to get wired for audio, with a lapel microphone and transmitter tucked into my waders, which have a pouch just under the chest part for storing a repair kit should the waders spring a leak. I wondered what would happen if my waders sprang a leak, since I was carrying a microphone transmitter and not a repair kit. I made a mental note to myself that, should I ever do a television show that required me being wired for audio in an inflatable raft, the repair kit stays where it belongs.

Once you got into your waders, you had to put boots over the stocking feet. Waders have stocking feet, reminding me a lot of some pajamas I had when I was pre-K. I checked to make sure the waders didn't have a flap opening in the behind. That would have been intolerable. Once you got your boots on, you were ready to go fishing. You jaunt on down to the stream and get into the water quietly, fishing upstream. The water is cold as the dickens, but that's how trout like it of course.

You throw your fly line into a thirty-mile per hour wind, and assuming it actually goes where you want it to, which is about one in every ten casts for people like me who fish stillwater and stay home when it's too windy, the current carries it toward and behind you in about three seconds flat, so you have to pick up line and do it all again, watching this churning water for this tiny little dry fly that might get taken by a trout.

Well, as it happens, it all works. Honestly and truly by some miracle, it all works and the next thing you know, a fat cutthroat is on the other end of the line, and well, to tell you the truth, it made all the wader issues, hiking issues, bear fears and possibility of butt flaps worth while.

I had two contingency plans. Three, actually. The first was that the show would turn out to be a rampaging success, and I actually looked okay and came off somewhat dignified. In that case, I would strut my way through the weekend like a rooster, all full of pride and arrogance. The second, again if the show was actually good, then I would be quiet and humble, honorably genteel, not a Philistine, the perfect example of the gentlemanly

Southern outdoorsman.

The third plan involved having my bags packed and a one-way ticket to Bolivia. I asked neighbors to please take care of my mother. She did her best to raise a good son, it wasn't her fault, I strayed from the path.

Oh, I had my new life all planned out, should the occasion demand it. It would be like entering the witness protection program, but instead it'd be the "Injun boy who makes a damn fool of himself on television trying to fly fish" program.

In the program, I would be secreted away in the dead of night wearing a fedora and heavy trench coat, wrap-around sunglasses on my face. And wing-tip shoes. I'd look like a shady character from *The Maltese Falcon*. They'd put me on a train which would pass through Texas, Mexico and the rest of Central America, eventually finding its way to Trinidad, Bolivia, on the Rio Mamore. They would set me up in a nice hacienda here, where I can fly fish for peacock bass in relative obscurity for the rest of my life. Militant Bolivian mercenaries would protect me from intruding eyes and smuggle crawfish, Community Coffee, Tony Chachere's seasoning and Abita beer to me illegally. Patches would take up residence in one of the hacienda's corner tower-rooms, where she can look out on the jungle surrounding us and snarl at the anacondas and jaguars.

Now and then some hunter or angler on a guided fishing or hunting tour of Bolivia would catch a corner-of-the-eye glimpse of me and report back to the *National Enquirer* or *The Star* that they saw "the notorious, maligned and publicly-shunned author Roger Stouff" but nobody believes it because they all think I am tending yak in Siberia. That's the cover story, you see.

Well, that's the three plans, anyway. I refused to have a get-together. I'm not a gambling man, so I figured I wouldn't play the odds that I wouldn't be shamed into a shapeless lump of skin, muscle and pretentiousness.

There's another fantasy I toyed with it. In it, I become an overnight fly fishing sensation, and to protect my privacy and that of my family I am spirited away in the middle of the night to Bolivia, to spend the rest of my days living in a glorious hacienda, waited on hand and foot by servants and blissfully fishing away each day in whatever river I choose, writing more books and doing public appearances on *Oprah* via satellite uplink because my schedule is simply too busy to make it to the studios in person, darling, have your girl call my girl, we'll do e-mail, okay?

There was, I guess, another alternative: the show airs, and nobody notices or gives a rip, and I just go on writing my newspaper column, fishing in the bayous and swamps, and have a lovely life here in dear ol' Lousy-ana.

Hmm...sounds great to me.

My father is surely looking down on me from the Great Mystery with my ancestors, shaking his head and saying, "I taught that boy everything I know and he still don't know nothing!" This was a favorite saying of my father's during our life together, until I was about ten when a light bulb suddenly went off and I asked, "But Pop, doesn't that mean *you* don't know nothing?"

"'Bout time," he grinned, and shook my hand.

My father taught me to fly fish. He was, make no mistake about it, a lethal weapon with a fly rod, no ifs, ands, nor buts about it. With a willowy old fly rod and a tiny yellow popping bug fly on a stretch of monofilament tied to the fly line, my dad would harass the bass and bluegill for hours on end, dozens and dozens of them falling prey to his talent in the course of but a single day. I fished the long rod until I was about fifteen, gave it up for some reason involving sports cars, high-school girls and cruising the streets of Franklin on Saturday nights.

Three years ago, I was looking through the old boat shed at my dad's house and there on a shelf, covered in dust, were two old fly rods. Mine and his. I took them home and though mine had been so severely chewed by rats it could not be salvaged, I rebuilt his to restored condition. That rod rekindled the spirit of fly fishing within me, and though I did it mostly for nostalgia in the beginning, I do it now because it just seems natural to me. It just seems right. I keep his old rod at home with my other rods now in tribute.

So truly, whatever the outcome, it's not riches, or fame, or even success that I hope for so much as doing the old man proud. I spent a lot of years not making him proud, years I wish I could reclaim now. We mended our fences and became father and son again before he left this world to join his Creator; to continue to make him proud remains among my most important tasks in the years remaining me.

There were drinks all around anyway. Despite my intention to endure it alone, we had a couple friends over. Just two. That was all I could stand. The clock counted down the minutes, the seconds, and then it was there on the screen.

Fly Fishing America, "Native Waters: Part 1."

"I look like a beached whale," I said.

"*SSSSHHHH*!!!" everyone reprimanded me.

I watched as we started out for Cutbank Creek and found our way to the creek. I watched cutthroat come to hand higher in the Rockies and Joe Kipp rib me about Crawfish bringing up mud from the ocean to make the land when any fool knows, as he pointed out, that it was Turtle who did that. I laughed.

The following week for the second part I laughed again as my hat blew off while explaining the pitfalls and the hardships of fishing for bass after a twenty-degree drop in temperatures from a cold front.

"Boat control is going to be an issue," I was telling Joe of the wind ripping across that pond. Right then, my hat blew off my head. Without missing a beat, I looked at Joe and added, "*Hat* control is going to be an issue as well."

I laughed again when the sheriff pointed out a time-honored Louisiana tradition.

"I got thousands of dollars in electronic equipment in this boat," David said to Joe and I. "You know how I check how deep the water is?"

He demonstrated by sticking his bait-casting rod straight down off the side of the boat to gauge the depth. This sent Joe and I rolling.

And I heard Joe standing along Bayou Teche telling the cameraman that, "He can't be Chitimacha anywhere else but here, just as I can't be Blackfeet anywhere else but there." There, in the aftermath of two hurricanes, his words were truer than any I had ever heard. Neither of us could be who we are anywhere else but the Backbone of the World and here in the Atchafalaya River Basin. But Hurricane Katrina and Hurricane Rita had brought the delicacy, the precarious nature, of our existence to the fore. We were paying for decades of decadence here in south Louisiana.

And when it all goes the way of memory, we might not be

able to be Chitimacha ever again. We are *people of the many waters* and without water, we will only be purple spots on the eyes of those who might remember us. The Great Sadness will end not with our extinction, but our eviction from paradise.

The Aftermath

Hurricane Rita wrecked the freshwater fishing. My usual haunts were completely unproductive and lack of rain only worsened the situation.

Instead, I have been venturing far afield in search of more productive water this fall. If things play out the way they did after Hurricane Andrew stormed through here, it'll be three years before any decent fishing returns. But Andrew cut a two hundred-mile-wide path with two hundred-mile-per-hour winds right where I'm sitting today. Rita made landfall one-hundred-and-fifty miles from here, but her storm surge inundated my freshwater fishing locales with saltwater. Bait fish succumbed and I while I didn't see huge rafts of dead fish like after Andrew, their absence verifies their demise. Reports from most of the coastal parishes are the same. Saltwater fishing is kicking tail, however, I'm just not set up for that kind of fishing and nobody's invited me lately!

That's not to say that there aren't a few spots that produce a few freshwater fish, but it's hit and miss, as if the fish are roaming heavily in search of food. I decided to make an exploratory trip to an area southeast of the Rez known locally as Quintana.

It was too far for me to paddle the pinou. Quintana is a series of oilfield canals cut into the coastal marshes. I reasoned that brackish water bass and panfish might have had a higher resistance to the salt than my exclusively freshwater quarry in other areas. I have a map of Quintana given me by a friend and, bracing my resolve, I put the boat over into the Franklin Canal.

The map illustrates the Quintana area very well, but what it does not show is how to get there. I knew that I had to turn into the a canal off the Franklin Canal, which I did, but then I got to a three-way intersection. I was confused and unsure of myself. I idled forward and grounded out in the middle fork. I backed the boat out and went right, and grounded out again. I backed out and went left and found ample water so throttled up to travel about two miles before I chickened out and turned back, making my way back to the Franklin Canal intersection. I got on my cell phone and called a friend and he told me I had nearly gotten to Quintana but turned around too soon.

However, he directed me to another area that was easier to find, but I had to cut through two miles of invasive accumulations. It wasn't water hyacinth, if was something we call "silver dollar" down here, a thick, matted plant that floats in great rafts. I had to stop several times to clear tons of this that accumulated between my outboard and transom, but finally got to a spot where the canal widened out and seemed promising.

I had with me an eight-foot five-weight. I don't fish anything lighter in these waters. I never know what I'll hook, big bass, monster catfish or bowfin, garfish. I know lots of folks who fish bluegill and the like with four- down to two-weight lines down here, but I just don't care for it. With a minimum five-weight I feel I've got enough backbone to fight the unexpected and still don't feel over-gunned for panfish.

My fly of choice was the cap spider. You can find this pattern on www.laflyfish.com if you don't know it. It's tied on a micro jig head so that the hook rides up, is very "leggy" and great for getting down there to larger, deeper fish. I had only two chartreuse cap spiders with a red spot at the head, and two blacks with a red spot at the head. I fished a chartreuse model under an indicator.

The very first cast saw the indicator settle in for a split second then plunge out of view. I lifted the rod tip and something yanked back, a side-slabbing, furious red-breasted 'gill big as my hand.

"Fluke," I thought to myself. "Can't be."

I let the big fella go and cast back to the same spot. I could see there was a huge stump remnant just under the surface of the water. No sooner had the VOSI hit the surface than it darted away and within moments a thrashing, frantic and very angry orange slab came to hand.

"Hmm," I thought. "Maybe not."

This fish went to the live well Another cast produced the last member of the triplets and I got disheartened. I moved the boat up a little and, for the next two hours, spot-cast and spot-caught, so to speak. Ended up with sixteen in the box, all beauties except one that I hooked too deeply to release conscientiously. I caught probably twice as many throwbacks.

It was the first good trip I had made all fall, and though that water was largely fresh it alternates with brackish throughout the year, so perhaps my theory on salt tolerance holds some merit. I have not been back to test it.

I'm estimating an eighty-percent reduction in freshwater fisheries along the coastal parishes by what I've been reading from other fishermen and reports in newspapers. Catches will probably continue to be spotty and roaming, as I believe these fish were also foraging for food or, at best, isolated enough and salt-tolerant enough to be a pocket of survival.

Road Trip

I often wondered what the people who were recipients of my father's crafts thought to themselves. How they felt, what they perceived, where their thoughts found a quiet corner to contemplate.

My father was a boat builder, jewelry maker, woodworker and woodcarver, among many other things. From a battered old shop with a dirt floor in the back yard, magic flowed in a ceaseless stream, most to be sold in the craft shop my grandparents ran out of a room in this old house I live in now. I would sit with him in that old shop, watch the boat or the watchband or bolo tie come together, see it leave, but I could not comprehend what the customer who might wander into the craft shop at my grandparents' house might feel, think, see there.

Even in my later years when, sadly, after my father's death I found the drive to build my own things of wood I could not imagine what really lurked behind the praise for a curly maple armoire, a bookshelf, a dresser of drawers.

Perhaps I am beginning to understand it, as I grow older, as I perceive from my own quiet corner at the side-edge of a life.

One Saturday morning, a pal and I headed north.

Winnsboro, Louisiana. I had never been there, though I passed nearby on a trek to Poverty Point when I was in college. Poverty Point is a prehistoric earthwork of staggering proportions and complexity nestled into the northeast corner of the state, past Monroe. But I had never been to Winnsboro.

This road trip was supposed to take place the weekend before, but a line of thunderheads passed from Texas into Louisiana that Saturday dropping up to three inches of rain and bolts of lightning across the state. A postponement was therefore in order until the following Saturday. A four-hour journey along featureless highways into the piney woods part of the state. I passed over many a muddy creek and small rivers, but the only one that struck me as truly beautiful was the Ouachita out of Columbia, Louisiana. At least on that day it ran clear and smooth, a fine little river nestled into the bottom lands near Winnsboro.

In his youth, Harry Boyd's mother took him fishing on the Ouachita River. Though raised in Monroe, he found his love for rivers and waters and fishing on that broad-backed waterway winding through northeast Louisiana.

There were several Native American nations living along the river in Louisiana and Arkansas before contact, including the Ouachita, who called themselves "wishita", along with the Caddo, Osage, Tensas, Chicasaw and Choctaw. The Ouachita called the water "the river of good hunting and sparking water." The Ouachita were nearly decimated by the Tensas before 1700, and destroyed completely by the Chicasaw just four decades later.

Silver water, sparkling water.

There's not a lot to see past Alexandria, Louisiana as one drives northeast and on through Columbia, into Winnsboro. Lots of pine trees, a few pecan orchards and plenty of red dirt set down by the Red River eons ago. But once in Winnsboro, a beautiful little town nestled in the northern piney woods, I started counting driveways on the street Harry lived on.

"One," I counted. "Two..."

"Maybe," my pal said, "it's that one right there, where that guy's standing in the driveway casting a fly rod?"

Sure enough, there was Harry Boyd and there was an awful lot of line in front of him; he was reeling it out of the way of my truck as we drove into the drive, smiling broadly.

We had met briefly a couple years before at the Acadiana Fly Rodders conclave in Lafayette, just long enough to exchange pleasantries then I had to get on the road to another commitment. We'd been in contact by email often ever since. Harry had wanted to ship me the rod when it was done, but I wouldn't hear of it. I was determined to pick it up myself. A fine craftsman's work is a pleasing, moving thing on its own, but to know the man behind the work creates levels of appreciation and resonance far greater. This would be my first modern bamboo rod by a man I greatly admired and respected. There was no way I'd let Harry trust it to the post.

Turns out the rod in Harry's hand with all that line out was not mine, but it was a close kin. Harry liked the taper so much he built himself one for bass and light saltwater, and he was casting his rod into the wind to a distance of eighty feet or so. Then he led us into the house and introduced us to the missus. Then he put the tube into my hand.

I used to wonder what people felt and thought and perceived when they took delivery of one of my father's wooden bateaus or calumets; one of my grandparents' river cane baskets or one of my piddlings in the wood shop. I used to guess at the emotions, the thoughts. Now I think I know.

I uncapped it and pulled the sock out slowly, then the butt section emerged from the sock. A burl reel seat spacer, shiny silver hardware, and amber cane, green wraps with black tipping, nickel silver ferrules flashed in greeting. I felt two tips in the bag and commented on it.

"All bamboo rods come with two tips," Harry chided, as if I should have known this. I did, but I was pretty flabbergasted by the beauty of the rod in my hand and not thinking very clearly. I was thinking even less clearly when I read that, in addition to Harry's signature, serial number and length-line markings, he had penned "Native Waters" on one flat of the bamboo near the winding check.

"I didn't want to put your name on it," he smiled, "because it'd lower the value if you ever sell it."

I laughed to myself. Sell it? The notion was unthinkable, but I grinned back, "I'll remember that when I put it on Ebay next week!" Harry laughed. He knew that wouldn't happen. From the moment I knew I wanted a Harry Boyd rod and made the commitment for one, I knew it was a lifelong bond.

What I have long loved about antique firearms, handmade furniture, bamboo rods and other such things was the mark of the craftsman. Men like my father, like my grandfather, but they were always detached. Distant. I didn't know the name or the face behind the rod, the old Damascus twist double-barrel that had been in the family for generations, the Edison Amberola in the den. Certainly I knew my father and grandfather and grandmother, but the detachment was still there, somehow. From the inside, looking out I still couldn't perceive the entirety of it.

To say that I was overwhelmed would be inadequate. I was completely blown away. Or so I thought, until we went outside to the driveway for a trial run. But as Harry led us back outside and I strung up the rod and before I knew it, threw an awful lot of line out--more than I had ever cast before with any rod--I saw from the corner of my eye Harry beaming like a proud parent. Like the way my father would grin widely when a boat left on a shiny galvanized trailer, or a violin cradled in the crook of an arm, or a turquoise and silver band on a wrist. I understood at last that the beauty of the craft is only half the story. The other half is that it moved directly from the maker's hand to the user's, the wearer's.

I've not had a lot of cane rods in my hand. I've never had a modern taper by a modern builder in my hand, to be sure. In general, when it comes to casting any fly rod, I'm a mediocre caster at best. My farthest cast—if such things mean anything— was about sixty feet.

But within three false casts with Harry's rod, I laid sixty-five to seventy feet of line out. Harry knew this by the length of the concrete sections in his driveway. I was not using the double-haul, a fly casting technique that adds energy and distance to casting. I'm not much good a double-hauling and in fact seldom need to use it, though I've been practicing more since my trip to Montana, the "land of winds as well as Big Sky" as I've come to think of it. But casting distance, while it impresses me and I enjoy striving for it, doesn't mean much in my local fishing. I am usually fishing within forty feet, fifty max.

"How's that feel?" the maker asked me, grinning.

I think I said something like, "It's exquisite," but Harry will have to tell you for sure, because I was in awe of the perfectly balanced and extraordinarily powerful rod in my hand, conjuring line behind and in front of me. I've never felt such wonder in a fly rod, and sometimes when I'm casting it in the yard these days, waiting for spring to actually get it out on the water, I wonder if I ever will again. Oh, I had to work on my timing.

The rod was far quicker in action than my Granger or other vintage rods. It was also lighter in the hand, being hollow-built. But I could tell right away it was a thing of purpose as well as beauty.

We retired to Harry's shop then, and got the grand tour of his domain. Harry Boyd's workshop is a magical wonderland, especially for someone like me who has built a few things himself, and would like to try his hand at a few others before going to Happy Hunting Grounds. Harry showed me planing forms and binders, planes and splitters, ovens and glues. He made ten or twelve rods a year at that time, and started down this road about eleven years earlier. He has become nationally known for his work, not only as a rodmaker but also as an author and exhibitor and teacher. Harry provides rod making classes to anyone whom wants to learn the art. He fishes prefers chasing trout these days. Winnsboro is closer to Arkansas trout than I am, and that's just one more thing I envy about Harry Boyd. As the son and grandson of craftsmen, I found myself within shops past and present, and the vision of the craftsman huddled over his work, satisfied only with the very best he could muster, unwilling to put his name on anything else, ran as true in my memories as it did that day standing there with Harry Boyd.

Before I knew it two hours had passed and it was time for me to hit the road back to the Rez. Harry also had an appointment to get to. We shook hands and promised we'd meet up again soon, probably at a conclave within the next few months. Back on the road for the four-hour trip home, I reflected along the way that it had been quite a year. Joe Kipp and I had fished trout in Montana and warm water in Louisiana. I had been from one end of the earth to the other, it seemed. With the new rod safely nestled beside me in the truck, heading south, heading toward native waters, I thought it was time to slow down and let the seasons lull me to rest.

October

October. Season of change and season of discontent, of moving, of harvesting and of stock and store. When the first gentle chill breath of winter nips at the nape of my neck, I feel it all over again: the coercion to move, to change landscapes. My feet grow restless with the need of October. I was born in October, and it runs through my bones like winter's breath.

The dog is the latest in a long line of October companions. Sometimes we sit along Bayou Teche and, nose lifted, nostrils flaring, eyes half-shut, she inhales October. I almost think she's dozing, but no, she is catching the scent of things that won't be here, won't happen, until tomorrow or the next day or next week, things that I can't sense but she inhales deeply and lets course through her lungs. October makes them more clear to her. October makes the scent of things far and away sharp and keen.

The water is high, but with this morning's front north winds will push it back into the bay. Last evening, garfish and carp swirled and left expanding rises in the bayou as we sat on the dock watching fallen brown cypress needles drift southward. A pair of wood ducks flew west, up the bayou, never diverting their path. The dog watched them pass, her black ears perched.

The trees are thinning, and I can see large nests that I forget about every summer when there's no October in the air. An owl perched nearby a couple of autumns ago, watched me for an hour or more, eyes wide and unblinking. It worried me, for a time, because I know the messages owls bring. But there was no death come to visit. Only winter, and promises.

Restless, I call the dog and we go to the truck. I put her in the back and drive for the levee, chasing October, white clam shell and limestone dust tailing behind. Because of civilization, because of responsibilities and deadlines and the cell phone hanging on the truck visor, this is the best I can manage: chasing my tail, so to speak, instead of moving and stocking and storing. I race after October for an hour, but at last, all I can do is helplessly turn for home, because in the end, October will move on and I'll still be here, confined in November. I can't imagine a more mournful existence no matter how hard I try.

I spy a little sparkle of black water and turn quickly, down the north side of the levee, to a tiny slough. I drop the tailgate and the dog leaps out, nose to the ground, tail beating left and right as she sorts and catalogs the scents of this place. I walk to the water and sit on an old fallen cypress. Water, again. It's all ebb and flow, Harry Middleton said. Things that come and go.

No surprise, really. It's always water lurking behind my eyes, black and green, water as primordial as the birth of the earth. If the Rockies are the Backbone of the World as the Blackfeet say, then these swamps and bayous are new skin, I guess, constantly changing, cells falling away and new ones emerging, shifting, transforming. Flowing and ebbing.

The dog comes and sits to my right, and, after a cursory request for a head patting, looks out at the little slough with me. She startles me when she does this, and she does it often: finds the focal point of my own gaze and joins in. Together we sit and watch October drift lazily by in the air, in the little blackwater slough, in drooping autumn-laden tree limbs.

When I was a boy, October was all mystery. Mystery and wonder, all at once. No less than spring; October was the antithesis to spring. The opposite of awakening. I had turned a year older earlier in the month, and, with the chill in the air and the browning of the world, I felt years past my age. Even as a boy, I knew it was time to move on, to make peace with autumn and ready for winter. But there was school to attend, and Thanksgiving was coming, then Christmas, and a boy can't move in October anymore, but that doesn't take away its mystery. Doesn't take away the cool wonder of its breath.

All things on earth point home in old October: sailors to sea, travelers to walls and fences, hunters to field and hollow and the long voice of the hounds, the lover to the love he has forsaken.— Thomas Wolfe

But it's growing dark and cooler. I stand and we make our way back to the truck. I'm not so hurried now, because I'm not going the same direction anymore. I'm going back, instead of moving with October, and it's rushing away behind me. Back home, nearly dark, the dog retreats to her yard, and I to the house. It's October, and there's a few bills remaining on the kitchen counter; the telephone sits guarding my escape, and it's unclear to me if the dead bolts on the door are keeping me in or October out.

Losing Home

I am thankful my father is not here to see it: the loss of home.

As much so as the little wooden house I grew up in on the Rez—with its green drop-lap siding, open carport and corrugated tin roof—home was that little cove out near the lake.

But it's going away faster. Vanishing, and one day it won't be there anymore. I hope I am not alive to see it. I hope I never have to bear that pain.

I grew up there, of course. In a little wooden bateau, a dozen feet long and born two years earlier than me. It, too, is ailing, and the mutual descent of the two leaves me desperately clinging for intangible cords to yesteryear.

He put me in that little boat when I was old enough, but as far as I can remember I was always there. On the bench seat, making the ride from behind the little green house all the way to *Co'ktangi*. *Co'ktangi ha'ne hetci'nsh*. The pond-lily worship place. When I was old enough, he'd let me slip over the side of the boat and wade along the hard-packed clam shell bottom. Once that place stood high above the water and stretched dozens of yards out into the cove, and Chitimacha from across the nation would gather there. Chiefs and nobles were buried there, their bones picked clean of flesh by the turkey-buzzard men and buried separately in split cane baskets. It was a place of power, as tangible and palatable as the water lapping at the bone-white shell at its margins.

I would wade around it, and pick up pieces of pottery with my toes and show them to my father. They were sometimes marked. Today I know some of the names that anthropologists have given the designs: Pontchartrain check-stamped. Manchac incised. Some even bore the thumb and fingerprints of their makers, fired into the clay for perpetuity.

The flat-topped lily, the American lotus, grew in abundance there, and droplets of rainwater would bead on their pie-plate surfaces, perfect gems. Their white flowers rose on spindly necks, opened their petals to the sun and shone like tiny fires.

I believe I caught more fish in *Co'ktangi* and Lake Fausse Point during the first half of my life than I shall ever see in the entirety of the second. He would paddle with one hand, cast with the other, and laugh in delight with every little bream and lunker largemouth bass. Yet even the fishing was not the essence of our love of the place. It was the power. Sweeping, undulating and cyclonic, the power saturated and uplifted us both.

The cove was larger, before the levee was built. The levee dissected it. The portion to the northeast side is nearly gone, just a flat puddle full of aquatic growth. In my portion of the cove, the lilies and the hydrilla made excellent cover for fish and kept the cove fresh, clean and thriving for years.

Then, about two decades ago, it was like someone threw a switch: the cove, and later the lake, stopped thriving. The fish diminished greatly. A few years later the lilies faded, then the hydrilla and finally we started turning up mud with the boat prop as we went through. It was clear: *Co'ktangi* and the lake were silting up, cut off from their natural flow by the levee.

It began to die then, but I go back, year after year. Sometimes there are a few fish. Most times not. Last time, the boat engine kicked up more mud than ever, and tapped on sunken debris as I went through, even though the water was high enough to be up into the woods at the shoreline. The bottom is coming up to meet the surface. A cancer, the siltation is claiming the life of home.

I cannot bear it. Can you imagine what it means to me? My heart and soul are there. Everywhere I look, I see myself, at different ages, with and later without my father, in this boat and that. I have always been there, but one day, soon, it will leave me, and I will be desolate. Lost.

Dreams, Black Elk noted, are sometimes wiser than waking. Can you begin to imagine the pain in my heart? It's just a place, to most of the locals that even know of the cove. Perhaps remembered as a great fishing spot, or a beautiful part of the state. But I am tethered to it. An umbilical runs between us. At any time, no matter where I am, I can close my eyes and face *Co'ktangi* by instinct, feel it out there, draw on its power. That power comes from deep inside the earth, from the radiating sunlight, from the whispering trees and the supercharged air.

Every year, it grows more thin. Can you imagine the loss? For eight thousand years I've been there, through the hot blood of grandfathers and grandmothers. I had thought once I would like to be cremated and have my ashes spread over *Co'ktangi*, but I fear now it won't be there to accept my remains, receive back all the power I've soaked from it over a lifetime.

Home. My mother and father gave me life, but everything I am was made there. Every moment of wonder in a rain shower from a cloudless sky; each restful gaze at a patch of irises along the black water's edge, and all the memories of a childhood fabricated there.

I'm thankful my father isn't here to bear the loss. Or my grandfather.

Here is yet another legacy left to me: regret. I must witness what none of my ancestors could at Charenton Beach, formerly the village *Ama'tpan na'mu*, where once you couldn't see to the other side; the emasculation of *Co'ktangi*, and the loss of so much of what made us Chitimacha, people of water, people of the lake.

I wish I had the courage to never go back.

I pulled the starter rope once, the engine fired faithfully, but I quickly shut it down. I thought I heard something. Looking up, I wasn't sure what it was. The birds there can cast their voices far, and the bouncing cries between the cypresses and tupelo can almost sound like words. Many times I swore there were other people down the canal I was fishing, but found only an old heron. And sometimes I don't know if I'm hearing my grandmother's stories reverberating in some corner, some crevice or niche, of my memory.

But for a split second, I thought I heard Ustupu just before the outboard rumbled to life.

The Indian boy was betrayed by his aunt, tricked into committing a heinous crime. His six hunting dogs were all turned to fire, and together with Ustupu they ascended into the skies. They say that sometimes a Chitimacha can hear him up there, calling his great dogs back to him for eternity:

Cins-kut! Tep-kani, apuk (Come!) *Kuc! Kapainch! Neka!, Ku-tep! Apuk! Apuk! Come back! Come back!*

They say only a Chitimacha can call Ustupu down from his banishment, but if he does, he will remain on earth as a killer of all Indians. No one remembers the words to call Ustupu or send him back.

With another pull, the engine roared to life. I idled out of the cove, and the motor skeg bumped ancient logs as I went.

Like the boy, I am betrayed. All my blood are betrayed. Sometimes, when I float on the thin, dying surface of *Co'ktangi* in a nearly half-century old wooden bateau, I wonder—if I knew the words to call down the boy and his six great dogs—what I might do.

Seven: Miles To Go Before I Sleep

The woods are lovely, dark and deep
But I have promises to keep
And miles to go before I sleep
(Robert Frost)

November. The woods and far-off places are calling, but I have Frost's affliction: duties, and distances.

What does it profit a man to sit inside concrete walls when autumn is turning the leaves golden, ocher, sunlit yellows and earthy browns? The Johnson grass is dying back, the grains fallen to earth, and the bobwhites, scarce as they are, pick at them gingerly.

I am getting old before my time. It's not the years accumulated on the road behind me; it's the burdens. In autumn, I always recall Havilah Babcock's declaration, "My health is better in November," because that was when the bird season began.

November, and the call of fall is persistent, deep and dark. Can you feel the world winding down, drowsy?

I love this time of year. It is the most magical, the most haunting of all. There is a sense of thinness within autumn, a feeling that the past, present and future are merging, time becoming meaningless. The age seems to fall away, though the colder air makes my joints hurt and burns my nose. More so even than spring, autumn moves deep in my marrow, and the little connections in my brain that tend to misfire and sputter from time to time are soothed, refreshed.

Somewhere in this time of year, in what Ray Bradbury called the October country, and beyond into November, is a world I so miss. I still see hints of it, like when the neighbor and his kids stroll through my back yard and near my old half-fallen oak tree. Because that's the way it was, no fences, and if there were, we climbed over or through them anyway, and it was fine, we were all a community, all a village. Now and then I hear shots from the bayouside nearby: someone dispatching a water moccasin slithering too near the house or the kid's swing set, and I take comfort in the sound, solace in the fact that there's still a place where it doesn't mean someone died.

There's more out there like me, men and women who are aging despite their years, sickened by a different kind of virus, a variant strain of despair. I read columns in magazines by Mike Gaddis and the late David Foster, and I know I'm not alone. In November, across this great industrialized nation of teeming masses of inspired shoppers, some of us are wondering why the Christmas season keeps coming earlier and earlier, and there are still folks like me longing for a simpler life and a greater satisfaction from it.

If I keep aging like this, in a decade I'll scarcely be able to survive all the wires strung high along the wooded margins, the trash in the prairie meadows, the sick film of slime over stagnant waters once bursting with fish. The changes in this world are forcing me to stoop; my knees don't extend all the way back anymore, and I am going deaf because what I've heard is too much to bear. A decade after that, I'll scarcely be able to open my door to find November, walk through the thin places within it.

So I leave work, go home and sit outside until dark, but it isn't enough anymore. And there's no way out of it. I'm locked up, shackled, have to work until I can afford to retire, because you can't live simply anymore. Sometimes, in the twilight of a weeknight when I'm regretting many of the choices I've made along the road behind me, I dream of a life that might have been as a gentleman farmer, a steward of the land and waters; or a rancher, or a park ranger. Silly, I know. But in my mind's eye, I remember trudging through corn stubble just off the reservation, looking for bobwhites, and the farmer would stop by, high on the seat of his tractor, his straw hat tilted back on the crown of his head, and he'd inquire about my mom and dad, maybe send me home with a few yellow ears, oh, so sweet. If I were smoking cigarettes behind a tree, or handling my gun dangerously, my dad would know about it before I got home.

Will I be too sediment-laden and thin to enjoy this Shangri La called retirement? Will I ever even make it there? There's no way to know. In autumn, I can almost reach out and touch it across the folded arc of time, where the ends have come much closer to each other and are far less viscous. I can smell coffee hand-ground in my gramma's old kitchen; elderberry wine uncapped from my grandpa's wine-making setup; horses back in the stables, and an old black tomcat sleeping under the pecan tree.

So I work, and I give, and I get paid, and in the end, I may have nothing to look back on but the work and the pay. The notion terrifies me. In November, I can feel the time slipping away behind me like melting snow.

"You're not old," I remind myself. "Wet behind the ears yet, some would say." But Frost's verse echoes in my ears, reminding me grimly: *Miles to go before I sleep...*

Better to live a pauper's life free and unfettered? Or trod on, against the odds, in search of the dream? The American Dream. My parents were likely the last generation to experience it, and even then in emasculated form. What's left to us? Wars, and rumors of wars; bloodbaths on military bases, in places of businesses; considerations of parole for a rapist who left his six-year-old victim in a frozen field nineteen years earlier; a gloriously ridiculously oxymoronic news article revealing that it's not necessarily lack of exercise making kids obese, rather its over consumption.

This is what is left to me. What none of my ancestors might have imagined.

November. I could just reach through it, punch a hole in its fabric, and wrench back the long-ago. The soon-to-be-gone. I miss the smell of horse blankets and saddle soap; fresh-sawn cypress and shellac; the sound, soft as kitten paws, of a wooden boat as it drifts among stands of cypress and tupelo in primordial green-black water.

Autumn-tinted leaves tumble across the back yard, toward the bayou; cedar smells resplendent when I crumble the needles in my hand; far and away in the distance, a shrill little call of some bird; November, and I could put a pack on my back and head some place half-real, were I not so exhausted.

December

Winding down of coils, tightened to the hilt in January, releasing their final twitch of stored power. As another year draws to a close, the world slows, churning in a spiraling descent toward renewal.

There are white pelicans on the lake, perched on old wharf pilings, the cross-planks long since rotted away. Most are white, their sleek, tan bills like blunt spears, but now and then the rare brown stands among them, accepted, unmolested. In December, pelicans on the lake are like messengers. They carry words of promise.

Cryptic vows, to be sure, and not easily decipherable. The words spoken by silent pelicans on old pilings along the lake shore are puzzles that only the wise can solve. I have not garnered sufficient wisdom to fully comprehend them, but I know that for decades of my life there were no pelicans here. Their return marks something important. Something about promises.

Even the lake itself is calming, winding down like some exhausted phantom. Though the world does not heed the calendars of man, and December is but a label placed upon time to organize our harried existence, the world knows the shades and shadows of December. It feels the winter solstice, the shortest day of the year, and as the minutes are added to each day to come, the world, and this old lake, recalls spring, summer and brilliant rain.

It is ancient and thoughtful. I know this in December. Laid down by the Mississippi River tens of thousands of years ago, the land here is but a babe compared to the glacier-scarred terrain of the north. Yet this old lake is ancient, and I wish I could hear its words clearly. It has been said that human beings have come to live too hastily. Because our time on this earth is so brief, we rush through it in a mad dash to make each moment remarkable. In this way we have forgotten how to slow down enough to hear ancient lakes, which speak more slowly than we can discern. Water, earth and stone speak in geologic rhythm, and to hear them we must slow, slow our ears, slow our spirits, reject the brevity of life in favor of the eternalness of wisdom.

Because in December, with the earth nearing slumber and the old lake growing sullen and thin, I know there are volumes written in the heart of the earth that I cannot read. Perhaps I have skimmed their contents, picked out a word or two in translation, but the secrets and wisdom still unread encompass all time.

Given the time, and the freedom, I think I might hear what this old lake is saying so slowly. With sufficient leave, I think I could at least glean a spark or two of erudition, if I could devote my life to hearing it. But I don't have the time to slow down, to listen to the lake and the stories it might tell me. I am throwing myself at deadlines, racing toward appointments, thrashing madly like a drowning man within a cyclone of responsibilities, bills to pay, obligations to meet and many, many more things not worth having or knowing.

In December, cold rain feeds the lake and the ground around it, though we fuss about the mud on our cars and the stains on our shoes, as if rain should abide by our calendars and dress codes. Rain speaks, too, as slowly as lakes, but we hear it no better. I remember, when I think back on the hastily passed years, waking at night to thunder and rain, lightning and wind. The old house I lived in with my parents soaked it up, but kept us dry, shuddered around me and whispered back to the world. I'd lie in bed and try to understand their conversation, talk of Christmas and winter, tales of the Earth and thunderbirds.

December. Pelicans on pilings on the lake. I wonder what they think, why they stand there so silent and still. Perhaps they are listening, their lives slow enough to hear. Tangled up is how I feel in December. Like an owl's nest, like the recipient of a message that can't be comprehended. Bits of twig and string and tiny, fragile feathers, downy and sparse. *Listen.* The world is saying something, but I cannot hear it. I live too hastily. It has been said we all do. We can't slow enough to hear the world: the whisper of rock, the murmur of water, the sonnet of rain. Our lives are so brief we try to wrench gratification from each instant, and in so doing fail to hear the geologic-paced words within.

Tangled. Knots and loops. That's how I feel in December. I pick at them with the close-cut fingernails of a professional in an office, try to free the wraps, loosen the coils, but they are pulled tight. Within the center of each snarl is a composite year. Like a prisoner counting the seasons of his confinement by tying knots in a length of string; each holds a year within the center of the knot, bound there, completely intact, but no amount of picking with fingernails and teeth will free it. Once knotted and pulled tight, the years can never be unraveled.

Winter moves, stealthily, across the splinter of land outside my window. Winter tangles. Winter tightens knots. All things slow even more, speaking at a pace so leaden now it would take an entire lifetime to discern but a single word. The earth blinks, and I am born, live out a hasty life, and am gone by the time the blink is done, having heard nothing.

Inside the tangles are chairs at the Thanksgiving table which now sit vacant; within the knots are smiles and laughter and overwhelming presences gone silent, thin. Winter forbids me even the water, pulling tight the cold, drawing the tag end of autumn taut. If not for winter's grip, I would be drifting down the back end of dark canals, reaching into thin places where there are no knots, no barriers. If not for the cold, I would seek silence on the lake at dusk, on water suddenly lit with golden fire and blue-jay feathers, watching the orange eye of the sun retreat below the cypress horizon. I think that there, if I listened slowly enough, I might hear a word or two. Words of black-masked yellow finches that swarmed in great flocks numbering in the hundreds, dancing in midair around me like they once did, suddenly darting away in unison when I began to live too swiftly, leaving them behind in knots I can't untie.

Wooden boats, bamboo fly rods, old houses and sundered live oaks ask me to slow down, start to hear. They draw me out of the circus cage where I am a restless captive, pacing behind iron bars. They let me hear echoes, at least. Under the tangled canopy of cypress limbs covering dark canals, there is erudition, wisdom. Yet in the back of my mind I worry about the time, obligations and expectations, all these coercions push me along too quickly to garner all the things I might learn there. Of turkey-buzzard men and Spanish galleons; of river cane and beaded purses; of dances, and songs, palmetto huts and dugout canoes. If not for the pushing shove of morning alarms, scribbling on calendars, there might be glimpses of rows of blue corn, muscadines on arbors, greetings and farewells.

The old workshop behind my father's house beckons, and I step over collapsed thresholds to study the disembowelment within. From here magic flowed like wild, silver fire. Turquoise, alligator teeth, abalone, silver, wood, beads and garfish scales. Decades of art were born here, streaming outward across the globe. Time has claimed the debt owed it. There are tangles everywhere. Tangles of scraps of hard maple lying on the dirt floor; tangles of tools, rusting, cold; tangles of old guitar parts, covered with dust; tangles of alligator bones, bleached white and silent, and knots of years, held firmly within. His old workshop is drawing tighter, and before long will never be worked loose again.

The mass of men, Thoreau said, lead lives of quite desperation. This is December, desperate and still, and like an owl's nest and the great feathered bird within, there are messages grim and joyful to be heard. At the middle of the long length of cord there is a span of straightness. A portion without coils and loops, without knots. I sit here in the living room of the old house, and there are no tangles here. This part of life, at least, is unwound. Behind it are the knots of the past, ahead of it the knots of uncertain days to come, but here in the middle, in this old house, my fingernails and teeth can rest for a brief moment. This old house speaks a little more urgently, just by a fraction, and I can hear it a little better than the earth, the lake, the old oaks and the rain. It tugs at my senses, reminding me that my grandfather returned here, my father returned here, and now I have returned here. Wayward sons all, we were drawn back to this old house, these lands and waters. To untangle knots. To work loose the snarls. It called from hundreds of miles away and lured my grandfather home, later my father, and finally myself. They had a purpose here. I suppose I do as well.

To untangle knots. To listen slowly enough to hear. Owl's nests and wide-eyed, unblinking word-bearers. Bluebird feathers and gold finches blanket a fire-engulfed lake at sunset. They all hold tangles to be unfurled, comprehended and sown in other ears and hearts. This is what has been left to me. It is my inheritance, these knots and tangles. My fingernails take up where my father left off, working loose the tight winds his father picked at. At the ends of the length perhaps there are no more tangles, but I do not know if I shall see it. Perhaps the owl will call my name before I am done.

Outside my door, temperatures are in the forties at night, just about sixty degrees during the day. While to a trout fisherman this may not seem to be a call to cease and desist, I know the warmwater species of the Atchafalaya Basin are moving to whatever deep water they can find, likely in the main river channel, closing the season with jaws shut tight. It's time to wrap up the year. There may be a span or two of warm weather and I might head to a pond to search for fish again, but the lake fishing is done until spring.

First I clean my boat, add fuel stabilizer to the tank and cover it for winter. Another year, another season passed, and it has served me faithfully yet again. It glows warm and amber, the varnished deck clean and soft, satin. I stand much taller now, much heavier than the oh, so young boy who first sat on its bench seats with his father paddling around Lake Fausse Point This vessel, small and low-sided, is a tome of memory.

I look across the yard to the fig tree and it is bare now, its leaves browning on the lawn; the chill of winter's first kiss forced it to shed. There would be no *kich* this late in the year, but I look anyway, wondering how I failed it. The little brown bird of my people's memory did not come this spring and I wonder if I will continue to fail the things that are left to me. This little boat, the lake itself, what other treasures will fall away because of my lack of strength?

The little boat is covered and stashed away, safe and dry, to weather yet another winter until spring returns at last. I turn my attention to my gear: rods are cleaned and grips brightened, my graphite tools happily in their bags and tubes. My bamboo rods sparkle amber, like the boat, under the sun. As I touch a soft, damp rag under the feet of the guides to wipe away any dirt or grime, I think of the big redears this one took out of the lake this spring. They were nested there in a circle of cypress trees and the Granger delivered a Jitterbee under an indicator to them time after time, bringing fat, strong redears to my hand without fail. Later it brought the season's best largemouth—four pounds—to the boat at a small pond far inland from the lake. The nickel silver flashed at me in the sun as I dried it and slid it back into its sock and tube. It will rest in my rod rack in the house until spring as well.

Each reel comes out of my tackle bag and cleaned carefully. I run each line through a pad to clean and treat them with line dressing, I take off the leaders and store them in their little plastic zip bags. The click of the Medalists also reminds me. Reminds me of a small canal off an industrial waterway where, in May, my cousin Jim and I got into a swarm of big red-breasted 'gills, reels clicking cheerfully as those hand-sized fish made startling, frantic runs toward the deep center of the canal. We were picking them out of the center of a huge cypress stump barely six inches below the surface, like a volcanic caldera, they made it their home. I think also of the morning my lady and I spent in a borrow pit near the levee harassing *sac-au-lait* and the fish fry that night.

The reels back in their pouches and tuck into my bag, I make sure my fly boxes are free of the brown cypress needles that are now falling across the basin, responding to autumn in a way I can somehow sense but not grip, not touch. I make a mental note of what I need to tie this winter, as opposed to what I need to purchase to be ready for the spring to come. The bag then goes next to my rods in the piddling room and, not ready to close the door to the outside, I take the dog out of her yard for a walk to Bayou Teche behind my house.

She romps across the yard, a black Lab of some years, still spry and frisky with cooler weather. I trod slowly behind her, somehow tired. It's been a long year, really. A year of many surprises, many accomplishments and many vanishings. I think again of *kich* and wonder if spring will be as lonesome again. The bayou has suffered from the north winds this cold front brought in, and there are mudflats two dozen feet from each bank, the water pushed out to the gulf by the front. Daisy won't swim as she normally would, the mud keeps her away. She trots alongside the channel, sniffing for animal scents, rolling in the weeds and chasing the few bugs moving in the chill.

The water does not move. It's still clear, though, or as clear as water gets in the bayou. Bait fish swirl here and there and I imagine I could catch a catfish if I loaded a bait casting rod with a big hook and offer of night crawlers. I entertain that notion for an instant then let it go. I'm tired, I guess. It's been quite a year.

A gust of wind rips through the trees. Cypress needles fall like brown, dry snow and the bayou suddenly trembles and shivers, a spasm of chill working its way downstream as if across gooseflesh. I shudder and turn my back against it but the dog leaps for joy and spins triumphant circles. She is a Labrador, and her kind thrives in the cold but I am a Chitimacha and a Cajun. We are people of summer now.

I stay longer, though, because the dog has not had a chance to get out and exercise in a few days and the wind has died down again. My neighbor's dock is looking near death, knocked about and saturated with soupy mud when Hurricane Rita forced the waters of the Gulf of Mexico far inland. I walk across it carefully, making sure I only step where the deck boards are nailed to the larger joists. Instead of water below me there is a mud flat detailed with bird tracks. Clams lie in the mud, suddenly stranded, castaways. If the water does not come back soon, they will bake under the sun and pop open like overripe figs. Across the mud is a slick, sinewy trail, a snake most likely, heading for a place to weather the winter.

But another gasp of cold shocks down the bayou channel so I call the dog and we head up the ridge for home. All is good. The boat is safe, the rods are safe, and this old house will keep me safe and warm until spring, as it has all my life, as it has my family for one hundred and sixty years. Susan asks me how my day is going and I smile and tell her it's great. Winter is coming and we'll watch a lot of movies, spend a lot of time talking of spring and waiting for warmer weather to return.

The holidays are nearing. This year, she'll learn how my mom's Thanksgiving dinner comes together, a family tradition that doesn't involve turkey, cornbread dressing or cranberry sauce. A little something that will survive the erosion from my life. The family has increased by one now, and there's joy in that. We sort through old photographs sometimes, Susan and I, and I tell her my stories. I find photographs of my grandparents, my father, of my uncle.

"I wish you had known them," I say, choking back how much I miss them, but what I really mean is I wish they had known each other. She bakes pumpkin bread and hangs curtains; the signs of a woman's presence are everywhere and the house seems to settle some, soothed. We kick through leaves in the yard, hands in pockets, and Daisy leaps at the chill, delighted. We pass by the fig tree, and it is bare, bereft of leaves, empty of little mottled-brown birds bearing messages, and my heart sags low again, feeling the failure. Some evenings I rush home, only an hour of daylight left, and we put the dog in the bed of the truck and race to a pond to await the sunset. A corner of it has erupted in yellow flowers, a thick mass of sunshine but everything else is browning, dying back. The water level in the pond is lower than I have ever seen it, and we talk about rain as we walk along its margins. The dog finds a suitable spot and dives in for a swim. As we walk, we pass empty cigarette packs, beer bottles and shotgun shells. I remind myself to bring a garbage bag with me, though I am weary of the world's uncaring. Tired of its neglect. Susan and I circle the pond, the dog leading or scurrying to catch up, and we take a cutting from the explosion of yellow flowers in the corner for I fear they, too, may not return next year. Whatever dull spirit leaves trash around quiet, beautiful little ponds also destroys yellow patches of flowers and circumvents ancestral messengers.

Yet I wonder what spring will bring to this world of mine. There are months of winter ahead and though Louisiana's cold season isn't usually very severe, I'll be longing for spring by Christmas, for green-black water and whispers. By summer, when the forecasters start eyeing the tropics again, all our dreads will return, sulking, menacing. We'll wonder what the warmer months hold for us, breath held, dread on our spines.

Co'ktangi Dreams

Dreams, my father's people believed, are windows not only to the soul but to the unseen world around us.

It is exceedingly rare that I remember my dreams. I can go months and months thinking I've never dreamed at all, though those who study the mind and its function will say we dream during sleep all the time, we just don't remember them. I don't know that I believe that: perhaps dreams aren't meant to be analyzed, scrutinized and categorized.

It was early Sunday morning I awoke from this one. I was on the shores of Co'ktangi. In my arms, clutched close to my chest, was a wooden footstool, I think, maybe more like a small step stool. I don't know why I was there, but I plunged myself into the water, struggling to keep hold of the little wooden stool and tread water.

In the dream, I kicked my way from just east of the mouth of the main channel of Sawmill Bayou to below it's south fork, and I was exhausted, fearful I wouldn't make it. I let go the stool so I could struggle more deftly against sinking and at once, there was a slope beneath my feet, a sudden upward thrust of bottom. I climbed it, and then I was standing, knee deep, on a hump of silty bottom in the cove. That's when I awakened.

What to make of it? I've had silly, seemingly meaningless dreams, of course. Dreams where absurd things happen, or terrifying things, and maybe they have some tap root deep into my psyche. More often than not I forget them by midday after the night of the dream. But this one stuck in my head all Sunday as I piddled in the workshop.

Sometimes dreams are wiser than waking, Black Elk said.

Where did it come from? When I was a little boy, I had a little red step stool. My grandmother gave it to me, and I was very, very proud of it. On the top of it in white letters was a little rhyme:

This little stool is mine
I use it all the time
To reach the things I couldn't
And lots of things I shouldn't!

I actually still have that little stool. I found it in my grandmother's house, my house now, when I moved in. She kept things like that: small treasures, little victories. But the stool in my dream was unpainted, felt like cypress to my hands. Yet I know I cannot be too literal in those sleeping moments.

Still, for some reason I clutched a step stool and plunged myself into *Co'ktangi*, the ancient religious center of the entire Chitimacha nation. I struggled to hold onto it and swim, nearly losing the struggle. And when I let it go, the bottom of the pond-lily worship place swelled up and saved me.

What is myth? Is it a word we have contrived to disguise things we cannot verify? Or is it a description of things we cannot cubbyhole, cannot fit into a practical, well-ordered life?

Is it myth, then, that a family of Chitimacha were once punished for eating a white deer they killed along the lake shore—somewhere very near to my dream's location—and then, as if in a trance, all walked into the lake together never to be heard from again? Later, a group of Indians were struck by misfortune in the lake and, about to drown, saved by what the oral tradition describes as a hut rising from the bottom to support them until help arrived. Now and then Indians would see lights over the lake, four of them, reputed to be the souls of that Indian family. I've seen those lights myself, many times.

Do my dreams harness myth, or history?

That little red stool was important to me. With it, I could stand at the kitchen counter and watch my grandmother dice onions for a stew; I could—under her watchful eye—fetch things for her that were previously out of reach, though I know the sense of accomplishment it gave me was her true objective. If nothing else, I could sit on the little stool, at my grandfather's feet while he told me stories.

And there was *Co'ktangi*. In every way my home as much as the little house on the reservation. My father would take me there and we'd fish its nooks and crannies, its secrets. Now and then he'd let me get out of the boat where the shell mound used to be. The one that they dredged in the 1930s for the value of its shell, and the skeletons of *na'ta*, chiefs, and holy men and Honored People rolled out of the dredge buckets, to be picked out of the valuable shell material by hand and tossed into the muddy bottom of *Co'ktangi*. Skulls, sailing like cannon balls. Femurs, ribs, whizzing through the hot, humid air like war cries. I'd slip over the side of the little boat, and I remember—oh, do I remember, or is it myth?—my little feet swinging below the surface as I balanced myself there on the gunwale. Feet swinging in the water, searching for firmness, and I'd lower myself a little more, a little more, certain if I let go I'd plunge in over my head, but my father was there, he knew better, and finally I'd touch the hard, shell bottom of the mound and it would support me. I'd wade around on the mound, pick up pieces of broken pottery with my toes. Broken, like the worship place itself. Sacrificed.

Ah, maybe it's hard to understand. Hard to comprehend, if we've spent the majority of our lives on concrete, wearing rubber soles and synthetic socks. Hard to know if it's true that *Cok'tangi* touched my feet and sent power through my bones. Hard to know such things, if we're insulated from our ancestors by dogma, pragmatism and cold concrete.

I don't know what my dream was trying to tell me. The danger is in trying to interpret it. The meaning will be made known to me in time, I'm sure of it. I rarely remember my dreams, often believe my sleep is dark and empty. But when they come to the light of wakefulness, rattle around in my head like stones in a clay pot, there is a reason.

For now, I stand knee-deep on a mound of water bottom near *Co'ktangi*, where my people gathered for countless generations. My wooden foot stool is floating nearby, bobbing in green-black water. I'll stand here and wait to see what comes. What it means. What power taken in through the soles of a boy's feet still exists in my bones.

If a man does away with his traditional way of living and throws away his good customs, he had better first make certain that he has something of value to replace them.—Robert Ruark, quoting a Basuto proverb in *Something of Value*.

Perhaps there's no moral standard that can be applied to what a civilization or a culture values. Perhaps, in the end, the moral standard is established by the importance and emphasis the culture sets forth. In a universe where all generalities are generally false, who's to know?

How some of you have looked across the span of your long lives without weeping, I don't know. I'm half the age of some of my dearest friends, and when I look into their eyes, I see a world I wish I had known. Even the landscape of my childhood pales in comparison.

I love reading stories about the South from around the turn of the twentieth century. Despite the blatant and unforgivable bigotry, the South was also a place of romanticism, tall tales and gallantry.

Oh, the landscapes they roamed! Havilah Babcock writes of a South Carolina where the quail swarmed like mosquitoes, where the woods were tall and old and stretched on for miles and miles and miles and you could walk them forever.

In Babcock's world, "Every country boy is entitled to a creek. If no creek's handy, maybe a meandering branch will do for a while. But it must have a few holes that he can't see the bottom of. That's an absolute requisite, and there's no getting around it."

I read again and again Fielding Lewis' *Tales of A Louisiana Duck Hunter* and though I've never shouldered a shotgun to track a duck in my life, my departed friend lived in such a world as Babcock, a world that was right here, under my very feet. A world where flocks of mallards blocked the sun, where marsh—like woods—went on for miles and miles and there was, above all, a sense of sportsmanship.

But I'm not just speaking from an outdoorsman's perspective. I am talking about something of value. At some point the government urged farmers to plant "fence row to fence row" and the quail lost their habitat. At some point, the engineers moved water from here to there and the waterways dried up or stagnated. In every case, the value was money, and the most of it that could possibly be obtained.

Those of us who value a meadow of so-called "idle land" understand its value. Those of us who value a hardwood forest with hardly any underbrush understand the value of its wildlife, its solitude and its ancestral wisdom, more so than its lumber and fertile soil as a field plot.

I wonder, sometimes, how we made the transition from peas and beans and corn and squash that had been in the fields that morning and in the market by afternoon...to vegetables stuffed into an aluminum can. How we went from fresh fruit to dried, from real lemon juice to artificial. Didn't it just feel wrong? Did the convenience overshadow the lost taste, the lousy texture?

All that's of value any more are belching smoke stacks, thousands of monoculture acres of farmland to feed our seething cities. Living in the city has become something of imagined value, because that's where the money can be made. A city is not sustainable—it must be spoon-fed all its resources, its food, its water, its building materials, everything. These things are trucked in, moved by rail, delivered by cargo planes in quantities that stagger the imagination. Cities are unable to tend to their own needs, so we must ravish small communities and wilderness to support their existence. They provide nothing in return except money, violence, smog and loneliness.

I read an interesting thing about cell phones the other day: it seems that something good has come from those damnable devices after all. For several years now people like me have bemoaned a world where parents arm their children with cell phones to track their every movement, keep them somewhat safer in a world gone amok.

But there was a study that says this maneuver on the part of moms and dads has had an unexpected benefit: Kids are actually going outside more. The cell phone, a technological concoction, has loosened the tether, and kids are actually realizing there is a fascinating world beyond the game controllers. There may be hope, after all.

Someone said to me that "driving is not a right, it is a privilege" and that struck me as oddly fatalistic. Driving is a privilege only because it generates cash for government coffers. By that same reasoning, then, watching television, cutting grass, washing the car, listening to music and all such things are not rights. Fishing and hunting have become privileges, too, rather than rights.

In an odd way, government determined there was something of value in globbing some earthworms on a hook, or bagging a rabbit for supper: cash, in the form of fishing and hunting licenses.

Progress has redefined value, and like sheep we accepted it. Personally, I'd prefer my fields filled with quail again, my lakes and rivers unmolested by engineering, my woods full of wildlife and adventure. Despite the inevitability of the life I've come to accept, deep inside me are still the powerful stirrings of wooden sailboats crashing through waves at sea, mountains with cold, fast water, vast prairies full of fair game.

But like it or not, something of value is now money. It is the means to an end that has by osmosis adapted its own phony value: retirement. Nice stuff. Credit. Savings. Good schools for the kids. Something of value is based on how much we can consume, believing it makes us happy. I sit here with my fancy-dancy new cell phone on my hip, my mega-fast computer before me, and realize I'm as callused and indifferent as anyone. I struggle through fifty weeks of work in a year, aching for the two weeks I can take to the water, to the wild places where value is defined entirely another way. There is no true wilderness anymore, Harry Middleton noted. That's why you often find me referring to the places I go like he did, as "wildness." That's all that's left, really.

I tell myself, if I had it to do all over again, things would be different. Maybe I would be so lucky, but chances are the inescapable trap of modernity will ensnare me all over again.

Simon Peter said, I go a'fishing: and they said, We also will go with thee. (John 21.3.) One day, we might go a'fishing and not come back. Don't worry about us, if we do. We'll have found something of value, some place where there's no good spot to hang a clock. All you'll find to mark my passing is my cell phone, abandoned. The cities can crumble, their skyscrapers turn black and desolate, their overpasses cracked and leaning; their glass windows can shatter and their lights go dark, but there was no value there, anyway, to some of us. No value at all.

Spots of Time

I couldn't find a single pair of shorts at four that morning, half-awake, holding a cup of coffee in one hand and searching with the other. Worried about deer flies and such, I opted for jeans, though I knew it would be hot as the dickens by noon during an uncharacteristic warm spell in January. But by then I was standing in temperate water somewhere far, far south of Morgan City on a shell reef. The water was up to my thighs, and I was able to wade out a good yardage from the reef.

It was the latest installment in my quest to catch redfish on a fly rod. Not just any fly rod, mind you, but a bamboo fly rod. I was there to christen my new rod built by Harry Boyd.

It was more than an hour's ride from the Berwick boat landing down the Atchafalaya River to where I stood. My fishing host, Lamon Miller, had deposited me there on the reef where he said the "bull reds" can often be found. A "bull red" is a redfish of enormous proportions, literal juggernauts, freight trains on the end of a fishing line. He had taken off in the boat to investigate other places while I happily waded around on the reef.

A couple of other boats had shown up after Lamon departed, anchoring off a few hundred yards away to fish, and I'm sure they were perplexed by the guy in the fedora standing up to his zipper in the Gulf of Mexico, fly fishing, wondering how the devil I got there. I paid little attention. The wind was low, not slack, but not bad. Harry's rod performed like a champion thoroughbred even in my mediocre hands.

I caught two "rat reds" or small redfish where the water was breaking over a point of the shell reef, and felt encouraged. Those were my first redfish on a fly rod, even if they were small. I was using a fly called a "golden bendback" tied by my friend Gary Henderson from Florida, his favorite for speckled trout and redfish.

Standing there on that white shell reef, casting blindly to potential fish, I was elated. Over the past year or so I have grown restless of spirit again, uneasy and suffering wanderlust. Far off the coast, these magnificent shell reefs, lightly dotted with shrubs and washed-up debris, are often pristine, often trashless and always beautiful. I could nearly imagine what the whole coastline of Louisiana looked like a century ago when these reefs numbered a thousandfold what they do now, before they were nearly dredged into extinction for the value of their shell.

Those reefs had protected Louisiana from hurricane surges for thousands of years. Great stumbling blocks to tidal surges, the

reefs would diminish any wall of water to very little at the edge
of the coast and marsh, and virtually nothing inland. But the
greed of Louisiana politicians won over, and all those shell reefs
were dredged and sold to line the pocket books of corrupt offi-
cials and businessmen. Fragments of them remain, such as the
one Lamon left me on while he went scouting for signs of
schooling reds.

I made a great cast, which for me is about sixty feet, right at
the edge of the breakwater. Gathering line in my hand I gave it
my usual retrieve after letting the fly settle a moment or two.
Strip-strip-strip, quick jerks taking in line, then let it settle. In my
mind, I could see the fly rush forward, rush forward, rush forward, then settle like an exhausted bait fish for a moment. The
process was then repeated.

At the end of one settling of the fly, I pulled line for another
strip and the line slipped through my fingers because it wouldn't
come forward. I pulled again and—being a freshwater fisherman
and accustomed to numerous snags such as cypress knees and the
like—I was surprised when the snag pulled back.

All at once the world seemed to shrink around me. The boats
anchored away from the reef were gone. Somewhere in the boat
searching for another fishing spot, Lamon vanished. Even the
reef behind me was gone.

I don't know how long what follows took. Later I told Lamon it was about ten minutes. It might have been twenty. It
might have been five. I have no idea because time suddenly became meaningless.

The fish broke water when I set the hook, but I didn't see it.
Only a mighty swirl of something big suddenly disturbed the
surface there in the shallows over the reef edge, and awful unhappy about it. He took off, and I'll say it was a redfish because
of the reputation this area has for bull reds and the fact that I
caught two small ones in the same spot, but the fact is I never
saw it.

He made a swift but not amazingly fast run away from me,
and before I knew it he was at the end of my fly line, one-hun-
dred-and-ten feet. Behind that line I had a one-hundred-and-fifty
yards of braided line for a backing. The way that fish was running I knew the backing would vanish fast, so I said a prayer to
the fishing gods, and to Harry Boyd (who is a Baptist minister by

profession in addition to being a rodmaker) and I "put the wood to him" as we bamboo rod fishermen say.

I made sure my rod stayed at about forty-five degrees to the water's surface but I leaned on the big red, the rod arching over in a studious curve. And I felt him twitch his head in annoyance, then turn toward me. Now I was scrambling to get line back on my reel as the fish meandered back in my direction but at about fifty feet out I had him back on the arbor and, again unhappy about it, he made another run this time to my left.

This time he took me well into the backing, shrugging off the drag on my fly reel as if it were nothing. I leaned on him again, hard, reminding myself that the monofilament leader tied to my fly line had a breaking test of seventeen pounds.

And to my great pride, I turned him again. I was raised Baptist but kinda fell by the wayside a couple decades ago. I silently promised Harry I'd move my letter soon as I got home.

All this time I'm slowly walking sideways and sometimes backwards toward the reef and more shallow water for when I got him close enough to grab. His run to my left was less vigorous, but no less determined, and now he was more or less a dead weight out there about eighty feet away, and I carefully pressured him toward me.

That was all he was going to tolerate.

At that nudge, he took off toward the breakwater where I had hooked him, my spool spinning and my backing line vanishing quickly.

Grimacing to no one except those far off anchored anglers who may or may not have even noticed my personal battle unfolding, I leaned on him again.

And suddenly the weight and the freight train and the irresistibility were gone.

I stood there, rod in my hand at my side, for long moments. Out there, somewhere, I could imagine the bull red meandering off with my gold bendback in his mouth. But when I finally reeled in my line, there was the fly at the end of my leader. The leader had not broken, my knot had not slipped. The hook had simply pulled out the third time I put the wood to him.

Lamon returned about twenty minutes later and I told him the story, with the caveat that, "I got no witnesses, I could be lying through my teeth."

I could be, but I guess you'll just have to take my word for it that I'm not.

It was the fish of the day, to be sure, but I won't say it's the fish of a lifetime. That one remains to be caught, and I haven't given up yet. I learned two things that disappointing but exhilarating afternoon: Louisiana redfish like gold bendbacks, and Harry Boyd's bamboo rod will handle 'em just fine.

Nothing much else to do. I decided to go to the little pond. Prior to the drought we experienced after KatRita, it was full of small to medium bass and bream and the occasional eye-popping largemouth. The drought caused the little pond to diminish from about four feet to less than one in some places. I doubted anything at all survived, but when the rains returned and the water level with them, I was surprised to find a fair population of feisty, if small, fish.

Always the thinning. Always the losing.

The cat, Patches, who stays in the house, eyed me suspiciously as I gathered up rod, bag, hat and made for the door. She used to be accustomed to my puttering around prior to a fishing trip, but I've been so home-bound that when I start clattering rod tubes and shaking tackle bags, she gets edgy, panics, and runs away to hide.

My favorite companion on trips to this little pond is Daisy. Daisy is showing her years a bit, slows down faster than she used to, but she loves that little pond much as I do.

I have to help her up into the back of the truck now. She used to be able to jump in, just after the hurricanes. A little later, I little hoist of her backside was all she needed. Now she makes a hearty, spirited effort and I quickly put my arm under her belly and lift her the rest of the way, where she spins a tail-wagging, huffing dance of delight that we're going on a fishing trip.

Off we go, and in my side-mirrors—both of them—I can see Daisy, tongue flapping pinkly in the wind, doggy slobber streaking along the sides of the truck, as she moves from side to side to see and smell as much as she possibly can. I remind myself I'll have to wash the truck that evening.

The land around the pond is overgrown with grass, taller than me. It'll all be roll-casting, something I don't think a six-foot bamboo banty rod will excel at. I brought a double-taper line, though, which should help.

Daisy knows when I lower the tailgate that she must wait until I am done setting up my rod and loading the pockets of my shorts with a fly box, hemostat and a cigar. I help her down, and she makes me laugh as she darts toward the trail to the pond, kept relatively subdued by the four-wheeling kids that have found the shallow end of the pond is delightfully four-wheelable. The pond is big enough that it doesn't really muddy up the rest when they have their fun.

I find one of my favorite spots. I can't even see the truck back at the road. It's nearly a hundred yards away. While the pond was in drought, all manner of brush sprung up on its revealed, fertile edges. Access has become hard to come by, and it's too soft-bottomed to wade. So I find a good spot, such as it is, and wiggle out a few feet of line, leader and black foam ant with rubber legs.

The little rod will roll cast, but not far. I have to raise my arm pretty high, but I can do twenty, twenty-five feet. Daisy has found a spot to my right, a couple dozen feet away, to wade. I taught her that early on: when I'm fishing a pond, she always wades to my right, theoretically over water I've fished already or, in this case, have left for her to enjoy. I fish to my left and walk that way if I can, and she stays behind me. We don't fish where others are fishing, so I never have problems.

Second cast and the foam ant is lost in a swirl. I have to strip-set, fearful that too vigorous a rod-lift at such short distance will send my fly into the jungle growth behind me. No hook-up. The 'gills are finning it, or swiping the fly with their tails. It's closer in, but I take up slack and let the ripples die. Another swirl, no hook-up, so I roll it out as far as I can again, waiting with the line as slack-free as I can manage. It takes a monumental conjuring of will to not even twitch the rod until I see the line twitch itself, but it pays, and soon a medium-sized green sunfish is in my hand, thrashing.

Daisy is there, at my side, ears perked. I didn't hear her arrive. She knows that she'll get one little bream out of the trip, which she'll toss around for awhile then roll on for a bit longer and finally crunch happily.

"Too big," I tell her. "You only get the really little ones." I toss it into the water, and the retriever in her rises and she makes a halting lurch forward before she catches herself and, pouting, turns back into the high grass to explore.

I hear her rustling around nearby. I make another cast and the same routine continues, swirling, slapping, finning, and finally a take. Not much better, but this one is a bass, maybe five inches. I'm pleased with my little banty rod. The shaft was dark cane, very brown, but straight. The butt section had a split ferrule, and I didn't need any more nine-foot bamboo rods. I was surprised how well it cast when I was done. That's the thing about building banty rods: unless you tape on some guides and a reel to a bare blank, you don't really know what you've got until you're done, days and weeks later. I like it a lot with a DT4.

I reel in and set the fly n the hook keeper, call for Daisy. She's at my side in a couple minutes, huffing.

"Come on, old girl," I smile, and she sits by my side for a rest and ear-rubbing, and I note the graying around her muzzle, faint, but getting more prominent as the months pass. I give her a few minutes, then we make our way through the tall grass again until I find another suitable spot to cast. She lies down behind me, content to give herself a rest.

The next little 'gill, also a greenie, is tiny. I flip it to the dog, "Here, my sweet," I say. She pulls herself up easily, takes the little gill in her mouth and stalks off through the grass, presumably to the trail where there's more room to play.

I fish on for an hour or so, until the sun is getting high and the bite is slowing. I've caught nothing large enough to even matter, but with each little splashing, accompanied by a grunting and rustling behind me as Daisy plays aerial games with the little bream and then flops on her back to roll on it, I'm quite satisfied with my morning.

Soon I hear the tell-tale crunch of a black Lab devouring a green perch. I take in my line and make my way to the trail, where Daisy is licking her cheeks happily.

I take the little Punch cigar out of my pocket and light it, and we sit there for little while, by the little pond, watching the morning mature. I put my hand on her back, almost without thinking about it, and she lifts her head a little higher, prouder.

We make our way back to the truck. She's just at my heel now, and halfway there she's lagging a few steps behind, so I slow a little, just enough to let her catch up, and the swing of her tail indicates I've restored her pride. She waits patiently while I put my tackle away, dry the rod and tube it, then help her into the truck, curling my nose.

"You *stink*," I say, and she grins at me toothily, so I just have to laugh and rub her ear again. Not just the truck due for a bath this evening.

In my mirror, on the way home, she's facing into the wind, ears and tongue flapping, tail swinging. We make it to the garage, and I help her down. The bath can wait, she's tired. She follows me to her fenced-in yard and I let her in the gate with a pat on the head. She nibbles on a bit of her food and curls up on the ground for a rest, but her head is up. Proud. The Lab in her will never diminish, and she is, I think, gloating over the trip with her human, satiated, enjoying the scent of fresh green perch on herself as a reminder of the day.

I head for the house for a change of clothes and cleanup, and I think not for the first time how much I'd have liked to known her when she was a pup, even a young adult. She was about ten when she came to stay with me, and I know that despite her good health, she's not a youngster anymore. Whatever time we have on a pond catching midget perch is time well-spent, though, between good friends.

The mercury is flip-flopping. Cold as the dickens one week or two weeks, then warms for a spell, then back to cold. We've had frost this year, but no real freezes. Normally I'd worry that without a couple of dips into the twenties, the vegetative growth of last summer would not be killed off in the shallows. But we've had so little rain over the last few months water levels all over southern Louisiana are extraordinarily low. This has killed most of the intrusive vegetation already, yet not washed out the salt deposited by the storms, which is badly needed.

I suffered through three weeks with a cold. There's no sense even going out in the boat, though on warm days when my head is cleared from the congestion and I'm not coughing my lungs out the urge is strong. I'd likely crash my lower unit into a log or stump with the water as low as it is now. The dog and I walk behind my house, along Bayou Teche, and mudflats extend three dozen yards from either shore to where the channel suddenly deepens in the center of the bayou. I've never seen it this low.

We need rain, and plenty of it.

The dog is exuberant. During my illness she hadn't gotten out of the fenced-in yard enough, so I was sure to bring her for a walk soon as I felt up to it. She finds scent after scent in the brown carpet of cypress needles, follows one to the shoreline edge and halts at the flat of mud beyond. She cocks her head curiously at the path the scent continues on.

Some critter walked through the mud from the bank to a cypress tree ten feet out. Normally the tree's trunk is in six or eight inches of water, but it's exposed now. I can't tell what kind of small animal it was that walked out to that tree because the silty mud holds no definition in the tracks, but the animal must have climbed into the tree and vanished into thin air, because there are no return tracks and I see nothing in the tree.

This lot, and the house upon it, were my grandparents' abode, but the house was built in about 1840 by Alexander Darden, a great-great-great uncle of mine. He was chief of the tribe at the time. I grew up with my parents nearby, and we had perhaps six acres between us. This bayouside was my haunt as a child. Now there are two other homes between mine and what is now my mom's, so I don't trespass between the two. But in my youth it was my wonderland. We kept horses here, two quarter horses named Tee-Boy and Kate, and a Tennessee Walker named, aptly enough, Walker. Kate and I shared the exact same birth date, and she was the fastest horse on the Rez, bar none. My first was a pony, a Shetland named Nancy. Even after I outgrew her, we kept Nancy around as a beloved member of the family.

But all that was a long time ago. I walk part of that land, perhaps seventy-five yards of it, now with the sweet old lab Daisy. She is really my fiance's dog, and sometimes I'm not sure if my girlfriend's sharing Daisy or Daisy's sharing Susan, but that's how it goes. She's brisk and energetic for a twelve-year-old, lean and fit, with the disposition of a lamb and great obedience but a menacing growl and roar for suspected intruders. She would have made a great bird dog, to be sure, but she's an even better companion walking the bayouside in January, thinking about years gone by and the flats left behind.

I realize most folks don't have such attachment to the land they were born and reared on, and I know I am blessed. Those of us who do, we take its changes and movements in stride, but there are memories around every tree trunk, ghosts behind each ridge, voices on every breeze. Daisy rolls in the grass playfully and for a moment she is a German shepherd named Lady, or a Springer named Shadow, an old hound named Bootsie. Now and then I pass an old water oak and the horizontal scars precisely spaced up its trunk level with my chest remind me of the barbed wire fence that used to be there to contain the horses.

Were I still a hunter, and there were still enough quail to shoot without feeling remorseful, I'd be in the fields. And yes, it'd be good to be in the basin, in the wild, near water however shallow and dingy. But I count my blessings that at least I don't live on some cramped municipal street, or in some apartment complex or even on a sprawling acreage without nearby neighbors yet still far from water. I'm don't mean to seem critical of those who live in such places. But I know that being there would diminish my spirit like some crippling disease, if not drive me mad.

Across the bayou from where the dog and I stand is a cypress tree from which a thick rope hangs by one of the topmost branches. Generations of Chitimacha children have learned to swim from this tree. It's a stout and strong old tree and at its base is a deep hole in Bayou Teche suitable for jumping from the rope or diving from the branches. The kids still come to it now and then. Sometimes they irritate me with their language or their loud music or just because I'm trying to tight-line a spinning rod with a glob of earthworms for catfish on a hot summer day. But I'm sure I irritated my elders too, so I just let it go.

Let it go. That's what it seems like to me, here on the edge of Bayou Teche, where I've lived for more than four decades, where my family's lived for at least one hundred and sixty years and where my people have been ages. It seems like the rivulets and eddies of time and space converge here, at least for me. The dog comes and nuzzles my hand and I scratch behind her ear. We both sigh in contentment at the same time, and I laugh at the coincidence. The sound of it makes her leap away, spinning joyous circles around me. I throw her a stick and she goes for it, brings it back, wide-eyed and ears perked for a replay. We throw sticks and retrieve them, making our way back to the old house, and the timelessness within.

For Want of A River

After Montana, I thought my stream-fishing days were done. It wasn't an easy realization. Though my love of streams and rivers wasn't nearly a full-blown, all-consuming obsession then, there was a sort of dull sadness that I probably had done all the fly fishing in fast, wild water that I would ever do.

But then I met Pete Cooper Jr.

Pete Cooper, author, magazine article writer, holder of several Louisiana records in the fly fishing division, was to me just a name on an internet bulletin board for fly fishing in our state. But Pete was talking about something I had never heard of: streams, streams you could wade in, streams with rocks and gravel and sand...and these streams were in Louisiana.

I made Pete's acquaintance first when I reviewed his book *Fly Fishing the Louisiana Coast* for an online magazine. Later, reading his board posts regarding these surely mythical streams in the bayou state, I asked him for some directions. What ensued was a complicated series of instructions that me, a backwoods bayou boy, understood little of, but in the end I was able to comprehend the most important points: several hours away I could be in wild water again.

Part of me didn't believe it. I knew there were hills in central and north Louisiana, a few scattered pieces of sandstone. But fast, cold streams? Bah! I had to see it for myself.

The trip had been in the planning stages for weeks, months even. Susan and I would escape to reputed hills and an allegedly rocky, meandering stream atypical of most in Louisiana.

We took off in the morning and, after a long drive and a rough, bumpy run on an unpaved, red dirt road, to the creek.

It was just a few feet to the edge of the bluff, and there was white sand under our feet even there, evidence of the tremendous antiquity of this stream, and the depth of the ravine witness to its former might. Twenty or more feet down there it was: a sing-song stream, leaping over rocks and sandstone terraces, chortling and laughing, murmuring and grumbling.

It was beautiful. Fall colors were glorious, golds and reds, yellows and browns, and leaves of every color shot down the stream, hurtling over smoothed rocks. I silently apologized to Pete Cooper and promised I'd buy him a beer.

I rigged a fly rod and decided on size eight black wooly bugger with a small bead of splitshot to get it down. For the lady I equipped a spinning rod with a blue-and-white beetle spin, a favored color of freshwater fish statewide. Pete told me the creek was mostly only ankle- or knee-deep, but there were deeper holes to be found, where fish might linger, as well as beneath the undercut of banks and fallen trees dangling in the flow.

In fact, our chances of catching were slim, I also knew. The stream was low, and it was dead winter. A cold front at that very moment was crossing east Texas and moving toward us. It would arrive the next day. But the fishing is never disappointing, only the catching can sometimes be.

Lacking waders—what use are waders to a boat fisherman, as I was back home?—I wore shorts and sandals. I loaded my vest with fly boxes I thought I might need, an extra leader and fisherman's hemostats—pure optimism, there—and slung a water bottle and camera over my shoulder. I slid a knife into a sheath on my belt, put my fedora on my head and, on a whim, opened the face of my cell phone to read the message flashing on the tiny screen:

No Signal.

Ah, yes. Who could ask for more?

I let the rod stretch out behind me in case these flatlander feet lost their balance, then we sidled down the ravine.

It was well after noon, dusk but a few hours away. I stepped out onto firm sand and the water was cold, catching me by surprise and further convincing me that the catching might be beleaguered. I headed upstream and Susan moved downstream. Remembering what I learned from my Blackfeet cousin Joe Kipp in Montana, I looked ahead of the rapids singing and chanting around me to what looked like a flat expanse of more slowly moving water. A pool, of course, a place where fish would not need to expend as much precious energy to simply stay put. The water seldom reached more than mid-calf as I made my way across the rapids and to the first pool.

Positioned near to the center of the west side of the stream, I was able to cast at undercuts in the bank and fallen trees in the water, but no bites resulted. Didn't matter, I was in heaven, remembering how to mend my fly line when it laid out three dozen yards ahead of me and immediately began coming back in the current. I worked up the second set of rapids, crossed to the east side of the stream and cast back to the west again. The fourth such cast was a bit high and twisted around a pine limb just over the water, so I had to negotiate back to the rapids, cross them on foot, and find a shallow route to the pine to unravel it successfully.

After several turns of the waterway upstream I decided to make my way back to my access point and fish southward, the direction Pete had tried to guide me. My girl had returned and elected to sit ashore and relish the beauty of the creek, so I continued downstream. Here the sandstone diminished and the sandy banks were by turns firm and easily passable or treacherously shifting, sinking or flowing under my feet unnervingly. The creek moved more slowly here, and the ravine deeper. At the lapping edges of the stream great rocks squatted beneath two dozen feet of sand bluffs. Deadfalls of great tree trunks were almost everywhere, and the next bend in the stream revealed a few broken stumps in the water.

At the base of one of these, a solid weight on my line took me by surprise and I lifted the rod tip to make a good hook set. The weight pulled back and after a short debate on the matter, a beautiful sac-au-lait of respectable size was spinning at my feet in the clear, copper-tinted water. I took a quick photo and let the fish go, an unexpected gift.

Around the next bend, the forest grew thicker and the great white bluffs blocked the sun. Long twilight stretched out downstream, and I cast at fallen logs and dark green spots of deeper water. From the shadows under huge, smooth rocks, in the crevices of tree trunks, in the gentle murmur of the creek's eons-long undulation, were hints of welcome. I reeled in my line and sat respectfully for a time on a white sand bar, along a stretch of the stream darker than the rest, as if dusk was a little nearer here than upstream or down. Deep as the ravine was there, I could have been sitting in some era of the distant past, perhaps a thousand years or more earlier than those at the summit of the gulch. I won't say what I heard or saw there, but I was sorry that I had not brought tobacco to return the greetings of cousins long, long passed from this special waterway; their voices mixed with that of the stream and spoke even then, if one but listened for them.

In time, I picked up my rod with regret and made my way back upstream where I could climb the sandy side of the gully.

We broke down our fishing rods and put away our gear, and I changed back into jeans because a few of the holes I stepped into were deeper than I expected and the hem of my shorts were soaked.

I promised myself—and the whispers along the dark bend of the stream—that would not be the last time we would visit that special, magical place.

On the drive home, as we talked nonstop about what we had found there, our surprise that it was in Louisiana of all places, I felt a hollow spot of longing, scarce and faint, open in my chest. It was a feeling I would come to know intimately in years to come.

Epilogue: Kich

I woke in a cold sweat, thinking suddenly of *kich*. Purple spots of memory danced across my eyes in the dark, phantoms. Memories of water lines high on cypress trunks and sheet-rocked walls, helicopters and splintered, jagged holes in rooftops, purple recollections of a voice from my youth, drifting across dead black water.

The entire spring had passed, then summer, and *kich* never came to me. I feared I had lost it, failed it somehow, and that ancient messenger, that fragile link to my people's faded greatness was gone forever, along with so many other things suffered during the year, the purple patches and the way of memory.

But I woke that night, sweat beading on my forehead, and I heard my grandmother's voice, with great clarity, drifting along the back ends of dark canals, whispering to me from thin places across a span of decades:

"If there will be a flood," my grandmother said to me when I was a boy, "the little bird will circle in the sky, afraid to come down, and will make no sound."

You have been blessed, boy. Thirty years. A lifetime ago.

I fish where my forefathers hunted mammoths with bone points; where brown-skinned people with river cane baskets moved enough soil and clam shell to create ceremonial mounds a hundred feet tall. I am descended of a line of *na'ta*, chiefs so powerful they were called Great Suns, carried about on litters so their feet would not touch the earth lest they destroy it. I fish where there may still be magic in old, sacred trees and thin green-black water; where I still believe in little mottled-brown birds and the places where God lives.

About the Author:

Roger Emile Stouff is the son of Nicholas Leonard Stouff Jr., last chief of the Chitimacha Tribe of Louisiana, and Lydia Marie Gaudet Stouff, daughter of a Cajun farmer. He has been a journalist for more then thirty years and writer of the award-winning column "From the Other Side" in the *St. Mary and Franklin Banner-Tribune*. He was featured on the television show "Fly Fishing America" in 2006, and was writer and narrator of the documentary "Native Waters: A Chitimacha Recollection" on Louisiana Public Broadcasting in 2010.

Visit the website for more books and blogs:
www.shadowfirebooks.com

Made in the USA
Charleston, SC
14 May 2012